New England Dogmatics

New England Dogmatics

A SYSTEMATIC COLLECTION OF
QUESTIONS AND ANSWERS IN DIVINITY BY
Maltby Gelston (1766–1865)

EDITED BY
Robert L. Boss
Joshua R. Farris
S. Mark Hamilton

FOREWORD BY
Kenneth P. Minkema

PICKWICK *Publications* · Eugene, Oregon

NEW ENGLAND DOGMATICS
A Systematic Collection of Questions and Answers in Divinity by Maltby Gelston
(1766–1865)

Pickwick Publications
An Imprint of Wipf and Stock Publishers
199 W. 8th Ave., Suite 3
Eugene, OR 97401

www.wipfandstock.com

PAPERBACK ISBN: 978-1-61097-931-3
HARDCOVER ISBN: 978-1-4982-8603-9
EBOOK ISBN: 978-1-5326-3776-6

Cataloguing-in-Publication data:

Names: Gelston, Maltby, 1766–1865, author. | Boss, Robert L., editor. | Farris, Joshua R., editor. | Hamilton, S. Mark, editor. | Minkema, Kenneth P., foreword.

Title: New England dogmatics : a systematic collection of questions and answers in divinity by Maltby Gelston (1766–1865) / edited by Robert L. Boss, Joshua R. Farris, and S. Mark Hamilton.

Description: Eugene, OR: Pickwick Publications, 2019 | Includes bibliographical references and index.

Identifiers: ISBN 978-1-61097-931-3 (paperback) | ISBN 978-1-4982-8603-9 (hardcover) | ISBN 978-1-5326-3776-6 (ebook)

Subjects: LCSH: Gelston, Maltby, 1766–1865 | New England theology | Calvinism | Edwards, Jonathan, 1703–1758—Influence | New England—Church history | Reformed Church—Doctrines | Theology—United States—History | Theology, Doctrinal

Classification: BX7260.E3 G25 2019 (print) | BX7260.E3 (ebook)

02/11/19

To
Ken Minkema
Robert Caldwell
&
Gloria Thorne

Contents

Foreword

WITHIN CONGREGATIONAL CIRCLES DURING the colonial and early republican periods in North America, a trained and qualified ministry was considered essential for the perpetuation of thriving churches and of a godly society. Thus, seminaries for the training of pastors were established— Harvard in Massachusetts Bay, Yale in Connecticut. After the Revolution, more such seminaries multiplied. These nurseries of learning and piety were hallmarks of the society.

But there were other, less institutional settings for ministerial formation, perhaps the most important being the "parsonage seminaries" or "schools of the prophets" set up by local pastors. It was common practice for a student, having finished his baccalaureate work, to supplement or extend his training and experience, either before going on for a master's degree, or while pursuing it. This period was called "rusticating." The student would identify an established pastor who ran a school of the prophets with whom he wanted to live for a time—usually a year or so—during which he would be part of the minister's family, try his hand at preaching, visitation, and other pastoral duties, and witness the domestic, social, and professional life of an ordained leader in all its aspects. He would also, under his mentor's direction, engage in further study.

Jonathan Edwards, the famous theologian and revivalist, was one of the figures of the colonial era who rusticated seminarians-in-training, as was Jonathan Jr, the only son of the senior Edwards to become a minister, during the post-Revolutionary period. Edwards Jr did not accept as many students as did his own mentors and former students of his father, Joseph Bellamy and Samuel Hopkins, but many of the ones he did accept went on to illustrious careers. Consider, for example, his nephew Timothy Dwight, who became president of Yale College and member of the literary circle known as the Connecticut Wits; Samuel Austin, pastor of the influential Fair Haven church in New Haven; Jedidiah Morse, geographer and founding member of Andover Seminary; Edward Dorr Griffin, pastor of the prestigious Park

Street Church in Boston and faculty member at Andover; and Samuel Nott, pastor of Franklin, Connecticut, for an impressive tenure of seventy-two years (that has to be some kind of record), successor to Edwards Jr. as the president of the Connecticut Missionary Society, and himself the mentor of several hundred ministerial candidates.

In the manner of his father, Edwards Jr crafted a list of questions in divinity for his students to answer. Still another of Edwards Jr's students was Maltby Gelston—hardly a household name, at least up until now. Gelston has left us his notebook containing his responses to all 313 questions posed to him by his mentor. Here we have a wonderful index of the nature of theological education in late eighteenth-century New England; of the evolution and points of controversy within Reformed theology generally; and of the continuities and changes occurring within Edwardseanism specifically. Hopefully, other such notebooks, whether by students or teachers, will emerge to help fill out some of the issues raised by Gelston's personal version of a systematic theology. But Gelston's notebook in and by itself is a valuable and informative source whose availability we can welcome and whose content we can plumb.

Kenneth P. Minkema
Jonathan Edwards Center
Yale University

Preface

Preparation of the Text

THE TEXT OF MALTBY Gelston is reproduced in this edition as he wrote it in manuscript form. That it may be presented in manner faithful to the original and in a way sensible to modern readers, a number of minor, technical alterations have been made:

1. Spelling is standardized to *Webster's Third New International Dictionary*. This means little more than excising unnecessary vowels from certain words like the "u" from "colour" or normalizing words like "indifferency" to "indifference" or "compleat" to "complete."

2. Punctuation in Gelston's manuscript is erratic and often inconsistent, particularly with respect to the use (or overuse) of commas—something quite common to this historical period. Such overuse is regularized. In addition, the editors have taken care to maintain all of Gelston's sentence structures and paragraph divisions.

3. Gelston's citation of Scripture requires minimal standardization. This means little more than completing abbreviations to biblical book references.

4. Minor typographical errors or obscure markings on the page, of which there are few, are also corrected without annotation. Those sentences and paragraphs that are crossed out in Gelston's manuscript are provided in the citations where they clearly contribute to the development of the author's thought(s).

5. Gelston references a number of secondary sources without citation. Insofar as they can be traced, they are cited in the footnotes.

6. Gelston's manuscript contains a substantial supplement to the main text containing extended answers to certain questions he thought

required further explanation. For the sake of the reader all supplemental material is cited in the footnotes.

7. Finally, all questions have been keyed to the corresponding page numbers in the original manuscript and appear in brackets as follows: *Question 1. [2]*.

Acknowledgements

We owe a monumental debt of gratitude to a number of friends and colleagues who helped us produce this work: Robert Caldwell, Oliver Crisp, David Kling, and Doug Sweeney. We are particularly grateful to Ken Minkema of the *Jonathan Edwards Center* at Yale University, who gave of his time and unmatched expertise to help shape this project and who also kindly agreed to author the preface for this work. Special thanks also to Gloria Thorne of the Sherman Historical Society who secured a considerable number of important manuscript resources for us and whose enthusiasm for the project carried us through in the final stages of editing. Finally, we would like to thank the staff at Yale University's Sterling and Beinecke Library's for their kind assistance in procuring Gelston's manuscript with great punctuality, precision, and care. Our families were an immeasurable source of support throughout this project. To them we owe far more thanks than could possibly be expressed here. Many thanks to the editor's of the following journals for generously permitting select portions of the following articles to be republished here:

S. Mark Hamilton and Joshua R Farris, "The Logic of Reparation: Contemporary Restitution Models of Atonement, Divine Justice, and Somatic Death." *Irish Theological Quarterly* [online first: http://journals.sagepub.com/doi/10.1177/0021140017742804] 83.1 (Feb 2018).

S. Mark Hamilton, "Jonathan Edwards, Anselmic Satisfaction, and God's Moral Government." *International Journal of Systematic Theology* 17.1 (2015) 1–22.

S. Mark Hamilton, "Jonathan Edwards on the Atonement." *International Journal of Systematic Theology* 15.4 (2013) 394–415.

SMH, JRF, & RLB
January 2019
Soli Deo Gloria

Editor's Introduction

JONATHAN EDWARDS' NEW ENGLAND theology represents "the single most brilliant and most continuous indigenous theological tradition that America has produced."[1] Despite its brilliance, the collected works of Joseph Bellamy, Samuel Hopkins, Jonathan Edwards Jr, Nathaniel Emmons, amongst others, rank as perhaps the most ignored body of theological literature in the history of theology.[2] In the most recent decade, however, interest in Edwards and his successors, particularly with respect to the reception of Edwards' ideas, has accelerated.[3] Amongst those of the New England theological tradition to excite such interest is Jonathan Edwards Jr and in particular, his doctrine of the atonement.[4] And while this otherwise limited interest has traditionally come more from historical theologians and church historians than any other source, there has emerged something of a sustained, and uniquely systematic theological interest in the recent literature, primarily in the form of theologically constructive projects and so-called retrieval theologies. What has revived this interest, particularly amongst systematic theologians, is equal-parts patient research and a new sense that the New Englanders after Jonathan Edwards Sr had more to say that was theological substantive than has been previously believed. We say patient research because while the New England theologians offer researchers a trove of literature—much of it yet to be explored—it mainly consists in sermons and smaller treatises of either a practical or ethical variety, next to nothing systematic. With the publication of Maltby Gelston's (1766–1856), *A Systematic Collection of Questions and Answers in Divinity*, contemporary systematic theologians have access for

---

1. Ahlstrom, *A Religious History of the American People*, 405.

2. The collected works of the most prominent New England theologians are housed in the thirty-seven-volume series, Kuklick, *American Religious Thought of the 18th and 19th Centuries*.

3. The most recent contribution to this literature are the essays contained in Crisp and Sweeney (eds.), *After Edwards: The Courses of the New England Theology*.

4. Crisp, "Penal Non-Substitution," 140–68.

the first time to a concise, organized summary of the theological peculiarities distinctive to the second generation of the tradition that owes its origin
to the so-called Northampton Sage. This singular resource, with its 313 specific doctrinal questions and answers, provides insight into the intellectual
development(s) of New England theology that compare with such early semi-
nal works as Joseph Bellamy's *True Religion Delineated* (1750) and Samuel
Hopkins' *System of Doctrines Contained in Divine Revelation* (1793).

That Gelston's *Systematic Collection* has unique value for systematic
theologians, over and above (or at least complimentary to) the works of
Bellamy and Hopkins, is the chief interest of this editor's introduction
and proceeds in two stages to a conclusion. In the first stage, we lay out
a biographical sketch of Gelston's life. As a means of showing the value of
Gelston's work for contemporary systematic-theological scholarship, in
stage two, we offer up a case study of the doctrine of atonement in New
England theology, comparing Gelston's set of atonement-specific questions
and answers with those works on the atonement of his mentor, Jonathan
Edwards Jr. Our comparative case study develops in the context of the larger
developing New England Theological tradition from the perspective of one
recent and compelling argument for Jonathan Edwards Jr's "Penal Non-
Substitution" model of atonement, put forward by the British philosophical
theologian Oliver Crisp. We conclude with several suggestions for how a
resource such as Gelston's Systematic Collection might best serve the ever-
growing research into this rich and controversial theological period of history. Let us turn our attention first to a brief biographical sketch of Gelston.

I. Biographical Sketch

Reverend Maltby Gelston was born, the only child of Hugh and Phoebe
Gelston, on July 17, 1766 in Southampton, Long Island, New York.[5] His father was a farmer of no mean significance, being a son of what appears to be
a well-known and well-respected merchant and long-time magistrate, Judge
Hugh Gelston of Belfast, Ireland. His mother was the daughter of David
and Phoebe Howell of Southampton, New York. As a child Maltby Gelston
worked on his father's farm, presumably turning his hand at all-things

---

5. The biographical information for Maltby Gelston is gathered from the following sources: Harrison, *A Discourse Delivered . . . at the Funeral of Rev. Maltby Gelston*
(1857); Dexter, *Biographical Sketches of the Graduates of Yale with Annals of the College
History*, Vol. 4, *July 1778–June 1792* (1907), 708–9; Ogden, *An Address Delivered . . .
Union Hall, Jamaica, Long Island* (1842), 4; Franklin, *History of Long Island* (1839),
144–26, 397; Giddings, *The Giddings Family* (1882), 123; Verill (ed.), *Maltby-Maltbie
Family History* (1916), 342–432.

agrarian. At the age of nineteen, after what he later recalled as "prayerful deliberation" and admittedly against his father's wishes—having had desired "to retain his son on the paternal farm, to be the prop and solace of his declining years"—Gelston enrolled at what was then, Yale College. He graduated from Yale with honors in 1791, during the presidential tenure of the famous Edwardsian-antagonist, Ezra Stiles (1727–95).

Immediately following graduation, Gelston began a three-year period of study in practical theology, under the private tutelage of Dr Jonathan Edwards Jr (1745–1801), as was something of a common practice of the period for men seeking the pastorate.[6] It was during this three-year period that Gelston composed his *Systematic Collection*.[7] According to Harrison— Gelston's longtime friend and eulogizer—during the course of his study with Edwards Jr, Gelston "made a public profession of religion" before the Presbyterian Church of Jamaica, Long Island, where he remained an active member until 1794—the same year he apparently completed his *Systematic Collection*. On August 1, 1792, he became the first tutor of Union Hall Academy, not far from his church.

Just two years later, on June 3, 1794, Gelston was ordained to preach by the New Haven Congregational Association in Milford, Connecticut; an appointment he had been apparently seeking for some time. He preached before congregations at West Granville, Massachusetts, and Roxbury, Connecticut and West Rupert, Vermont, before he arrived in small township of Sherman, Connecticut in the fall of 1796, following a brief period of declining health.[8] Though they (the church in Sherman) were in "a low and divided

6. For a helpful resource on ministerial education in New England during this period, see: Gambrell, *Ministerial Education in Eighteenth-Century New England*. More recently, see: Warch, *School of the Prophets: Yale College, 1701–40*; Kling, "New Divinity School of Prophets 1750–1825: A Case Study in Ministerial Education," 185–206; Minkema, "Jonathan Edwards on Education and His Educational Legacy," 31–50; Bezzant, "'Singly, Particularly, Closely': Edwards as Mentor," 228–247.

7. Inscribed on the first page of Gelston's *Systematic Collection*, is a note which reads, "A copy by Maltby Gelston when studying divinity of the questions and answers of Dr. Edwards a son of President Edwards, when he gave instruction in theology in his study in New Haven to young men seeking the ministry—Mills B. Gelston, Ann Arbor, Michigan, 1887." Mills Bordwell Gelston was the seventh child of Maltby Gelston. He was born August 27, 1817 and died of a paralytic stoke February 28, 1903. Like his father, Mills Gelston was educated at Yale College and eventually became a Presbyterian minister to Ann Arbor, Michigan.

8. (Courtesy of Gloria Thorne) Gelston's ledger (c.1832) records some interesting details about the social affairs of the town and his own interaction with its various members, one of which was the town's 'shoemaker,' Willy Bertrum:

Tapping a pair of shoes .12 ½ (cents)

By mending shoe- .03

state, [and] containing only twenty members," Gelston was gladly installed
as minister to the Sherman Congregational church for "100 (GBP) and a few
cords of firewood" per annum on April 26, 1797. Interestingly, Sherman's
historical society records show that the vote to call Gelston occurred in the
early part of January that same year. More interesting still is that amongst
the eighteen individuals who registered to vote in this ecclesiastical proceeding of the "New Fairfield North Society," the final name to appear on
the record is none other than Jonathan Edwards, D.D. The society's decision
to call Gelston into "gospel ministry" was nearly unanimous.[9] Two months
following the decision to install him as minister—something formalized
the following month—Gelston composed two letters to "The people of the
North Society, in New Fairfield." In the first, Gelston clarifies some of the
details of the people's expectations upon him. The following is a portion of
the letter from March 14, 1797:

> Gentlemen,
>
> In all the transactions of a public nature, especially where the
> interest of religion is concerned, a clear and determinate under-
> standing of each other is doubtless esteemed highly important.

Making a pair of shoes-	.50
Mending shoes & boots	.16
Making small pair of shoes-	.40
Making small pair of shoes-	.30
Sole leather 4 pr. Shoes-	.35

The ledger also records a variety of details of Gelston's personal and church related
interactions:

P[ai]d. David Northrop for recording 2 deeds @ .20c ea.

Thomas Hall for repair of windows at Meetinghouse $1.50,

drawing away old steeple .75

Delazon Hungerford — 3 days worth threshing - $1.50

Cloth for pantaloons — $2.16

To John Appleby, a bull — $9.00

Cyrus Hungerford — making pair boots & mending upper leather — $2.75

Eggs — 10 cents doz.

15 pounds nails @ 7 cents # = $1.05

Use of team for the day = .50c.

2 days chopping wood — $2

1 gal. cider = .25c

1 broom = .17c

knitting mittens = .25c

9. We are grateful to Gloria Thorne for supplying us with a transcribed copy of this
document.

On this ground, I would beg leave to request some explanation of one article in the Call, with which you have honored me. The article, to which I refer, is the fifth. On this, one inquiry which arises is; whether in the case of death, the whole of the proposed settlement, or if death take place with a period less than three years from the time of settlement, the whole of what shall be received or may justly have been expected, previous to death, will not be considered as free from the terms of refunding? Another [inquiry], whether in the case of separation, the terms of refunding will not be relinquished, if you Minister, by a council mutually chosen, should be adjudged free from being the blameable cause of the separation?

In the second letter to the "North Society," signalling the council's agreeableness with his previous inquiries, Gelston addresses them no longer as "Gentlemen," but as 'Brethren' and salutes them with "Sentiments of Affection," rather than "Sentiments of Esteem." He writes,

Brethren,

You have thought proper to honor me with a Call, to settle among you in the work of the gospel ministry. It is an expression of friendship, and in its nature and consequences, highly important and interesting. In this view, it has been my endeavor, I trust, to take it into serious consideration; to seek counsel from the God of wisdom, and receive advice from men, in whose opinion and matured experience I have reason to place confidence. After man serious reflection on the subject, I feel ready to declare what, in my present view of things, appears t be duty. As duty ought to be the governing influence of our conduct, the appearance of it, from circumstances and prospects of usefulness, will be received, as are expressions of my feelings. Of your friendly Call, under present prospect, I profess a willingness with cordiality to accept. To my acceptance, I would add a sincere wish that you and myself may, in future, be governed by benevolence, that we may act, in all our proceedings with reference to our proposed union, from a real attachment to the general good; that we may walk worthy of the vocation wherewith we are called, with all lowliness and meekness, with long-suffering, forbearing one another in love; endeavoring to keep with unity of the Christ in the bond of peace.

With sentiments of affection,

Subscribes yours,

To serve in the gospel,

Maltby Gelston

New Fairfield. March 20, 1797.

Once elected, Gelston remained at the Sherman Congregation church, according to Harrison, as their "faithful and judicious servant" for the next forty-five years (and even beyond that as minister emeritus), until his death in 1856.

During Gelston's tenure, 249 persons were added to the church and by all accounts he served as a devoted (and despite his portrait's rather morose appearance) and cheerful minister. As a testimony to his devotion, Gelston left a cache of elegantly hand-written sermon manuscripts (nearly one thousand total),[10] various personal correspondence letters, and the following poem that he composed for the church at some (presumably later) point during his ministry.

Crucifixion

The Son of man they did betray
He was condemned and led away
Think O my soul on that dread day
Look on Mount Calvary.
Behold him lamblike led along
Surrounded by a wicked throng
Accused by each lying tongue
And thus the lamb of God they hung
Upon the shameful tree.

T'was thus the glorious sufferer stood
With hand, and feet nailed to the wood
From every would astream of blood
Came flowing down amain.
His bitter groans all nature shook
And at his voice the rocks were broke.
The sleeping saints their graves forsook
While spiteful Jews around him mock
And laughed at his pain.

10. Thorne estimates that Gelston preached well over two thousand sermons during his ministerial tenure, more than nine hundred manuscripts of which remain catalogued and preserved at the Sherman Historical Society. The remaining sermon manuscripts, Thorne speculates, were either lost or offered to family or other ministers for keepsake.

Now hung between the earth and skies
Behold in agony he dies
O sinners hear his mournful cries
Come see his torturing pain.
The morning sun with drop of light
Blushed and refused to view the sight
The azure clothed in robes of night
All nature mourned and stood afright
When Christ the Lord was slain.

Hark man and angels hear the Son
He cries for help but O there's none
He treads the wine press all alone
His garments stained with blood.
In lamentations hear him cry
Eloi lama sabachthani.
Though death may close his languid eyes
He soon will mount the upper skies
The conquering Son of God!

The Jews and Romans in a land
With hearts like steel around him stand
And mocking say 'Come save the land
Come try yourself to free.'
A soldier pierced him when he died
Then healing streams came from his side
And thus my lord was crucified
Stern justice now is satisfied,
Sinners for you and me.

Behold he mounts the throne of state
He fills the mediatorial seat
While millions lowing at his feet
With loud hosannas tell.
Though he endured exquisite pain
He led the monster death in chains
Ye seraphs raise your loudest strains
With music fell bright Eden's plains
He conquered death and Hell.

'Tis done the dreadful debt is plain
The great atonement now is made
Sinners on him your guilt was laid
For you he spilt his blood.

For you his tender soul did move
For you he left the courts above
That you the length and breadth might prove
And height of depth of perfect love
In Christ your smiling God.

All glory be to God on high
Who reigns enthroned above the sky
Who sent his Son to bleed and die
Glory to him be given
While heaven above his praised resound
O Zion sing his grace abounds
I hope to shout eternal sounds
In flaming love that knows no bounds
When swallowed up in heaven.[11]

Beyond these few historical facts and the testimony to the effectual ministration of his church duties, there is little extent biographical material about Gelston and even less about his time under the instruction of Edwards Jr. This is somewhat problematic at one level. For, we want to be careful not to read Gelston's *Systematic Collection* too far afield from the historical context wherein it was composed. With that in mind, and as there is so scant a record of Gelston's life at the time, his particular place in and value to the New England theological tradition has (for our purposes) a great deal more to do with the particular answers that his *Systematic Collection* supplies us with than it does with the circumstances of its composition. For this reason, let us briefly and more broadly consider the occasion of his composition, after which we will turn our attention to the significance of its content, paying particular attention to what it says about the nature of the atonement.

The occasion for which Gelston's wrote his *Systematic Collection* appears to be in keeping with those activities common to the early New England ministerial tradition, sometimes referred to as the "parsonage seminary." It was commonplace for college educated ministerial candidates, like Gelston, to receive the bulk of their practical instruction from an established local minister. In the case of Gelston, such instruction came from his time with the younger Edwards—a coveted arrangement to be sure. For, after President Edwards' death in 1758, scores of ministerial candidates (again, principally from Yale College), including John Smalley (1734–1820), Jonathan Edwards Jr (1745–1801), Aaron Burr Jr (1756–1836), looked to

---

11. We are grateful to Gloria Thorne for generously supplying us with a manuscript copy of this poem.

Edwards Sr's closest disciples for their private practical-theological educa-tion in the New England way.[12]

This post-graduate education, as it were, in most cases involved various (and sometimes voluminous) assigned readings (especially where a minister, like Joseph Bellamy, for example, possessed such a well-stocked personal library), the regular composition and delivery of sermons from that minster's "desk" (i.e., pulpit), and of chief interest here, the student's task of answering a sort of Edwardsian-specific, catechetically-structured lists of theological questions.[13] The first of these lists to appear was composed by President Edwards himself and was later developed and supplemented (exponentially) by his son, Dr. Edwards. One such list consisted of ninety questions that Edwards Jr expanded to a forbidding 313 questions. Not all of Edwards Jr's ministerial trainees were assigned the take of answering all 313 questions. The number of questions assigned to a candidate perhaps hinged on the degree to which Edwards Jr perceived to be the needs of each individual under his instruction. For what reason we do not know, but in the case of Gelston, all of them were assigned. The intent of this otherwise rigorous ministerial education was apparently both to prepare younger, in-experienced ministers with the demands that would be upon them by their various (socially and economically diverse) congregations and, perhaps more so, to fortify the future of the New England congregational tradition with Edwardsian ideals, the erosion of which had begun no sooner than with the loss of President Edwards himself.

Gambrell's careful study of eighteenth-century ministerial train-ing in New England makes it clear that the disciple who seemed to have most aggressively taken up (and certainly developed) Edwards' educational model was Joseph Bellamy.[14] From the late 1750s up until his death in 1790, Bellamy undertook the private ministerial education of over sixty

---

12. Bellamy undertook the private education over sixty men from the late 1750s almost until his death in 1790. For a comprehensive list of his ministerial students, see: Anderson, "Joseph Bellamy (1719–1790): The Man and his Work," 356–450.

13. Hopkins, *Life and Character of the Late Rev. Mr. Jonathan Edwards*. For example, Samuel Hopkins records that directly upon his assuming the Presidency at New Jersey College (Princeton), Edwards assigned a list of 'questions in divinity' to the senior class. Accordingly, these questions were "to be answered before him [Edwards]; each [stu-dent] having opportunity to study and write what he thought proper upon them. When they came together to answer them, they found so much entertainment and profit by it, especially by the light and instruction Mr. Edwards communicated in what he said upon the questions, when they had delivered what they had to say, that they spoke of it with the greatest satisfaction and wonder," 46–47.

14. Gambrell, *Ministerial Education in Eighteenth-Century New England*, ch. 6.

candidate ministers. Following the outline of his own famous *True Religion Delineated*,[15] Bellamy imbibed his students with a sort of Calvinistically-bent moral philosophy; on one occasion, explicitly entreating them, "to preach a morally reasoned Calvinism."[16]

Bellamy's "school of prophets," as it became known, was arguably the most significant development in the Edwardsian intellectual tradition until Nathaniel William Taylor (1786–1858) and his so-called "New Haven Theology."[17] So pervasive was Bellamy's influence on the subsequent generations of Edwardsians, that it is more likely the case that those who would eventually claim President Edwards as their theological patriarch were more indebted to Bellamy for their theological peculiarities than they were indebted to Edwards.[18] This is perhaps no more evident than by an examination

15. Bellamy's injection of Calvinism into the vein of popular moral and legal discourse was endemic to the New England church and society alike. In the short period following its publication, *True Religion Delineated* had been purchased (in one particular case, sixty copies by the same individual!) and read by nearly everyone in New England. According to Harriet Beecher Stowe, Bellamy's so-called, "Blue book," contained a catalogue of subscribers listing "almost every good old Massachusetts or Connecticut family name." Stowe continues, saying, "Its dissemination was regarded as an act of religious ministry, and there is not the slightest doubt that it was heedfully and earnestly read in every good family of New England; and its propositions were discussed everywhere and by everybody," Stowe, *Oldtown Folks*, 373–75ff.

16. Valeri writes, "According to the regnant moral discourse, doctrine was subject to a test of moral verification, so Bellamy was compelled to demonstrate how Calvinism satisfied the canons of natural law—observable, uniform, and universal principles that . . . upheld the virtue of benevolence. Bellamy assumed that by deducing evangelical doctrine from this moral law, he could meet the objections of his detractors without capitulating to Arminian soteriology and anthropology. He subsequently developed the doctrinal and practical emphases of his Calvinism in terms of moral and legal obligation. He thought that he could affirm the superiority of Calvinist theology without following the Antinomian path away from social and moral obligations," *Law and Providence in Joseph Bellamy's New England*, 56–57. Tryon Edwards (1809–94) later described as proof of Bellamy's "mental Samsonism" and his "almost unequalled power in the desk," was the centralization of the doctrine of God's moral government of all things within his theological system. Edwards, "Memoir," lxiv, lx.

17. For more on the significance of Taylor, see Doug Sweeney's excellent work: *Taylor, New Haven Theology, and the Legacy of Jonathan Edwards*.

18. There are at least three reasons for believing that Bellamy's contribution to the Edwardsian intellectual tradition exceeded that of any other New Divinity thinker, including Edwards' other principal disciple, Samuel Hopkins (1721–1803) and his codification of the so-called New Divinity theology in a *System of Doctrines contained in Divine Revelation*. First, all of Bellamy's most influential New Divinity works (E.g., *True Religion Delineated*; *The Great Evil of Sin, as it is Committed Against God*; *The Law, Our School-Master*; *The Wisdom of God in the Permission of Sin, Vindicated*; *A Blow at the Root of Antinomianism of the Present Age*, predate Hopkins' most significant works, of which there were few. From this it might not even be unreasonable to suppose that

of the continuities and discontinuities that persisted between Edwards, Bellamy, and their successors on doctrine of the atonement—hence our interest in a case study of atonement in Gelston and Jonathan Edwards Jr.[19]

For Bellamy's part, he argued that sin was an infinite insult to God's benevolence and the moral law that reflected it.[20] Thus, Christ's death for sinners was not intended to absolve them of their individual debts to a wrathful God. Rather, it publicly satisfied the unmet demands of the moral law, thereby restoring dignity and honor to a benevolent and merciful God.[21] This emphasis is what has traditionally signaled the supposed point of theological departure for Edwards' successors. For, consequent to such a theological alterations (amongst others)—that Christ satisfied the legal demands of the moral law for everyone—it has been long believed that Bellamy (and those after him) ultimately rejected such fundamental Calvinistic ideas as the doctrine of limited atonement.[22] Accordingly, Bellamy regarded these and other innovations in his moral governmental theology as the surest means to fortifying Calvinist thought in familial, ecclesial, and civic life throughout New England. Ironically, rather than warding off the liberalizing tendencies in New England's theology at the time, Bellamy's innovations, and in particular those developments he made to his doctrine of the atonement, have since been used to show New England theologies eventual undoing.[23]

Hopkins' System of Doctrines had something of a negligible effect upon the already established views of those who had previously studied at Bellamy's so-called, "school of prophets." Following from this is the second reason, namely that Bellamy's "school of prophets" was responsible for the education of the most influential New Divinity leaders of the next generation (For a list of Bellamy's students see: Anderson, "Joseph Bellamy (1719–90): The Man and his Work." 356–450; Third and finally, in the wake of Edwards' death, the correspondence between Bellamy and Hopkins reveals Hopkins' desire for Bellamy to be the spokesman for the New England Calvinists (see: Hopkins to Bellamy, October 8, 1758, HS 81268; Valeri, *Law and Providence in Joseph Bellamy's New England*, 72, n. 36). For a competing sentiment, see: Edwards Amasa Park, *The Atonement: Discourses and Treatises by Edwards, Smalley, Maxcy, Emmons, Griffin, Burge and Weeks, with an Introductory Essay*, lxii-lxiii.

19. Crisp, "The Moral Government of God: Jonathan Edwards and Joseph Bellamy on the Atonement," 78–90.

20. Bellamy, "True Religion Delineated," 345.

21. Ibid., 320–22.

22. "True Religion Delineated," *WJB 1811*, 390–92.

23 For two helpful accounts of conservative theology's descent into liberalism in New England from the mid-eighteenth century, both of which implicate Bellamy's work as a substantive cause, see: Wright, *The Beginnings of Unitarianism in American*; Smith, *Changing Conceptions of Original Sin: A Study of American Theology Since 1750*.

While Bellamy was perhaps the most prodigious producer of second-generation Edwardsians, Hopkins and Edwards Jr certainly played their parts in carrying on the tradition.[24] Hopkins—President Edwards' first biographer and proud purveyor the now famous notion of "Disinterested Benevolence"[25]—like Bellamy, was for a time mentor to Edwards Jr. In fact, it is in all likelihood that Hopkins, whose eventual attempt at the systematization of Edwardsianism (and who had been entrusted by Sarah Edwards with the bulk of her husbands manuscripts), most effectively imbibed Edwards Jr with the catechetical model of instruction that he so effectively carried forward in his own ministerial mentorship.[26] This is especially evident in his mentorship of Gelston. For, as we have already mentioned, during Gelston's three-year period of instruction he was assigned not a portion, but all 313 theological questions that Edwards Jr had compiled. This is part of the reason for Gelston's contemporary significance. Evidence suggests that he was the only one of Edwards Jr's students to have labored in tackling all 313 questions with full and detailed answers, thus making his *Systematic Collection* particularly valuable, in comparison to other (mostly partial) lists of answers that other sources might provide. Interestingly, Gelston appears to have spent the bulk of these three years composing his answers in New York while serving as a sort of interim minister himself, rather than in Edwards Jr's home, as was so often the custom for many parsonage seminaries of the time. Besides his being assigned the colossal task of answering all 313 questions, there are few details that are known about Gelston's particular interaction with his mentor. Perhaps Dr. Edwards' having registered to vote his former pupil into the Sherman church indicates the endurance of their relational interaction and closeness. That no extant personal correspondence—like that which Edwards Sr enjoyed from his friends Hopkins and Bellamy—between Gelston and Edwards Jr remains to seems to invalidate the idea of any perpetual closeness between the two. Toward the end of his life, however, Gelston intimated to Harrison his "high regard" for Dr. Edwards and his theology. Gelston also indicated to him, sounding much like President Edwards, that,

> He read three human systems of theology and one divine; that
> after reading the former he was in doubt which to follow, when

24. Conforti, *Samuel Hopkins and the New Divinity Movement: Calvinism, the Congregational Ministry and Reform in New England between the Great Awakenings.*

25. Ibid., 13. For more detailed treatment of Hopkins and Disinterested Benevolence, see: Post, "Disinterested Benevolence: An American Debate over the Nature of Christian Love," 356–68.

26. Ferm, *Jonathan Edwards the Younger,* ch. 5.

he determined to read the latter, which he did from beginning to end with pen in hand. After this, when a new question of doctrine arose, he went, not to [Samuel] Hopkins, Ridgeley, or [President] Edwards, to see what they said, but to the Word of God, to see how it compared with that.[27]

Such praise bespeaks not only a respect for the tradition that Gelston no doubt, self-consciously conscripted himself to under Edwards Jr. It also suggests the theological endurance of the early doctrinal summaries that make up his *Systematic Collection*. For this reason, despite the lack of further, more intimate, details about his life, Gelston's significance for our better understanding the development of the New England theological tradition is beyond question. Let us now turn our attention to the developments surrounding the doctrine of atonement in early New England Theology.

II. New England *Dogmatics?* A Case Study of the Atonement

There are a variety of ways we might consider and weigh the significance of Gelston's *Systematic Collection*. One particularly fruitful possibility is to treat Gelston's work as a principal resource in the following case study. To this end, in what remains of this introduction, we present a brief case study of the doctrine of atonement and its development amongst the New England theologians. This will be less of an exercise in historical theology, and more of a systematic theological inquiry. That is, our interest in Gelston's *Systematic Collection* has primarily to do with whether it might cast any new theological light on a recently rekindled discussion of the atonement in Edwards and his successors.

For those acquainted with New England religious historiography proximate to the theological legacy of Jonathan Edwards, the phrase "New England dogmatics" might sound like something of a contradiction. For, there may well be no other Protestant theological tradition that, having emerged from a single source, had so quickly and so erratically developed, and had yet come to such a sudden and still curious end. This is precisely what makes the ensuing proposal so interesting. For, there is more to the story that is

27. Harrison, *A Discourse Delivered*, 18. Bezzant rightly points the impertinence that such thinking would have been to Gelston's mentor at the time, were it to have been made public. According to Bezzant, "Such an attitude in [President] Edwards stood in stark relief to the later reputation of those in the New Divinity, who, it was said, developed quite hierarchical conceptions of master and learner, in which refusal to accept the received wisdom of the theological system was met with disapproval," "Edwards as Mentor," 237–38.

significant to warrant contemporary attention than has traditionally been be-lieved. In this way, we are not suggesting that Gelston's *Systematic Collection* somehow provides justification for our re-visioning the development of New England theology as a whole. Our proposal is far more modest. With this editors' introduction we want to join a growing number of scholars in etch-ing away at the still fairly entrenched historical narrative of so-called "decline and fall"[28] that still characterizes the trajectory of Edwards' thinking amongst his successors—something that has traditionally had a great deal to do with the doctrine of atonement.[29] In this way, the difference between our proposal here and the recent revisionist proposals about the doctrine of atonement in Edwards and his successors in contemporary literature amounts to simple difference in the angle from which we are looking, and Gelston's *Systematic Collection* provides just such a vantage.

With all this in mind, the remainder of this introduction unfolds in three parts to a conclusion. Following a brief sketch of President Edwards on the penal substitutionary nature of the atonement—a way of demarcat-ing the theological landscape, as it were, with which we are principally concerned—in the first part we lay out a sort of synthetic account of the so-called moral government model of atonement that has traditionally characterized Edwards' successors. Then, in part two, we consider a recent account of Jonathan Edwards Jr's moral government model offered up by Oliver Crisp. In the part three, we lay out evidence that suggests that Ed-wards Jr's model of what Crisp calls "Penal Non-Substitution" is doctrinally "thicker" than Crisp suggests. We then pivot to a discussion of the dozen or so questions and answers about the atonement that Gelston's *Systematic Col-lection* offers and consider how his answers to these questions bear upon our understanding of the atonement as it developed in New England around the time of the American Revolution. Here too, as with Edwards J., we will see evidence that some version of the doctrine of penal substitution, though diminished in part, remains a piece of the doctrinal furniture of this second generation Edwardsian. Let us turn now and briefly consider President Ed-wards on the atonement after which we layout our synthetic approach to the moral government model of atonement.

28. The *locus classicus* for the decline and fall narrative of New England theology is found in Haroutunian, *Piety Versus Moralism*. Arguably, the most helpful treatment of this dominant historiography is put forward by Brietenbach in "Piety and Moralism," 177–204. See also: Valeri, *Law and Providence*, ch. 2.

29. Various iterations of the development of an atonement theory in New England theology appear in: Evans, *Imputation and Impartation*, 101–2; Stephens, "An Appeal to the Universe," 55–72; Guelzo, *Edwards on the Will*, 134–5; Ferm, *Jonathan Edwards the Younger*, 114–16. Rudisill, *The Doctrine of the Atonement*; Foster, *A Genetic*; Boardman, *A History of New England Theology*.

II.1. Atonement and the Moral Government of God

Until recently, and for more than a century, scholars have maintained that President Edwards' musings about the atonement gave rise to a form of the moral government theory of the atonement that his successors embraced and developed, (roughly) according to which Christ dies in order to satisfy the rectoral rather than the retributive demands of God's moral law.[30] In this way, Christ performs the work of a penal example, whereby he vindicates God's moral law and government without vicariously substituting himself for particular individuals, as in the case of penal substitution. Christ thus satisfies the legal demands of the moral law for everyone, not as a means of releasing them from their individual and particular debts to divine retribution. Rather, Christ dies to satisfy the unmet demands of the moral law, which in turn restores dignity or honor to God—the lawmaker.

This atonement narrative has seemingly reached a point of argumentative entropy in the literature, what with evidence that has more recently been held out that recommends President Edwards' subscription to a version of the penal substitution theory of atonement. On this theory, Christ willingly assumes the legal responsibility for the sin(s) of human beings and by his substitutionary death pays their debt of punishment in order to satisfy God's retributive rather than his rectoral justice.[31] The recent suggestion that the so-called Northampton Sage may in fact have articulated such a doctrine has in part motivated a set of serious inquests into his successor's doctrinal formulations, the most serious of which have been put forward in two articles by Oliver Crisp.[32] In the first, Crisp directs his attention to Bellamy's doctrine of atonement and convincingly recasts the "decline-and-fall narrative" as a story of doctrinal development—a move that has motivated much of the ensuing analysis. In the second article, Crisp offers up a thoroughgoing and rigorously systematic analysis of Edwards Jr's doctrine of atonement. Crisp's

30. The Moral Government model of atonement comes in a surprising variety of expressions. Traditionally, though perhaps mistakenly, the first to articulate a Moral Government model was Hugo Grotius (1583–1645), the Dutch (Arminian) theologian, and jurist (this has recently been contested; see: Williams, "A Critical").

31. According to Packer, there is no single paradigm that accounts for all iterations of the doctrine of penal substitution. Nevertheless he locates certain features or aspects common to most accounts, aspects including: 1) the retributive demands of divine justice, 2) the necessity of the atonement, 3) the substitutionary and penal nature of atonement, and 4) the infinite, objective value of Christ's vicarious sacrifice; see: Packer, "What Did the Cross Achieve?" 3–46.

32. See e.g.: Crisp, "Penal Non-Substitution," 299–327 (hereafter, *RCPT*); Crisp, "The Moral Government of God," 78–90; Cooley and Sweeney, "The Novelty of the New Divinity;" Cooley, "The New England Theology and Atonement"

analysis of Edwards Jr ultimately distances him from the possibility—if his father did hold to some version of the penal substitution theory—that he carried on this aspect of the Reformed theological tradition.

So in order to distinguish, better still, isolate Edwards Jr's thinking about the moral government theory from his fellow Edwardsians, let us consider a sort of "core sample" of features of the New England version of the moral government theory.[33] By core sample we mean a sort of collation of ideas about the atonement that developed during the first, second, and third generations of Edwards' intellectual tradition. Such a survey will bring us close to the heart of our understanding what it means for New England theologians to have been harangued with a decline and fall narrative until recently. For the sake of brevity and clarity, we set out this core sample in the following series of numbered theses, interspersed with both primary source evidence and some explanatory comments. For a more detailed discussion of these some of these features, we direct our readers elsewhere.[34] We begin with:

1) God is the moral governor of the universe.[35]

That is, God is the supreme authority over all creation, including his morally responsible creatures. God's government is his power, according to which his infinite wisdom and unfathomable divine will are exercised over his creatures to direct them to their various appointed ends. God's moral government describes his specific interaction with rational creatures.

33. Joseph Bellamy was the first of the New England theologians to articulate what has been traditionally characterized as a full-scale moral government theory of atonement. His account was in many ways formulaic for many later Edwardsians, including Samuel Hopkins, Jonathan Edwards Jr, Edwards Amasa Park, amongst other. Bellamy's *True Religion Delineated* (1750) is commonly regarded as the first expression of the moral government theory in America. Its wild success is recorded in such works as: Stowe, *Oldtown Folks*, 373–75; Valeri, *Law and Providence*. For more on the relationship between Bellamy and Edwards and an explanation of the so-called "endorsement story," see: Crisp, "The Moral Government of God," 78–90.

34. Park, "The Rise of the Edwardian Theory of the Atonement." For some helpful and rather critical interaction with Parks essay, see: Cooke, "Edwards on the Atonement," 97–120. Works comparable to the value of Parks' essay, include: Bellamy, *True Religion Delineated*; Edwards Jr, "On the Necessity of the Atonement," 1–42; Edwards Jr, "Remarks on the Improvements," 481–92; Edwards Jr, "Thoughts on the Atonement;" West, *The Scripture Doctrine of the Atonement.*

35. "When moral creatures are brought into existence, there must be a moral government. It cannot be reconciled with the wisdom and goodness of God, to make intelligent creatures and leave them at random, without moral law and government" (Edwards Jr, "On the Necessity of the Atonement," 6).

President Edwards himself had a robust doctrine of God's moral government, commenting,

> Hereby it becomes manifest, that God's moral government over mankind, his treating them as moral agents, making them the objects of his commands, counsels, calls, warnings, expostulations, promises, threatenings, rewards and punishments, is not inconsistent with a determining disposal of all events, of every kind, throughout the universe, in his providence; either by positive efficiency or permission.[36]

This brings us to our second thesis:

2) God governs his rational creatures by instituting the moral law.[37]

For Edwards and his successors alike, the moral law is the means by which God displays the righteousness of his self-love, makes his moral perfection and holiness comprehensible to the creature, and threatens those who despise his general benevolence toward and authority over his rational creatures.[38] Again, consider Edwards, who writes:

36. Edwards, *WJE* 1:431 (Edwards discusses God's moral government at varying lengths throughout his works. For some of his more detailed discussion, see: "Miscellanies" nos. 13, 102, 119, 132, 137, 177, 346, 422, 525, 547, 651, 661 n. 5, 702, 742, 752, 760, 762, 954, 1039, 1183, 1196, 1299; "Concerning the End for which God Created the World," *WJE* 8:429, 488–99).

37. According to Park, "The moral law is a transcription of the divine perfections, and all God's government is designed to unfold his own true character, and exhibit a genuine picture of it to the world. Accordingly, we may forever expect to see his mind written, and his character as indubitably expressed, in what he does, as in what he says, in the government which he exercises, as in the law which he has given," *The Atonement*, lxvii). In this passage, Park quotes West, *The Scripture Doctrine of the Atonement*, 23, 25, 26, 66, 88, 112, 114, 150, 153.

38. Edwards writes elsewhere that "this was the grand rule given to Adam; and the command of not eating the forbidden fruit was only given to try whether he would keep God's commands or no, to try whether he would be obedient to the law of nature, or moral law. As the moral law was the grand law given to the children of Israel in the wilderness, and is often called THE LAW, and is spoken of as THE LAW given to them, and the time of the giving of the Ten Commands is spoken of as the time of the giving the law, as if that had been the whole of the law given—and indeed, it was virtually so—and all those ceremonial laws that were added were only for the trial of their obedience to the great rules of this law, as particularly "thou shalt have no other gods before me," etc.: it was to try whether they would keep that moral law, the rules of which required that they should love God with all their heart, with all their souls, and with all their mind, and all their strength, and regard his authority and glory, and submit themselves wholly to him, and yield themselves up to him, and obey and serve him as their God' ("Miscellanies" n. 884, *WJE* 20:144). See also: "Blank Bible," *WJE* 24:702, 1125.

The chief and most fundamental of all the commands of the moral law requires us "to love the Lord our God with all our hearts and with all our souls, with all our strength, and all our mind": that is plainly, with all that is within us, or to the utmost capacity of our nature: all that belongs to, or is comprehended within the utmost extent or capacity of our heart and soul, and mind and strength, is required. God is in himself worthy of infinitely greater love, than any creature can exercise towards him: he is worthy of love equal to his perfections, which are infinite: God loves himself with no greater love than he is worthy of when he loves himself infinitely: but we can give God no more than we have.[39]

By including references to President Edwards amongst these number theses we are intentionally trying to draw attention to the fact that are indeed doctrinal continuities regarding the moral government of God that are rightly labelled "Edwardsian." Given this, the following thesis is a fairly critical distinction that Edwards' successor made with some frequency is arguably the principal point of theological departure of the Edwardsians from their mentor.

> 3) God's moral government is revoked by sin, which, strictly speaking, is an offence against the moral law, not God.

By making the moral law the measure of sin's offence and thus ensuring that the problem that the atonement solves is a punitive one—an offence that requires the satisfaction of God's retributive justice—they end up supplanting the idea that Christ's work is in any way a substitutionary act.[40] Edwards Amasa Park explains:

---

39. Edwards, "The Great Doctrine of Original Sin Defended," *WJE* 3:141.

40. This move may well be as much an ecclesial manoeuvre as it is a theological one. Consider that the generation following Edwards' death was marked by ecclesial difficulties consisting chiefly in a lack of authority. Mark Valeri argues that Edwards' chief successor, Joseph Bellamy, in his *True Religion Delineated*, attempted to wed his theological determinism to the language of the "moral discourse of Enlightenment ethics," convinced that the only hope for the doctrinal rehabilitation of New England was to demonstrate publicly the indispensability of divine authority to the virtue of the moral law. See: Bellamy, "True Religion Delineated," 50, 51. See also: Valeri, *Law and Providence*, 42, 49, 51; Erskine to Bellamy: Jan. 26, 1753, HS document number 81199, Joseph Bellamy Papers, Boxes 187–90, Folders 2929–64, Case Memorial Library, Hartford Seminary, Hartford, Connecticut. According to Valeri, "Bellamy's burden was to elucidate this axiom in a way that rendered experimental Calvinism ethically compelling" (*Law and Providence*, 50).

Our Lord suffered pains, which were substituted for the penalty of the law, and may be called punishment in the more general sense of the word, but were not strictly and literally the penalty which the law had threatened. . . . The humiliation, pains, and death of our redeemer were equivalent in meaning to the punishment threatened in the moral law, and thus they satisfied Him who is determined to maintain the honor of this law, but they did not satisfy the demands of the law itself for our punishment. . . . The active obedience [of Christ], viewed as the holiness of Christ was honorable to the law, but was not a work of supererogation, performed by our Substitute, and then transferred and imputed to us, so as to satisfy the requisitions of the law for our own active obedience.[41]

This brings us to our fourth thesis:

4) Sin requires atonement in order to satisfy the penal consequences of retributive justice, which rectoral justice demands by the moral law.[42]

This too is quite an important point of distinction. For where penal substitution demands that the offender suffer a penalty, rectoral justice has clear penal implications and Christ must suffer these implications in order to restore the honor that is due God's moral law; the difference here being that Christ suffers this penal as an example, not as a substitute for any individual. And this leads us to our final thesis:

5) Christ makes atonement, not as a penal substitute but as a penal example, making it possible for God to forgive sin.[43]

41. Park, *The Atonement*, xiii–x.

42. Edwards Jr, "On the Necessity of the Atonement," 8–9. Compare with, "The atonement is the substitute for the punishment threatened in the law; and was designed to answer the same ends of supporting the authority of the law, the dignity of the divine moral government, and the consistency of the divine conduct in legislation and execution. By the atonement it appears that God is determined that his law shall be supported; that it shall not be despised or transgressed with impunity; and that it is an evil and a bitter thing to sin against God. The very idea of an atonement or satisfaction for sin, is something which, to the purposes of supporting the authority of the divine law, the dignity and consistency of the divine government, is equivalent to the punishment of the sinner, according to the literal threatening of the law."

43. Bellamy, *True Religion Delineated*, 60. See also, "The design of the incarnation, life and death of the Son of God, was to give a practical declaration, in the most public manner, even in the sight of the whole intellectual system, that God was worthy of all that love, honor, and obedience, which his law required, and that sin was as great an evil as the punishment threatened supposed; and so to declare God's righteousness, and

In other words, Christ's death for sinners was never intended to absolve them from their individual debts of punishment to God. Rather, Christ's death publicly satisfied sins impunities against the moral law, making the forgiveness of the sins of individuals possible.[44]

Now, insofar as these five thesis reflect a core sample of those ideas expressed by Edwardsians on the moral government, we can make three summary observations that puts initially seems to put greater theological distance between Edwards and his successors on the matter of the atonement. We shall limit ourselves to just three brief observations in order to bring sufficient shape to the foregoing theses, and to set up our discussion of Crisp's penal non-substitution.

First, we note that for Edwards and his successors alike, the atonement is a distinctly punitive matter. The precise reason for which Christ absorbs this penalty is, however, a question for which Edwards and his successors have markedly different answers. For Edwards, and his doctrine of penal substitution, Christ absorbs the penalty for the sin(s) of particular individuals through his vicarious suffering and death. For later Edwardsians, such as Bellamy or Hopkins or Park, and more specifically for Edwards Jr, the penalty that Christ absorbs is not person-specific, that is, Christ does not die for any particular person(s).[45] Second, we observe that for Edwards, Christ's death is directed primarily toward satisfying God's retributive justice. For his successors, on the other hand, it is principally rectoral justice for which Christ dies, not the rectoral justice that God requires, but that required by his moral law. Herein lies the apparent mechanism of the Edwardsian doctrine of atonement, which is our third observation. For the Edwardsians, sin appears to be an offence against the moral law, not God. This is perhaps the sharpest distinction between Edwards and his successors. A detailed account of this distinction is something that requires further consideration and is beyond the scope of our purposes here. It is a problem that certainly has more than one explanation. There are three things we ought to understand about this distinction. According to the Edwardsians: 1) God can somehow be entirely insulated from direct insult(s) to his nature; 2) God is chiefly concerned with rectoral rather than retributive justice; and 3) atonement requires that Christ dies as a penal example rather than a penal substitute. With all this in mind, having now a birds-eye-view of what is at stake for the

---

condemn the sins of an apostate world, to the end [that] God might be just, and yet a justifier of the believer. And this he did by dying in our room and stead" (Bellamy, "An Essay," 378; see also: West, *Scripture Doctrine of the Atonement*, ch. 2).

44. Bellamy, *True Religion Delineated*, 320–22.

45. Particular attention is paid to this observation in Crisp's, "The Moral Government of God," 85–90.

New England moral government model, we transition to Crisp's account of Jonathan Edwards Jr's doctrine of Penal Non-Substitution.

II.2. Crisp, Edwards Jr, and Penal Non-Substitution

According to Crisp, Edwards Jr puts forward a fairly robust model of atonement that deserves the attention of contemporary scholarship, not least for which, its having developed (though often unnoticed and certainly under appreciated) at such a unique period and place in the history of theology. In order to re-invigorate this otherwise diminished model, Crisp exposits the theory for contemporary analysis. Interestingly, in as much as Crisp's efforts to retrieve Edwards Jr's model for analysis, it is Crisp's analysis of Edward Jr that deserves further consideration. For, a wider look at Edwards Jr's works points both to his development of Crisp's so-called penal non-substitution model, and rather curiously, what appears to be a version of the doctrine of penal substitution model of atonement. Our engagement with Crisp's work serves the purpose of showing that the New England model of atonement is perhaps more complex or "thicker" (to borrow a term from Crisp) than Crisp's account boasts. Indeed, there is far more that is of profitable interest in the literature of the Edwardsians than is often recognized in contemporary theology, especially as it relates to the atonement, divine honor, divine justice, the moral law, and legal debts. Let us begin by considering Crisp's five components of Edwards Jr's theory of atonement:

A—Necessity of Atonement

Crisp begins by unpacking a common assumption of moral government theories, namely that they do not necessitate the atonement. According to Crisp, the Edwardsian version of the governmental model does in fact necessarily requires the atonement. Drawing recourses from Francis Turretin, Crisp explains the fine-grained distinction between to types of necessity: hypothetical necessity and absolute necessity. On hypothetical necessity, the atonement is, first, merely the most fitting way for to solve the problem of humanities sin against God, and, second, it is contingent on other divinely ordained features of redemption.[46] On absolute necessity, divine retribution is not necessary for penal non-substitution. According to Crisp, "Defenders of penal non-substitution regard the atonement as a means of vindicating the moral law and government of God, rather than as a means to satisfying

---

46. Crisp, "Penal Non-Substitution," 145–48.

divine retributive justice."[47] This leads Crisp to the conclusion that Edwards Jr's model could be developed according to either form of necessity.

It is true that the Grotian version of the moral government theory implicitly rejects an absolute necessity concerning punishment. Accordingly, rectoral justice is independent from retributive justice (where God's justice is penal in nature rather than his right governing of the moral order through the moral law). In this way, God's righteous governance of the world is primary in terms of his justice, and his retributive justice could be deferred. This is not to say that God would not also be just in his act of retribution, this act is not necessary—if he so deems. In a similar fashion, the Edwardsian theory can articulate the logic of the atonement, as fundamentally depending upon either atonement made for governing the world or retribution. The Edwardsian theory depends upon an absolute necessity in this sense. Accordingly, a contemporary defender of penal non-substitution can supply a rationale for God's ongoing governance of the world through Christ's act as a penal non-substitute. Human sin is acquitted, individually, based on the human response to the benefits made in Christ's act. However, as stated above, the theory could retrieve from the early nineteenth century Methodist theologian, John Miley, a hypothetically necessary atonement because it seems peculiar that God could not bring about atonement in another way in any possible world. Crisp summarizes what is at stake for the necessity of the atonement in three parts. First, "Atonement was necessary for the salvation of some number of fallen human beings." Second, as "Some act of atonement was necessary for the salvation of some number of fallen human beings." Third and finally, as "A particular act of atonement was necessary for the salvation of some number of fallen human beings."[48] On a hypothetical necessity understanding of penal non-substitution, atonement becomes necessary based on God's ordination to save the "elect" and to provide the atonement by one particular means—Christ's act on the cross. Thus, the atonement is neither random nor is it based on the divine will alone.[49]

Again, what we aim to show next is that not only did Edwards Jr (also represented in the tradition he inspired—Gelston) affirm penal non-substitution, but penal substitution with some elements of the governmental theory. Accordingly, we will see that retribution is fundamental for penal substitution and that rectoral justice is dependent upon it—retribution is necessary for the moral government of the world and God's moral

47. Ibid., 148.
48. Crisp, "Penal Non-Substitution," 148–51.
49. Ibid., 152.

government fits into his providential control. And with this we transition into Crisp's discussion of:

B—Divine will, moral law, and atonement

There appears to be a deeper problem with the moral government theory of atonement. The problem seems to amount to the notion that God is supremely free to save in the manner he chooses. This means that laws are always contingent upon divine arbitration—laws are mutable, and are not internal to God's nature—and as such not binding on God in any way. Some would call this "legal voluntarism" where the moral law(s) are rooted in an act of God's will alone. The contemporary defender of legal voluntarism can avert the challenge in two ways. First, he can defend a modified voluntarism. On a modified voluntarism, the moral law is based upon the divine will, this is true, but the divine will is somehow always reflecting of the divine nature in the human context. In this way, if God's moral law is primarily rectoral in nature, and this somehow reflects his nature, then it is perfectly within his right and just to relax the punitive consequences of the law, once again, so long as God has made right the moral order in which humans find themselves. The moral law, in some sense, then, is binding on God, once it is set in motion, because it reflects his nature and is contingent up what has already been divinely determined about the moral order in which he has created humans. In a similar way, a defender of penal non-substitution could affirm a non-voluntaristic doctrine of the moral law. By claiming that the law is not primarily based in divine volition, but that the law is an extension of the divine character where God must act in such a way as to satisfy the highest law—the goodness of the eternal law.[50]

The questions that most concern us here is the necessity and nature of divine justice and, more than that, the divine motivation as they relate to the moral law and human transformation. These important distinctions are fundamental to both New England theology and contemporary models of justice and the atonement. For, the apparent de-coupling the rectoral and retributive justice in the thought Edwards Jr is a crucial aspect for our understanding the Edwardsian doctrine of atonement. However, we understand Gelston and the Edwardsian tradition to affirm a penal substitution of a modified sort. What we mean by this is not that rectoral justice is fundamental, in a non-voluntarist or voluntarist sense, but that retributive justice is fundamental to God's moral governing of the world (within God's providence). So, Christ as a penal substitute becomes central in God's governance of human beings. Another question we raise, is whether rectoral justice or retributive

50. Crisp, "Penal Non-Substitution," 153–57.

justice are fundamentally a payment made to the moral law or is it a payment made to God himself? By differentiating within New England dogmatics, the atonement options are expanded for contemporary discussions. Rather provocatively, we think that within these discussions the atonement theories are a more complex, with several new vignettes than may have been thought to this point. For it seems that there are at least three models of the atonement at work in the Edwardsian tradition that have relevance to contemporary atonement. Let us move on to Crisp's next point.

C—Sin and Its Penal Consequences

The third component of the moral government model or penal non-substitution concerns the nature of sin and its penal consequences. Both penal substitution and penal non-substitution affirm that there is some debt of punishment required for re-establishing the sin-fractured relationship between God and humanity. Both Grotian and Edwardsian variants of the moral government model involve maintain that sin requires a penalty— "non-transferable" penalty. This is because guilt is not transferable either between humans or between divine-human and other humans. Penal substitution on the other hand, says that the penal consequence of a guilty sinner is transferable. Herein lies the mechanism of the atonement—the consequences from human sin are transferred to Christ and Christ pays the debt of punishment for those sinners (of the world or the elect). Distinctively, what is required is not a debt of punishment on penal non-substitutionary atonement, but a penal equivalent to satisfy the demands of the moral law. Atonement, then, is construed more communally in virtue of God's means of governing the world. An actual, individual payment to God for sins committed is thus not required. Instead, a "suitable equivalent" must pay the penalty for the disorder in God's moral order where humans have failed to honor God's means of governance. There is an imbalance in the force or the moral order hindering the means by which God has chosen to providentially orchestrate the world toward its proper end. Christ, then, brings about balance by paying the penalty as a "suitable equivalent."[51]

Several important questions emerge from this discussion that concern the relation between Christ and the moral law, and, for that matter, the relation the moral law has to the divine nature or the eternal law. We are led to think, contra Crisp, that Edwards Jr affirmed a variant of penal substitution where Christ's act of atonement brought about balance in God's moral order by transferring the penal consequences of human sin to himself on the cross. Below we signal some important data from Gelston that might be

51. Crisp, "Penal Non-Substitution," 157–58.

suggestive in this direction. The contemporary questions deserving attention that follow from this such a discussion include some of the following: Does Christ make a payment to the moral law, to God himself or to both in some sense? Is a non-transferable payment made sufficient for human atonement for sin? In what sense is Christ's payment truly penal in nature? Are there other options available like the possibility that Christ pay a penal payment to the law that somehow multiply repeatable rather than a discrete penal payment made individually?

D—The *Solutio Tantidem*

In the fourth part of Crisp's account of Dr. Edwards' penal non-substitution model, he offers some explanation of the concept of the so-called "suitable equivalence" of Christ's sacrifice. It is in this part where we can see what is perhaps the most significant difference between the Northampton Sage and his son. Suitable equivalence has to do with several tightly woven together concepts. Crisp fixes on two concepts in particular. First, whether the death of Christ is of a sufficient weight, as it were, to tip the scales on the penal demands of the moral law. Or put differently, whether Christ's death can be treated "as if it were the moral equivalent to the sin of humanity."[52] Second, whether or not the problems of (and therefore the solutions to) the retributive and rectoral demands of divine justice can be individuated one from the other. Upon reviewing the several explicit comments about the suitable equivalence of Christ's made by some of those later New England theologians, Crisp argues that on penal non-substitution, "Christ's suffering on the cross was not a species of penal substitution."[53] This, as the comments clearly show, is because while Christ was thought to have suffered a penalty of some sort, he suffered it specifically to meet the demands of the moral law, not as a substitute for individual persons. Crisp is careful to note, against several recent accounts of penal non-substitution, that for Dr. Edwards, Christ's work remained an objective, though not supererogatory act.

E—Suitable Equivalent and Acceptation

In a related point, Crisp thoughtfully goes on to show how Edwards Jr considers that Christ could in fact have suffered less than he actually did suffer and still have offset the penal demands for human transgressions against the moral law has some interesting links to the medieval doctrine of "acceptation." Here, Crisp distinguishes between what he aptly refers to as a "thin"

52. Crisp, *RCPT*, 314.
53. Ibid., 312.

versus a "thick" doctrine of Christ's equivalent suffering for sin. "Thin," because the accumulated penal consequence(s) of human suffering may in fact
not have required a corresponding infinite equivalent to offset their demands;
something he says is likely not the case for Edwards Jr. "Thick" because,
alternatively, it may be the case (and likely is for Edwards Jr) that because
sins against a being of infinite value require an infinite punishment, that the
only suitable equivalent for such offenses much be of corresponding infinite
value, and thus offered up by an infinite person, namely Christ. Following his
assignment of this latter account to Edwards Jr, Crisp further discriminates
between what he calls a "thicker" and a "plain thick" version of the "thick"
view of the equivalence of Christ's suffering. According to "thicker" version,
Crisp describes Edwards Jr's assertion that "any amount of suffering endured
by Christ is of a qualitatively different nature to any suffering that might be
endured by someone who is merely human"; something he says of Edwards
Jr is "counterintuitive."[54] The "plain thick" view, to the contrary, Crisp claims
avoids the fallout that seems to be entailed by the "thicker" view, which says
that Christ's hitting his thumb with a hammer, as it were, is an infinite suffering like his death on the cross appears to be. Crisp shows that Edwards Jr's
consideration of supposed thickness of Christ's equivalent suffering is not
discordant with his earlier assertions regarding Edwards Jr's thinking about
the necessity of the atonement.

Crisp is altogether correct to claim that the son of the Northampton
Sage contributed a great deal more to the development of the New England
theological tradition than he is often credited with.[55] The preceding should
no doubt make this point clearly. His account of Edwards Jr's doctrine of
penal non-substitution is thoroughgoing and convincing. It is, however, not
without its own vulnerability. For there is evidence that suggests that Crisp's
account of Edwards Jr's thinking about atonement is itself "thicker" than we
have been lead to believe. Upon this suggestion we transition to consider
several important comments that Edwards Jr makes about the atonement
that lend support to the idea that he had a place in his thinking for the
penal substitution model after all. By considering these comments, we are
not interested so much in how to reconcile this anomaly. It is enough for
us, as we move on to Gelston, to point it out in hopes of provoking more
systematic-theological research into this century-long debate. Let us turn
now our attention to two important sources in Edwards Jr's works.

54. Ibid., 316.

55. For more on his significance to the Edwardsian tradition, see: Ferm, *Jonathan
Edwards the Younger*.

II.3. A "Thicker" Reading of Edwards Jr on Atonement

Of the variety of theological writings that offer some additionally detailed insight into the development of his father's legacy regarding the atonement, there are two works in particular that shed some help light on Edwards Jr's thoughts about the work of Christ. It is here where we shall see that Crisp's account of Dr. Edwards' model of atonement is itself "thicker" than Crisp makes it out to be. The first work to shed more light on this matter is his *Thoughts on the Atonement*, echoes of which appear in a second piece by Edwards Jr, called "Remarks on the Improvements Made in Theology by His Father, President Edwards." In both cases, the younger Edwards makes several curious statements that point in the direction of his ascent to something along the lines of a penal substitution model of atonement. Let us consider a few such statements from the good Doctor's works, and then consider their significance to the larger account of his doctrine of atonement, after which we will turn out attention to Gelston. Dr. Edwards writes,

> By atonement, I mean something done or suffered, which, to the purpose of supporting the honor and dignity of the divine law and government, shall be equivalent to the punishment of the sinner according to law. Therefore, the atonement made by Christ implies his substitution in the stead of the sinner, who is to be saved by him; or that he suffered that in the sinner's stead, which as effectually tended to discourage, or prevent transgression, and excite to obedience, as the punishment of the transgressor himself, according to the letter of the law would have done.[56]

In another place he maintains,

> The atonement is the substitute for the punishment threatened in the law; and was designed to answer the same ends of supporting the authority of the law, the dignity of the divine moral government, and the consistency of the divine conduct in legislation and execution. By the atonement it appears that God is determined that his law shall be supported; that it shall not be despised or transgressed with impunity; and that it is an evil and a bitter thing to sin against God. The very idea of an atonement or satisfaction for sin, is something which, to the purposes of supporting the authority of the divine law, the dignity and consistency of the divine government, is equivalent to the

---

56. Edwards Jr, "On Necessity of the Atonement," 1–42; Edwards Jr, "Remarks on the Improvements," 481–92 and "Thoughts on the Atonement," 493–508.

punishment of the sinner, according to the literal threatening of the law.[57]

From these statements, it is clear that the idea of substitution goes hand in hand with the legal/penal aspect of the atonement in the way Edwards Jr thinks about Christ's work. The question for us is how Dr. Edwards can affirm both something that sounds quite like penal substitution and at the same time, the penal non-substitution model that Crisp labors (convincingly) to illumine. Part of the answer to this question has to do with the way that President Edwards and his son make sense of two aspects of the atonement. First, the nature of owing a debt versus owing a debt of punishment. Second, the direction of sins offense—whether it be an offense directed toward God or his moral law or both. So, before we turn our attention to Gelston's account of atonement, let us briefly consider these two aspects, as they appear first in President Edwards' works and then in the works of Edwards Jr.

II.3.1 Debts and Debts of Punishment

Penal substitution invites some of its greatest criticisms from the idea that Christ's death is equivalent to his absorbing the penalty for the sin of humanity. Or to put it differently, that the work of Christ is a payment of humanity's debt of punishment. This is quite a subtle and nevertheless critically important distinction from Christ's work being construed as payment for a debt *simpliciter*. Not understanding the difference between the nature of a simple debt and a debt of punishment is to miss the substance of penal substitution altogether. And the difference is this: to owe God a debt of punishment is to owe a debt specifically for an offence that requires humanity (the debtor) suffer loss by suffering a punishment equivalent to their offence(s).[58] This is the work of Christ on the penal substitution model, namely, to suffer loss by paying humanity's debt of punishment to God's retributive justice. To owe God a debt of any other sort is to owe God for something that requires that God (the creditor) not suffer loss. The work of Christ in this light fits more than one model of atonement. And it is in this distinction—between debts and debts of punishment—where the tension in Edwards' and his son's account of divine justice and atonement appears. This tension has two parts. The first tension we will see by way of a contrast between what a debt

---

57. Edwards Jr, "On the Necessity of the Atonement," 8–9.

58. Lewis, *RCPT*, 329 (emphasis added). According to Lewis, "in the case of a debt, what is required is that the creditor shall not suffer a loss. Whereas in the case of a debt of punishment what is required is that the debtor shall suffer a loss."

demands and what a debt of punishment demands and we will see the second by understanding the direction, as it were, of sins offence.

First, notice that a debt of punishment requires that transgressors (or more accurately, Christ) suffer loss. In this way, the penal substitution model is surprisingly anthropocentric in terms of its chief goal, in that the problem facing sinners is not a matter of their failed effort to restore anything to God, so much as it is with his exacting a penalty from them (or again, Christ). President Edwards says as much about this sort of judicial demand in several places throughout his work. For example, he argues that,

> God declares that those sinners that are not forgiven shall pay the uttermost farthing, and the last mite, and that all the debt [of punishment] shall be exacted of them, etc. Now it seems unreasonable to suppose that God, in case of a surety, and his insisting on an atonement made by him, that he will show mercy by releasing the surety without a full atonement, anymore than that he will release it to the sinner that is punished, by not insisting on the complete punishment.[59]

In other words, in the same way that the full punitive demands of God's retributive justice are to be exacted from sinners, Edwards says that they are exacted from Christ and this, because he is their representative and God should require no less from him despite his status as a divine person.[60] Notice that Edwards says nothing in this context of what Christ's work does positively, that is, positively for God. This is because restoring anything to God is not a problem that the penal substitution model endeavors to solve. Interestingly, in another place, Edwards argues that restoring to God the honor that is due him is precisely the work Christ undertook in making atonement, saying,

> The sacrifice of Christ is a sweet savor, [first], because as such it was a great honor done to God's majesty, holiness and law, and a glorious expression and testimony of Christ's respect to that majesty etc.; that when he loved man and so greatly desired his salvation, he had yet so great respect to that majesty and holiness of God, that he had rather die than that salvation should be

59. "Miscellany" n. 1076, *WJE* 20:460.

60. Matthew Levering offers a recent and helpful synthesis of Edwards' thinking about punitive nature of divine justice and its relationship to both spiritual and somatic death in: *The Ecumenical Edwards*, 134–40. Levering's argument lends considerable strength to the idea that Edwards did in fact support some version of penal substitution. It is worth noting that several of his references to the nature of human suffering (and God's providential role in that suffering), however, might well be read in support of a penal non-substitution or moral government model.

any injury or dishonor unto those attributes. And then secondly, it was a sweet savour, as it was a marvellous act of obedience, and so an expression of a wonderful respect to God's authority. The value of Christ's sacrifice was infinite, both as a propitiation and as an act of obedience; because he showed an infinite regard to the majesty, holiness, etc. of God, in being at infinite expense from regard to it. (See Nos. 451, 452).[61]

To make the distinction between owing a debt and a debt of punishment clear, consider the following analogy.

Imagine that you get a call one day from "Easy Eddy," the notorious Chicago gangster Al Capone's bookkeeper. Eddy calls to talk to you about some massive unpaid debt that you owe Capone after losing a few hands of poker to Capone a few weeks ago.[62] Eddy reminds you that you owe Capone a hundred-grand and that if you don't pay up soon, the next call you'll be getting will be a "house call," from none other than Capone's so-called "Enforcer," Frank Nitti, and a few of his leg-breakers—only they won't be breaking legs, they will be coming to finish you. Desperate to avoid a thrashing by Nitti-and-company, you quickly hang up on Eddy and phone your brother, Jake "Greasy Thumb" Guzik, who happens to be a close-confidante of the Capone family. After telling your brother what you've done and that you don't have the money, he arranges a meeting with you and Capone to make a deal. To your great surprise and relief, in the meeting, your brother promises to pony-up the hundred-grand to pay your debt to Capone. The problem, however, is that having brokered the deal and bought your debt to Capone, your brother Guzik is now out a hundred-grand (provided he pays-up of course). What is interesting is that by discharging you of your debt to Capone, and assuming it himself, Guzik is now in a position to either forgive your debt to him outright and absorb the financial loss or exact the same sort of retribution from you, as would have Capone and company. Buying up your debt gives him that right. In this way, Guzik can either pay your debt or your debt of punishment.

Now, if we stop here we could cash out this analogy in terms of either a payment of a debt of punishment or payment of a debt. To owe Capone a debt—in this case, a debt of honor—means that he may neither lose money nor his honor and thus remains both vigilant and patient until these things are restored to him. To owe him a debt of punishment means that getting back the money means less to Capone than killing you, perhaps in order

61. "Miscellany" n. 449, *WJE* 13:497 (emphasis added).

62. For a recent and interesting account of Edward O'hare and the Capone empire, see: Eig, *Get Capone*.

to show that he is not one to be trifled with and that he will inevitably and eventually settle all accounts of those offences against him.[63]

It is the Capone-like exaction of a debt of punishment that is precisely the problem that the death of Christ solves on the penal substitution model. God's punitive action for offences against him is the actualization of his retributive justice. And according to exponents of penal substitution, it is the retributive demands of divine justice that Christ takes upon himself to meet for humanity's sake. Divine retributive justice is that which God visits upon the unrighteous for sins against him.

For Edwards' part, Christ is somehow depicted as paying both a debt simpliciter and a debt of punishment. For Christ to perform both of these works is a problem on several levels. But before we show how this is a potential problem—because it is so intimately bound up with the direction of sins offence—let us consider a second aspect of a debt of punishment.

II.3.2. Retribution and the Direction of Sins Offence

The second aspect of a debt of punishment that demands our attention here is the underlying assumption that sins offense is directed against God himself, and not, say, against his moral law. According to Edwards,

> Sin is of such a nature that it wishes ill, and aims at ill, to God and men, but to God especially. It strikes at God; it would, if it could, procure his misery and death. It is but suitable that with what measure it meets, it should be measured to it again. 'Tis but suitable that men should reap what they sow, and that the reward of every man's hands should be given him.[64]

In this way, exponents of penal substitution make much of the fact that divine retribution for offenses against God are private legal affairs—that is, they are offenses against God himself by individual, morally responsible creatures, in contrast to say, a public offense, which is an offense against a society. Consider that if someone commits a crime against another, that person is liable for the offense and punishment will likely befall the offending

---

63. We are aware that this later arrangement could lend equal support to a moral government model of atonement in the sense—following our analogy—that Capone appears interested in little more than making a penal example of you. It seems to us that introducing the idea of substitutionary atonement is the razor's edge of difference between the moral government and penal substitution models. That Christ is punished for sin is the point. The reason for his punishment is the distinguishing factor and something controlled in large part by the particular designs of divine justice.

64. "Miscellany" n. 779, *WJE* 18:436.

party. The individual, who sins against God, so they argue, is thus justly liable to the punitive measures of God's retributive justice as an individual. Such exponents also make much of the fact that private or individual offenses require individual reconciliation. This is, so they claim, what Christ does in making atonement, namely, effect personal, individual, and legal reconciliation between persons and God. That sins offense is against God and that it is something with individual implications is evident from the previous quotations. However, Edwards says elsewhere that,

> 'tis requisite that sin should be punished, as punishment is deserved and just, therefore the justice of God obliges him to punish sin: for it belongs to God as the supreme Rector of the universality of things, to maintain order and decorum in his kingdom, and to see to it that decency and right takes place at all times, and in all cases. That perfection of his nature whereby he is disposed to this, is his justice; and therefore, his justice naturally disposes him to punish sin as it deserves. The holiness of God, which is the infinite opposition of his nature to sin, naturally and necessarily disposes him to punish sin.[65]

He then goes on to argue that,

> God is to be considered in this affair not merely as the governor of the world of creatures, to order things between one creature and another, but as the supreme regulator or Rector of the universality of things, the orderer of things relating to the whole compass of existence, including himself, to maintain the rights of the whole, and decorum through the whole, and to maintain his own rights, and the due honor of his own perfections, as well as to keep justice among creatures. 'Tis fit that there should be one that has this office, and the office properly belongs to the supreme being. And if he should fail of doing justice to him[self] in a needed vindication of his own majesty and glory, it would be an immensely greater failure of his rectoral justice than if he should deprive the creatures, that are beings of infinitely less consequence, of their rights.[66]

A close reading of these two statements alongside the one in the previous section reveals that these statements are actually incongruent. The problem here is that if penal offences are both criminal and punishable, they are not, strictly speaking, private or individual, so much as public or societal affairs that are punishable by the authority of a system of laws, not an individual

---

65. Edwards, *WJE* 18:437 (emphasis added).

66. "Miscellany" n. 779, *WJE* 18:440 (emphasis added).

lawmaker. In other words, a coherent picture of penal substitution seems to require that sins offence be levelled against the moral law and not God himself, and that this is a problem facing all persons collectively, not as individuals, as it is so often thought to be the case. For Edwards' part, he seems to conflate the two.

It might be helpful to think of the difference between the offences that are tried in a United States district or civil court versus those tried in a United States criminal court. In a United States district court, someone might be sued, for example, for a breach of contract. Strictly speaking, this is not a criminal offense. This is a personal, (and therefore private) offense—one person versus another (even another individual group, as in a class action suit)—that is resolved by the offending party's restoring or making reparation for the offended party. United States Criminal courts, by contrast, try criminal offenders. If someone is on trial for murder, say, that person's offense is, again, strictly speaking, not against the one they killed (though I am sure we would all agree that murder is, if not the most, among the most egregious personal offenses that human persons can perpetrate against one another). Rather, their offense is against the laws of the society to which both parties have presumably assented and which demand that murderers pay a debt of punishment to society upon the commitment of such a crime. And in the United States judicial system, this debt is paid by incarceration or sometimes, in some states, death. In this way, murder, or any such criminal offense, is a public matter between the murderer and the society at large, not, strictly speaking, the murderer and the one that was murdered.[67] To put it differently, there's a difference between offenses against Capone himself and those levelled against the rules of his club.

Now, carrying this line of thinking over to the more recent suggestions of Edwards subscription to penal substitution, if Christ is said to pay a debt of punishment on behalf of others, then, the debt is actually not a private offense against God—like in a district court—requiring that something be restored (via reparation) to God, despite those claims of his being the privately offended party.[68] To put it rather bluntly, nothing is restored to God on the penal substitution model. Instead, and quite to the contrary of the apparent demands of God's retributive justice, penal substitution seems only to make provision for God to restore righteousness to humanity,

67. We are grateful to Patrick Murphy and Christ Wolf for this analogy.

68. We suppose, were one to construe the three-ness of God in terms of a "society" of persons in the God-head, as well as construe human persons as some sort of collective "moral whole," rather than morally responsible individuals, then it would consistent to think of sin as a public offense that issues in debt of punishment owed to a society. We are not conscious of any such theological argument having been made.

leaving God dishonored and his Son, crushed (as the prophet Isaiah says) for this dishonor, and what is more, all of this being of no apparent benefit to himself. And this is in contrast to Edwards' apparent thinking that the work Christ does in making atonement restores honor to God—something that belongs to owing and paying a debt of honor. The problem, as we have suggested before, is that Christ cannot perform both works. He cannot suffer as a penal substitute and a non-penal substitute. So, the question for us then is whether Edwards' commitments to the rectoral demands of divine justice are at odds with his commitment to the role of retributive justice issued by penal substitution. Our answer is yes, they are at odds, and they are in no less than two important ways.

First, because Edwards construes sin as both a private offense against God for which humanity is liable to pay a debt of honor and as a private offense against God for which humanity is liable to pay a debt of punishment (which as we have seen previously is itself something of a contradiction, that is, if we understand a debt of punishment to be a public or societal offense)—both acts of which cannot be done simultaneously by a penal and non-penal substitute. In other words, Christ cannot absorb divine wrath for sin as a penal substitute, when he is at the same time (collectively) deferring or delaying that wrath until the consummation by making reparations on behalf of all humanity. The second way they are at odds, is because Edwards construes the nature of Christ's substitutionary work in what we might call "personal" and then "meritorious" terms. By personal substitution, we mean the substitutionary work he performs by "standing in," as it were, for individual persons upon whom are the retributive demands of God justice. By meritorious substitution, we mean the substitutionary work he performs by accumulating the reparative merit of honor that offsets the infinite demerit of sin. For, because God is infinitely holy, sins against God accrue an infinite demerit, as it were, that requires some infinite merit to offset.[69] It seems to that, at least with respect to the mechanism of the atonement, these are not complimentary accounts of substitution so much as competing ones. For, no honor is restored to God by his meeting out retribution against the Son—paying a debt of punishment does not necessarily pay a debt of honor. In these two ways at least, there is a tension in Edwards' account of Christ's

---

69. This is referred to in the literature of contemporary philosophical-theology as the status principle. The status principle says that the degree of an offence is measured by the "status" of the one offended. So, a transgression against a being of infinite value accrues an infinite offence. For this reason, and because God is infinitely just, he cannot simply set aside or (ultimately) pass over offences against his nature. God's justice is inexorable. He must punish sin. For further discussion of the status principle, see: Kvanvig, *The Problem of Hell* and Crisp, "Divine Retribution," 35–52.

atoning work. Against this detailed backdrop, let us consider some Edwards Jr's thinking on the matter.

Of the variety of theological writings that offer some additionally detailed insight into the development of his father's legacy regarding the atonement, there are two works in particular that shed some light on Edwards Jr's thoughts about the work of Christ. The first is his "Thoughts on the Atonement," echoes of which appear in the second piece called "Remarks on the Improvements Made in Theology by His Father, President Edwards." In both cases, the younger Edwards makes a number curious statements that point in the direction of his ascent to something along the lines a penal substitution model atonement. What is interesting—what makes this evidence so curious—is that Edwards Jr has never been attributed with articulating anything but a so-called penal non-substitution model of atonement, where (roughly) the work Christ accomplishes is claimed to be that of a *penal example*—repairing the dishonor done to the moral law by humanity's transgression(s) against it. The following two statements, each one represent a sort of core sample of ideas in which are resident both Dr. Edwards' clear out-working of the penal non-substitution model and the presence of substitutionary language in keeping with his father. Dr Edwards writes,

> By atonement, I mean something done or suffered, which, to the purpose of supporting the honor and dignity of the divine law and government, shall be equivalent to the punishment of the sinner according to law. Therefore, *the atonement made by Christ implies his substitution in the stead of the sinner*, who is to be saved by him; or that he suffered that in the sinner's stead, which as effectually tended to discourage, or prevent transgression, and excite to obedience, as the punishment of the transgressor himself, according to the letter of the law would have done.[70]

In another place he maintains,

> *The atonement is the substitute for the punishment threatened in the law*; and was designed to answer the same ends of supporting the authority of the law, the dignity of the divine moral government, and the consistency of the divine conduct in legislation and execution. By the atonement it appears that God is determined that his law shall be supported; that it shall not be despised or transgressed with impunity; and that it is an evil and a bitter thing to sin against God. The very idea of

70. Edwards Jr, "Remarks on the Improvements," 481–92; see also: "Thoughts on the Atonement," 493–508.

an atonement or satisfaction for sin, is something which, to
the purposes of supporting the authority of the divine law, the
dignity and consistency of the divine government, is equivalent to the punishment of the sinner, according to the literal
threatening of the law.[71]

Clearly, from these statements, the idea of substitutionary atonement is
part of the way Edwards Jr thinks about Christ's work. Whether we can
call this a full-blow doctrine of penal substitution remains to be seen. At
most, we are left wondering just what Edwards Jr actually believes about the
atonement, and specifically, how a substitutionary work plays into a non-
substitutionary model of Christ's work. It seems to us there are (at least)
three possible answers. Consider that both the good Doctor was simply
unconscious of the impact of the commitment they was making by trotting
out such a claim—a case of category confusion. Given the relative precision
of Edwards Jr's account, this seems highly unlikely. If so, then perhaps he
actually saw a theological way forward—a way that make the New England
model of penal non-substitution unique to the rest of the moral government tradition—that we have yet to discover—a way that Christ can be
both a substitute and a non-substitute that avoids what is an obvious logical
contradiction. The most likely possibility, it seems to us, has to do with his
construal of the nature of substitution. Notice that Dr. Edwards says nothing about Christ being a substitute for individuals. Notice also his emphasis
on Christ's substitutionary work as having a direct impact on the demands
of the moral law, which, as we saw in the case of President Edwards is a
public or societal matter—humanities offence is against the moral law, not
God, strictly speaking. By implication, it looks like the solution (atonement)
to the problem (transgression of the moral law) effects all humanity. How
can this be? The answer may be that he augmented individual substitutionary atonement to some account of universal substitutionary atonement, in
keeping with Crisp's relatively recent suggestion that we ought to understand two things: First, the New England theologians were interested in
doctrinal development and ought to be seen in this light (rather than some
sort of doctrinal decline and fall, as has been the earlier trend). Second, their
developments as it relates to the atonement tended toward expressions of
some sort of hypothetical universalism, according to which Christ's work
extends in some sense to all persons—like we see here from Dr. Edwards.
What then about the President Edwards? How do we make sense of the
anomalous appearance of both substitutionary language, moral government
language, and the oddities of his account of rectoral and retributive justice?

71. Edwards Jr, "On the Necessity of the Atonement," 8–9.

Perhaps looking further down the historical road to Gelston will enable us to look back at Doctor and President Edwards with some greater clarity.

II.4. Gelston on Atonement

To this point we have challenged the idea that says that the moral government or penal non-substitution model of atonement was the atonement model of choice amongst the New England theologians from Dr. Edwards onward. Interestingly, our findings reveal that not only should we think of President Edwards' account of the atonement as "thicker" than has hitherto been thought, but that we should also think of Dr. Edwards' model of atonement as "thicker" than his most recent interpreter has made out. In what remains of this introduction, we aim to show that there is some data suggesting that Gelston himself inherited this otherwise odd, amalgamated tradition of holding to some aspect of both a penal and non-penal substitution model of atonement. To get at Gelston's thinking about these matters, we have isolated the following list of atonement-specific questions and answers from his *Systematic Collection*:

> Question 152 [201]. Why was a satisfaction or atonement necessary to the dispensation of pardon?
>
> Question 153 [202]. Why was a satisfaction or atonement so great as that of Christ necessary to the dispensation of pardon?
>
> Question 154 [203]. In what consisted the essence of the atonement of Christ? In his obedience, or his sufferings, or in both?
>
> Question 155 [204]. In what sense did he satisfy divine justice by his sacrifice?
>
> Question 156 [205]. Was God under an obligation of justice to provide an atonement for sinners?
>
> Question 158 [207]. Did Christ redeemed all men alike, elect and non-elect?
>
> Question 171. [233]. Did Christ suffer and die in the stead as well as for the benefit of his people?
>
> Question 172. [234]. Could he have made atonement without suffering in stead of his people?
>
> Question 173 [235]. Did Christ pay the debt for the elect, so that they can claim salvation on the foot of justice?

Question 174 [236]. Where the sufferings of Christ to the purpose of supporting the divine law equivalent to the endless torments of the sinner?

Question 175 [238]. Do the sufferings and obedience of Christ proved to the divine law to be a just law?

Let us take each question and answer in turn, offer some brief commentary, after which we will conclude with a series of implications from our findings along with some suggestions for further research. Gelston asks, in Question 152, "Why was a satisfaction or atonement necessary to the dispensation of pardon?" His response is as follows:

> Answer 152. In order to the dispensation of pardon and atonement, satisfaction is necessary because without this the law and the moral government of God must fall into contempt. If a law be made, and the penalty be not executed when broken, it is of no more consequence than if no penalty had been annexed. Indeed, the law is of no mere importance than mere advice in the view of all rational beings. It would be more contemptible than advice. For, it pretends to something which is not supported. Not only the law, but the character of the lawgiver must fall equally into contempt. This is the case in human governments, and this would be the case in the divine. If the honor of the law be not supported by a proper execution of its threatenings, the moral government of God would be subject to constant disorder and confusion. In this case, the rebellious may go on with impunity and with increasing wickedness. Nor would there be anything to deter others from the like. In this way, infinite mischief may be produced and be forever experienced without any diminution or relief.
>
> Either, therefore, the full penalty of the law must be executed or some atonement must be made which, in support of the divine law and government, will answer the like purposes with an infliction of the punishment. No pardon of consequences can be obtained without an atonement or satisfaction which is equivalent to the full demands of the law.

There are several points worth highlighting here. Clearly Gelston is committed, like his mentor, Dr. Edwards, to the idea of the necessity of atonement. Notice also that Gelston frames the problem of the moral law's demands in the context of divine honor. It interesting that he links these demands so intimately with the demands of the lawgiver. "If the honor of the law be not supported by a proper execution of its threatenings, the moral government of God would be subject to constant disorder and confusion." This is quite a telling statement. For, either a payment must be rendered or atonement—a suitably equivalent payment—supporting the divine law and government be made. That said, it not altogether clear from Gelston's answer what mechanism is explicitly at work in atoning for human sin. His use of the term "equivalent"—reminiscent of penal non-substitution— might be a clue. That he says, "Either, therefore, the full penalty of the law must be executed or some atonement must be made" is confirming of the same. However, notice the subtle distinction of the either-or clauses at play here. Gelston seems to be affirming that Christ's atoning work assumes that Christ never actually paid the penalty of the law. In other words, his "suit-ably equivalent" payment is a sacrifice of a non-penal substitution, which is yet something new altogether. That said, his thinking of sin as an offense against the moral *and* God pulls in a different direction.

In question 153, Gelston considers "why was a satisfaction or atone-ment so great as that of Christ necessary to the dispensation of pardon?" His answer is as follows,

> (Answer 153) The evil of sin is infinite, and in its nature and consequences tends to produce infinite mischief in the moral government of God. No atonement, therefore, could wipe off this evil, but that which is also infinite. The sinner would make no atonement by repentance and reformation, for they are al-ready do. He cannot suffer a punishment of the temporary kind which will be adequate to the crime; for it would be but finite. Nor could any creature, however great, atone: because what ever he should suffer would still be finite. It is allowed, however, that a creature more excellent than man might have made an atonement proportionally greater. But to render an atonement completely adequate, the person must be infinite in dignity and excellence, or suffer and infinite evil fully equal to the sins of those for whom he makes atonement. Hence, it was that an atonement so great as that of Christ was necessary.

Gelston makes the case for explicit support of the doctrine of the neces-sity for atonement, something made much of in Crisp's analysis of Edwards Jr. He writes, "The evil of sin is infinite, and in its nature and consequences tends to produce infinite mischief in the moral government of God. No atonement, therefore, could wipe off this evil, but that which is also infinite. The sinner would make no atonement by repentance and reformation, for they are already do." Gelston goes on to make clear that a divine person is necessary to make atonement. Gelston's emphasis on the necessity of the atonement represents a token of the Anselmian tradition (which echoes the non-penal substitution found in the final part of his response in the previous question), and yet still does not commit Gelston to either a view of penal substitution or non-substitution.[72]

In question 155, Gelston pushes further toward this distinction when he asks, "In what sense did he satisfy divine justice by his sacrifice?" What he says about how the atonement is answerable to divine justice and for whom it is answerable will reveal a great deal about Gelston's theological commitment. He argues,

> (Answer 155) Christ so completely answered the demands of the law as that, the believer may be saved from the curse of it, and yet the honor of the law and the dignity and authority of the divine government be fully supported. The penalty of the law, however, may still be executed to the full extent upon the finally impenitent. Justice therefore, has received no satisfaction with respect to them. And indeed, the believer, were it not for the constitution and promises of God might, notwithstanding all Christ has done and suffered, experience the full punishment due to his sins. The believer, therefore, would not demand a release from punishment, as a debtor might demand a release from his debt when a third person had paid for him the full demand of his creditor. Justice, therefore, is not satisfied with respect to the believer as it is with respect to the debtor. God was under no obligation from justice to accept the atonement which Christ has made: and if he actually does except of it, it must be from sovereign mercy and free grace.

There are several important observations that might be made here. First, notice that Gelston appears to think Christ's work solves a problem related to the law that entails a solution to problem of offenses against God himself; something we will see again in his answer to question 175. Second, notice that the solution to the problem is not collective, that is, not for all humanity. "Did Christ redeem all men alike, elect and non-elect?" His answer is quite telling, pushing directly against Crisp's suggestion that hypothetical universalism was a doctrine that developed amongst the New England theologians. While it may have developed so for Bellamy, but perhaps not for Gelston. He argues that "[t]he believer, therefore, would not demand a release from punishment, as a debtor might demand a release from his debt when a third person had paid for him the full demand of his

---

72. Answer to Question 154 is regrettably missing in from Gelston's notebook. Question 154 [203] reads as follows: 'In what consisted the essence of the atonement of Christ? In his obedience, or his sufferings, or in both?'

creditor. Justice, therefore, is not satisfied with respect to the believer as it is with respect to the debtor." In other words, the work Christ was somehow in Gelston's mind accomplished only for the elect. With his repeated reference to "believers," this suggests a substitutionary act on the part of Christ, which again hints in the direction of his subscription to something like a doctrine of penal substitution.

Next, in Question 156, Gelston considers whether God was "under an obligation of justice to provide an atonement for sinners?" To this he responds, rather briefly, that

> (Answer 156) If God had been under an obligation of justice to provide an atonement for sinners it must be on account of his law. For, surely if the law of the holy, just and good, is so far from requiring God to provide an atonement, strict, distributive justice requires the actual punishment due to the violation of the law. Since, therefore, the law is thus holy, just and good, as is evident from the nature of it, and the declarations of God's word, if an atonement be made for the violation of it, it must proceed not from justice, but the goodness, mercy and grace of God.

There are two rather interesting elements to this answer, chief among which is Gelston's introduction of the concept of distributive justice. This category often assumes two other (sub)species of divine justice: remunerative justice—having to do with rewards, and retributive justice—having to do with punishment.[73] As we have already seen, the penal substitution model of atonement is mostly often directly associated with overcoming the problem of divine retribution. That Gelston speaks here of distributive justice, makes at least some logical room for our thinking that the aspect of remunerative justice must play into the way he conceived of Christ's work. How it factors in is the question. What is clear from the previous section is that functional role played by Gelston's affirmation of remunerative justice puts him at an increased distance from penal substitution. The second point of interest here is Gelston's seemingly intentional link between divine mercy and divine justice. That atonement is made by virtue of God's mercy rather than by some judicial precedent lends support to idea that God has some notion of substitution in mind. What is substituted? is the question. Is this a substitution of one for particular individuals, as in the case of penal substitution? We might well think so, especially in view of his answer to question 156. Perhaps this is merely a nod to the notion of suitable equivalence. It is not entirely clear.

---

73. For some helpful discussion of the distinctions of divine justice expressed in the Reformed tradition, see: Owen, *A Dissertation on Divine Justice*, 494ff.

Without really supplying us with answer, Gelston moves on to question 157, where he asks "Does the appointment of a Mediator prove that God is already reconciled to men?"

> (Answer 157) If the appointment of Mediator prove[s] that God is already reconciled to men, then it will prove that he is so without the execution of the office as Mediator. If so, then, there was no necessity of Mediator. But surely a God of infinite goodness and compassion would never require any thing of this kind, unless absolutely necessary. The design of the Mediator is to lay a foundation, so that he may become reconciled to mankind in a consistency with his law and moral government. But to say that reconciliation takes place previous to the undertaking and accomplishment of the Mediator's work is to place the effect before the cause.
>
> Besides, none are interested in the benefits of the atonement until they are possessed of those qualifications which are made the necessary prerequisites. Nor are any sinners reconciled to God until they are interested in the benefits of this atonement.

Here we see that Gelston has in mind that the design of the atonement is such that it makes restitution between humanity and the divine according to both his moral law and moral governance; something we saw in answer 156. Notice his appeal to the necessity of the atonement. His suggestion that the Mediator "is to lay a foundation" hints at some interesting points. What is this foundation? Whatever it is, it appears that it is something definitive, that is, something from which God is able then to execute his retributive and/or remunerative justice. It also appears that by this work of mediation, God is able to deal in an effective way with both believers and non-believers. Notice, finally, that reconciliation to God, as Gelston sees it, is not something which those prior to Christ's work enjoyed the true privilege of.

In question 158, Gelston asks whether "Christ redeemed all men alike, elect and non-elect?" To this he responds:

> (Answer 158) The atonement of Christ is sufficient for all mankind would day, but accept of it upon the terms proposed. The invitation of the gospel is in universal terms, "whosoever will, let him take the water of life freely." Revelation 22.17. So far, the elect and non-elect are alike. But the application of this redemption will be made to the elect alone. Nor was it the design of God. From eternity that any but the elect should actually accept of the proposed atonement and enjoyed the happiness of the redeemed. It is the elect who are chosen of God in Christ before the foundation of the world. Ephesians 1.14. It is the elect who

are "Justified by his grace freely through the redemption that is
in Jesus Christ." Romans 3.24. It is the elect who are redeemed
from the curse of the law. Galatians 3.13. And it is the elect who
"seen a new song, saying, Thou art worthy to take the book, and
to open the seals thereof: for thou wast slain, and hast redeemed
us to God by thy blood." Revelation 5.9.

Redemption, when used with reference to Christ, seems to
mean the application of the benefits and blessings which he has
procured to believers in this world, and the actual introduction
of them to happiness in the world to come. But this is a happiness which none but the elect experience.

Had the atonement of Christ been designed to be extinguished, the guilds of a certain number of sins, as a man liquidates a debt of a certain fixed and determinant sum of money, he
doubtless would have had the sins of the elect in view, and would
have extinguished the guilt of these, but this does not appear
to have been the object of the atonement. Strictly speaking, the
atonement has extinguished. Neither the seems of the elect nor of
the non-elect. But it has laid a foundation so that the punishment
due to the sins of those who are interested in it, may as completely
be removed as if they never had been guilty. Here, then, lies, the
distinction: the elect will experience this. But the non-elect, in
consequences of their neglect, will not experience it.

Here Gelston seems, rather strangely, to affirm something like hypothetical universalism, which more naturally fits with either Moral Government
or Anselmian satisfaction, and echoes Crisp's notion of doctrinal development. Gelston's reference to the sufficiency-efficiency distinction of Christ's
work hints in this direction. That said, such thinking also might fit with a
version of penal substitution, provided he construe the payment as one for
sin, corporately construed, rather than individually construed where Christ
pays a debt of punishment for the consequences of sin. It is not entirely clear
to this point that this is what he has in view.

In question 171, Gelston asks: "Did Christ suffer and die in the stead as
well as for the benefit of his people?" His answer is as follows.

(Answer 171) Christ suffered a punishment which would fully
support the honor of the divine law and the dignity of the divine
government, though his people be released from the punishment they personally deserve. Indeed, the object of his atonement was that they might thus be released. Still, however, it does
not appear that they can demand this release as a debtor might
insist upon a discharge when a third person had fully paid the
demand of his creditor. Christ, therefore, did not suffer and die

in the stead of his people so as to lay God under obligation to accept of the atonement, whether he chose or not. He, however, suffered and died so far in their stead. That day will not actually experience that punishment, which otherwise, they would have experienced. By his sufferings and death. He completely atoned for the sins of his people. They will not, therefore, be required to undergo any farther punishment.

Here Gelston raises the question as to whether Christ suffered in "instead" and as a "benefit" for his people. His answer is interesting, but, once again not entirely clear. In fact, the following may be the most confusing aspect of Gelston's thinking. "Christ suffered a punishment which would fully support the honor of the divine law and the dignity of the divine government, though his people be released from the punishment they personally deserve." However, Gelston does not clearly articulate penal substitution. Gelston supports the notion of Christ bearing the penal demands of the law, but this does not necessarily suggest a substitutionary act, even more, a substitutionary act for individuals. In other words, it is not apparent that Christ absorbs the penalty for individuals. Gelston states, "therefore, did not suffer and die in the stead of his people so as to lay God under obligation to accept of the atonement." He proceeds immediately to say something seemingly contradictory, namely, that "He, however, suffered and died so far in their stead."

In question 172, he asks the related questions: "Could he have made atonement without suffering in stead of his people?"

> Answer 172. It is not conceived that any thing without suffering would have constituted an atonement. Nothing but this could have shown the awful and tremendous consequences of sin. Nor could anything else have shown the incident evil and instructive tendency of sin. Nothing else would properly have been a penalty of the law. Obedience was already due from every creature, and could, in no sense be considered as a penalty. It does not appear, therefore, that the honor of the divine law or the dignity of the divine government could have been supported except by suffering, either personally, or having a substitute. This substitute must, to make an atonement which would be complete and satisfactory, suffer instead of his people, so far as mentioned above.

Here again, Gelston is clear that Christ's suffering is necessary, yet it is an open question as to the priority of retributive justice or rectoral justice. Even where there is a place for retribution, it is not entirely clear that it amounts to (1) the absorption of a penalty or (2) that Christ's act is committed on behalf of the individual. These fundamental tenets are essential elements of standard penal substitution theory. It is true that Gelston uses the language of "suffering" and "substitution," yet he also uses the language of "satisfaction" and atonement for a collective whole, "his people". In the quote above, Gelston suggests moral government or penal non-substitution when he says, "Nothing but this could have shown the awful and tremendous consequences of sin. Nor could anything else have shown the incident evil and instructive tendency of sin. Nothing else would properly have been a penalty of the law." Gelston's use of the word "substitution" seems to amount to a different kind of substitution than that found in penal substitutionary atonement. Rather, Gelston states that this "substitute" must "suffer instead of his people" not on behalf of his people or in their penal stead. With the variations of atonement theory swirling around during the time of New England theological development, it is not surprising that New England theologians, like Gelston, might use language reflective of penal substitution theory, moral government, and even the satisfaction theory. While the evidence points in favor of interpreting Gelston as a defender of moral government his language lends itself to some ambiguity.

According to question 173, Gelston inquires: "Did Christ pay the debt for the elect, so that they can claim salvation on the foot of justice?"

> (Answer 173) When one man pays a debt for another, where a sum of money is due, this other on the principles of strict commutative justice may justly demand a release from his creditor. The reason is, because the creditor has received his full demand, and justice in no case demands more than the law points out, as due. But in matters of distributive justice. The law does not point out the punishment of one man as due for the crime of another. It has no right to demand this. And the one man should consent to suffer for another, the executive authority is not obliged to accept of the substitute. It is against the breaker of the law that it is threatenings are leveled, and it is to him alone that the law looks for satisfaction. Originally, therefore, it knows of no substitute. If then, one man actually suffers the punishment due to another, the demand of the law, according to strict distributive justice, still remains in full force. If the sovereign accept of this punishment as a substitute, it is not because this kind of justice requires his acceptance.
>
> Similar is the case of the elect. This kind of distributive justice will never support any claim for salvation. To a matter like this, the punishment might still be executed.

The general good or general justice, however, admits of their salvation, and by virtue of God's promise, on the ground of this, they have a right to expect it.

It seems clear from the above that Gelston has in mind rectoral satisfaction rather than the absorption of penal consequences. Christ does not so much assume the penalty of individual sin, but he honors God or the moral law in a way that creates a surplus benefiting humans. The notions of "credit" and "creditor" are clearly at home with Anselmian satisfaction, or, possibly, moral government. Whilst the discussion on whether the payment is paid directly to God or the moral law by which God maintains moral order is an open question, but what seems clear is his rejection of a certain variant of penal substitution that says that Christ suffered a loss on behalf of the elect so as to pay the debtor (as is clear here: "The law does not point out the punishment of one man as due for the crime of another. It has no right to demand this."). Rather, Christ pays off the debt owed to God the creditor. In other words, he pays a positive demand.

For question 174, Gelston responds to the question of "Were the sufferings of Christ to the purpose of supporting the divine law equivalent to the endless torments of the sinner?" His answer is quite illuminating.

(Answer 174) The sufferings of Christ were not infinite in duration. Nor were they incident in quantity or degree, for it was his human nature, which suffered, and that was capable of only a finite degree of suffering. The infinite dignity of his person, however, gave value to his sufferings, which was fully equivalent to the endless torments of the sinner. Reason teaches us that the sufferings of a king's son, especially if he possesses every amiable quality of a man, are of more value and importance than the sufferings of one of his lowest subjects. And in proportion, as the son is more elevated in station and character, his sufferings will be of proportionably more value in every respect, but especially to the support of the law and the dignity of the government.

We may be sure that the sufferings of Christ are equivalent to the endless torments of the sinner, from God's actually accepting it as such. He would not accept of that which does not answer the demand of the law. This he fully intimates, when he says, "And ye brought that which was torn, and the lame, and the sick; though ye brought an offering: should I accept this of your hands? saith the Lord." Malachi 1.13. That the sufferings of Christ were accepted as an equivalent is evident from what is abundantly asserted. "Who his own self bare our sins in his own body on the tree." 1 Peter 2.24. "As Christ also hath loved us, and hath given himself for us, and offering and a sacrifice to God for a sweet smelling savour." Ephesians 5.2. "For he hath made him to be sin for us, who knew no sin." 2 Corinthians 5.21. Who gave himself a ransom for all." 1 Timothy 2.6. "For by one offering he hath perfected forever them that are sanctified." Hebrews 10.14.

Here Gelston again takes up and defends an aspect of suitable equivalence, this time by addressing the value of Christ's sacrifice—a discussion that is often ignored or misconstrued by contemporary atonement theoreticians. That Christ's sacrifice was suitably equivalent to the "eternal torments" is not the same thing as say that he endured the actual torments of hell for anyone. This seems to point away from Gelston's subscription to a penal substitution theory. And at the same time, Gelston links humanities offense to both God and the moral law. It seems to us that despite the lack of clarity on these various comments of Gelston, that a fairly strong cumulative case can be made that he did not espouse a doctrine of penal substitution. So, what did he subscribe to in the end?

Finally, in question 175, Gelston asks, "Do the sufferings and obedience of Christ prove the divine law to be a just law?"

> (Answer 175) It does not appear that the nature of the law is, in any instance, to be determined merely by its sanctions. The will or character of the lawgiver, the tendency of the law, and the nature of the trends rations against which its penalties are leveled, more properly give complexion to the law. Whenever, therefore, the justice of a law is questioned, the character of the lawgiver is equally questioned. And though he should execute the full extent of the threatening, this would not achieve the difficulty with respect to his law or character, for we know that an unjust and rigorous sovereign may commit the greatest injustice in this way, and be at proportionably greater distance from rectitude of heart. Something more than merely suffering the threatening of the law is necessary to vindicate its justice. Nor would mere obedience alone determine the law to be just. One of the contrary nature may be as punctually obeyed as if perfectly just, and it is injustice remain undiminished.
>
> But if we take into consideration the true character of God and of Christ, we have the fullest assurance is law is holy, just and good. Without this, what ever be the sufferings in support of it, or however punctually obeyed, we would have no certainty of its justice.

In this final atonement-related question, Gelston further affirms his commitment to something other than penal substitution. The key phrase here is when Gelston says, "Something more than merely suffering the threatening of the law is necessary to vindicate its justice." In this way, Gelston is saying that Christ must do more than merely suffer by absorbing the penal consequences. He must honor the law and its requirement, which in turn honor's the Father. Notice again, as with his previous answer, the link between the moral law's demands and the demands of God, the legislator. Although, these finer distinctions do not allow us to make a simple and easy categorization of what Gelston actually believed. The difficulty is parsing out his understanding of the specific mechanism at work in the atonement and how this relates to God and his moral law, particularly the specifics of meting out the requirements of the law beckons a serious scholarly return to the New England theological tradition, Gelston offering us one window into what remains a veritable trove of rich, under-researched theology. The complexity and depth of insight amongst New England theologians and the intricacy of doctrinal developments that have emerged from it are reflected here in the reading of Gelston.

Conclusion

To speak of New England dogmatics still remains something of a contradiction. Our introducing Gelston and his doctrine of atonement is but a modest contribution to this untapped and underdeveloped field of research. The doctrine of atonement reflects a wider and deeper conversation needing to occur with New England theology. So also is the relationship of Reformed dogmatics at large with their New England brethren.

Having been almost exclusively a matter of historical interest, and motivated primarily by questions about the nature of President Edwards' doctrinal relationship to his intellectual progeny, contemporary systematic and constructive use of Edwards' intellection tradition remains very much in its infancy. The atonement is but one example; one that still requires serious or sustained systematic theological inquiry. While penal substation theory was swirling around in New England discussions, it is apparent that it is not the dominant theory of the day—unlike what we find today in Reformed evangelical churches. How penal substitution assumed the dominant place in contemporary discussions depends on the social, cultural, and theological mores leading to its acceptance. During Gelston's time and location, the moral government and Anselmian satisfaction are live, even popular, and robust options for New Englander's. They, too, should be live options for contemporary theologians, as we have shown above. Through a process of retrieval, New England thought helps us raise new questions, in our social and historical context, about God's relationship to his creation, the law, and Christ's relationship to these doctrinal loci. Again, Gelston leads us to raise these questions.

Our brief investigation into Gelston provides one way in which the theologian might find it useful. What you have in your hands is a lens into the New England tradition and its influence on Reformed theological developments in America. Certainly other doctrines deserve our reflection. Gelston advances some interesting thoughts on the nature of revelation, natural knowledge of God, God's Trinitarian nature, and the study of last things. These thoughts may or may not be novel insights from Gelston. Even still, they too reflect the New England tradition of theological development.

Theological Questions

THE SCHOLASTIC CHARACTER OF theological education in New England during the eighteenth and early nineteenth centuries is reflected by a variety of surviving lists of theological questions. These lists offer insight into the program of theological education in New England before and during its institutionalization, beginning with Andover Seminary (1808). These lists vary in content, length, and intent. More than a pedagogical devise, these list provide unique insight into the transmission of those theological sensibilities distinct to the Edwardsian intellectual tradition.

What follows are three lists of theological questions. The first list, entitled, *Questions on Theological Subjects* (c. 1746) is composed by President Edwards and consists of fifty-one questions, mostly of a controversial variety.[1] It is not clear what Edwards had in mind by generating this list. However, references to his *Miscellanies* (e.g.: question 4, 34, and 37) indicate that the list may have been the record of particular theological problems that Edwards was attempting to work out during this period of his Northampton tenure. It is also possible, indeed, probable, that Edwards composed this list expressly for tutoring ministerial students.[2] The second list, entitled, *Theological Questions of Jonathan Edwards Sr*, also composed by the Northampton sage, consists of ninety questions.[3] Less concerned with any theologically controversial subject, Edwards' design for this second list of questions seems to be fixed more on particular aspects of an array of fundamental doctrines, ranging from arguments for the existence of God to the

1. A similar list, entitled, *Questions for Young People* (c. 1730) consists of approximately 139 (different) questions, apparently designed to test the biblical knowledge of the youth in Edwards' congregation. Edwards, MS, BRBL, Box 21, f. 1263, "Church and Pastoral Documents" *in The Works of Jonathan Edwards Online, Vol. 39,* http://edwards.yale.edu/.

2. Minkema, "Jonathan Edwards on Education and His Educational Legacy," 38–39.

3. Park, "Questions of the Two Edwardses for Their Pupils in Theology." For digital access to both lists of questions, see: Jonathan Edwards, "Church and Pastoral Documents" *in The Works of Jonathan Edwards Online, Vol. 39,* http://edwards.yale.edu/.

nature of the atonement. The third and final list, often accompanied by his father's ninety questions belongs to Dr. Jonathan Edwards Jr and consists of a formidable 313 questions. It was composed expressly for educating those who sought their practical ministerial instruction from those belonging to Edwards' New Divinity.

Questions on Theological Subjects[4]

1. Upon what accounts was it necessary that Christ should satisfy for the sins of men?

2. How is it inconsistent with the perfections of God not to fulfill his threatenings of eternal damnation to impenitent sinners? Or, how can we prove from the perfections of God that he will fulfill, etc.?

3. How is Christ said to be risen again for our justification? Rom. 4:25.

4. How does Christ's death fulfill that threatening of that law, "the day that thou eatest [thou shalt surely die?" (Gen. 2:17)]. ["Miscellanies," nos.] 281, 357, 506.

5. Is it possible in the nature of the thing that there should be any law that don't require perfect obedience?

6. Wherein did the sufferings of Christ differ from the sufferings of the damned?

7. Seeing there is so much that the damned suffer that Christ did not, how can his sufferings be equivalent?

8. What evidence is there that it is the will of God the first day of the week should be kept as a Sabbath?

9. In what sense did Christ bear the wrath of God for our sins?

10. What is that which most probably would have prevented Adam from eating of the Tree of Life before the time of probation was ended, seeing it was in no respect forbidden?

11. What was the special end of the Tree of Life?

12. Whether it can ever be said to be contrary to the attribute of God's mercy for him to execute the most strict justice?

13. How is it said that Christ redeems us to God by his blood?

---

4. Edwards, MS, BRBL, f. 1246 "Church and Pastoral Documents" *WJEO 39*.

14. How can that act of obedience in Christ be accepted for us, which the law never required of Adam?

15. Whether God's certain foreknowledge of future events is not as inconsistent with the Arminian notion of liberty as God's absolute decrees?

16. Whether the notion of a self-determining power in the will of man, or the will voluntarily determining all its own acts, don't imply a contradiction?

17. In what sense is God said to be necessarily existent?

18. Questions concerning the part that the three persons of the Trinity sustain in the work of redemption.

19. In what sense will Christ deliver up the kingdom to the Father?

20. Whether there be[ing] no succession in the knowledge of God weakens [and] takes away the force of the argument for the necessity of events from God's foreknowledge?

21. Whether it be possible that the foreknowledge of God should be an effect of events not yet in being?

22. Whether Adam's posterity be liable to all the punishment that Adam was liable to in his own person for his eating the forbidden fruit?

23. Whether the death threatened to Adam for eating the forbidden fruit was annihilation?

24. Whether a person's being absolutely assured of their salvation be inconsistent with a being yet continued in a state of probation?

25. How can we prove from reason that God maintains a moral government over the world of mankind?

26. What is the most proper course to be taken in order to growth in grace?

27. Cannot God's decrees be demonstrated by his foreknowledge?

28. Don't God's being incapable of having his happiness added to by any knowledge or respect of his creature argue that his end in creating the world could not be his own glory?

29. Are there not many inconsistencies in the Arminian notion of freedom of will?

30. How far the voice of reason concurs with the voice of revelation in the doctrine of a public, general judgment at the end of the world?

31. Whether there are not good reasons, without divine revelation, by which we may argue that the world will come to an end?

32. How far the unity of the Godhead may be argued from the manner of the creation?

33. Whether the unity of the Godhead can be demonstrated a priori?

34. In what respects is Christ God's elect? ["Miscellanies,"] no. 769.

35. Whether there is not good evidence that the saints in heaven know what is done in the church on earth?

36. Whether the saints in heaven be n't in a state a preparation for and proficiency towards another state?

37. Whether there be n't good evidence that the death spoken of in the threatening denounced be something more than annihilation? ["Miscellanies,"] no. 785.

38. Whether any probable conjecture can be made concerning the occasion of the fall of the angels?

39. Whether Satan before his fall was not the highest of all creatures?

40. Whether any prophecy of Scripture are properly fulfilled in more events than one?

41. Whether or no it will not follow from the principle of the Arminians that God in no respect excites or assists to acts of virtue, any more than to acts of vice?

42. In what sense was faith in Jesus Christ necessary in order to salvation under the Old Testament?

43. About the faith of miracles.

44. Why that active unition of soul is called by the name of faith?

45. Whether the corruption of heart can in any respect be reasonably looked upon as any ground of the imputation of Adam's first sin?

46. What will be the order of the events and proceedings of the day of judgment? "Miscellanies," no. 949.

47. What good reason can be given why God, who is infinitely and unchangeably happy in him[self], should seek his declarative glory and make that his last end in his works?

48. How far does inability to any disposition or act, render a person incapable of obligation to such disposition or act?

49. Whether or no it don't imply a contradiction to suppose that any-thing is an effect of some cause, and yet is not necessarily connected with its cause?

50. Whether we can have any certainty of any existence, past, present or future, but only our own present ideas and consciousness, upon sup-position that 'tis possible for that which is not necessarily existent to be without a cause?

51. Is not there reason to think that those that live and die in sin under means, are generally given up to judicial hardness before they die?

Theological Questions of Jonathan Edwards Sr.[5]

1. How does it appear that something has existed from Eternity?

2. How does it appear that this earth and the visible system are not from eternity?

3. How does it appear that the existence of man is derived and dependent?

4. How do you prove the natural perfections of God, viz. his intelli-gence, infinite power, foreknowledge and immutability?

5. How do you prove his moral perfections, that he is a friend of virtue, or absolutely holy, true, just and good?

6. How do you prove that the Scriptures are a revelation from God? And what are the evidences, internal and external?

7. How do you prove the divine Mission of Christ?

8. How do you prove the divinity of Christ?

9. How do you prove the personality and divinity of the Holy Ghost?

10. How do you prove that the persons in the Trinity are one God?

11. Whence arose the Manichean notion of two Gods, and how is it confuted.

12. Whence arose the polytheism of the pagans and how confuted?

13. Whence was it that the knowledge of the one true God, in which Noah was instructed, was not preserved among his posterity in all ages?

---

5. Park, "Questions of the Two Edwardses," 367–81.

14. Why are not mankind in all ages (their internal faculties and external advantages being sufficient) united in right sentiments of the one true God?

15. Were the moral character of God and the moral law understood and loved, would there be any objections against revealed religion?

16. What is the true idea of God's decrees?

17. How do you prove absolute and particular election?

18. Did God decree the existence of sin?

19. Why did God decree sin?

20. In what sense did he introduce sin into the universe?

21. How do you reconcile this with the holiness and goodness of God?

22. What is necessary to constitute a moral agent?

23. Are men moral and free agents?

24. What is the difference between natural and moral power and marginal inability?

25. How is absolute moral necessity, or inability, consistent with the free agency of man?

26. How is the doctrine of universal, absolute decrees consistent with the free agency of man?

27. How do you prove a universal and special providence?

28. What is the covenant of redemption?

29. If man was created in original righteousness, how is that consistent with moral agency, it being said that a necessary holiness is no holiness?

30. What was the constitution under which Adam in innocency was placed?

31. Was Adam under the same necessity of falling that we are of sinning?

32. Are all intelligencies bound to love God supremely, sinners and devils?

33. Is the law holy, just and good, and how is it proved?

34. Are they who are under its curse bound to delight in it?

35. How great is the demerit of sin?

36. Are the torments of hell eternal?

37. How do you reconcile them with the justice and infinite goodness of God?

38. How do you reconcile them with those texts which say Christ died for all men, that God will not that any perish?

39. How does it appear that human nature is originally depraved?

40. Whence comes that depravity?

41. How is it proved to be total?

42. What is the covenant of grace?

43. Are the law and gospel inconsistent with each other?

44. Why was an atonement and one so precious as the blood of Christ necessary?

45. In what manner did Christ atone for sin?

46. To whom does it belong to provide atonement, God or the sinner?

47. Did Christ redeem all men, alike, elect and non elect?

48. Can the offer of Christ be made with sincerity to the non elect?

49. How is redemption applied?

50. What is the office of the Holy Ghost in the work of Redemption?

51. What is regeneration?

52. Whence arises the necessity of it?

53. What is true love to God?

54. What is true benevolence to man?

55. What is true repentance, and how distinguished from legal?

56. What is true faith?

57. What is pardon and justification? what is their foundation and what is the influence of faith therein?

58. How are full satisfaction and free pardon consistent?

59. Is the sinner forgiven before he repents?

60. Is sanctifying grace needful at all to any man, unless to that which is his duty, and in the neglect of which he would be without excuse?

61. What is the sum of man's duty, and what the effect produced by the sanctifying influence of the Holy Spirit?

62. Can that holy volition in us, which is the effect of divine power be wholly our act or our duty?

63. How is it proved that unbelief is sin, and that all errors in moral matters are of a criminal nature?

64. Will the wicked heathens, Jews, Infidels, and errorists of every kind be without excuse at the day of judgment?

65. What is the essence of true virtue, or holiness?

66. Is there no virtue in the exercise of natural conscience, the moral sense, natural compassion and generosity?

67. Is not self love the root of all virtue?

68. Do not the unregenerate desire to be regenerated and can they not properly pray for regenerating grace?

69. Do they not desire the heavenly happiness?

70. What is the utmost the unregenerate do in the use of the means of grace?

71. Is any duty done by them therein?

72. Do they grow better in the use of means?

73. To what are they to be exhorted?

74. What is the real advantage of the assiduous use of means to the unregenerate?

75. How do you prove that the institution of the Sabbath is of perpetual obligation?

76. How is it that the sabbath is changed from the seventh to the first day of the week?

77. How do you prove that public worship is to be celebrated on the sabbath?

78. What is the foundation and duty of prayer, since God is omniscient and immutable?

79. How do you prove that family prayer is a duty?

80. To whom are the promises of the gospel made, to the regenerate or unregenerate?

81. Are no encouragements given to the unregenerate?

82. How do you prove the saints perseverance?

83. What is the nature of a Christian Church?

84. Who are fit for communion therein?

85. What is the nature and import of baptism?

86. How do you prove infant baptism?

87. What is the nature of the Lord's Supper?

88. What are the rules and ends of Church discipline?

89. What is the character of a good minister of Christ?

90. In what does the happiness of heaven consist?

Theological Questions of Jonathan Edwards Jr.[6]

1. How does it appear that something has existed from eternity?

2. How does it appear that this earth and the visible system are not from eternity?

3. How does it appear that the existence of man is derived and dependant?

4. How do you prove the natural perfections of God, viz. his intelligence, omnipotence, omniscience, immutability, omnipresence, and unity?

5. How do you prove the moral perfections of God, that he is a friend to virtue; absolutely holy, just, good, and true?

6. What do you understand by the light of nature?

7. For what purposes is revelation necessary?

8. Is not the light of nature sufficient to direct mankind to their duty and happiness?

9. In what sense is the light of nature sufficient to direct men to the knowledge of their duty?

10. Is the light of nature so plain to every man that it is impossible to be rendered more plain by revelation?

11. If the light of nature were sufficient to direct mankind to their duty and happiness, if they would make a right use of it, would divine revelation be useful and worth while?

12. If mankind should become ever so well disposed after they had sinned, would the light of nature ever discover the way of pardon?

---

6. Park, "Questions of the Two Edwardses," 367–81.

13. If a revelation be necessary must it not be given to all mankind in all ages?

14. How is it consistent, that a revelation should contain mysteries, as it is said that mystery is no revelation?

15. Are we to give up our reason, receiving a revelation which is inconsistent with reason?

16. If we are to receive no doctrines, under the pretence of revelation, which are inconsistent with reason, do we not make the dictates of reason the test of a true revelation? And if so, what advantage is there in a revelation, since we are to try that by the test of reason?

17. Is not the law of nature perfect? If so, what need of a revelation?

18. What, according to the light of nature, was the end of the creation of man?

19. If the end of the creation of man, were his own happiness, whence so much misery in the world?

20. On the supposition of no future state, what rational account can be given of the creation of man and his state in this world?

21. What do you say to the maxim, that all, who are equally sincere in their religion, are equally acceptable to God?

22. Is it a matter of indifference, what religion a man entertains, provided he be moral?

23. Will bare repentance and subsequent observance of the laws of nature secure pardon to the sinner?

24. Can God make positive institutions, which are not founded in reason and the nature of things?

25. Is the light of nature sufficient to enable us to judge in all cases what is subservient to the good of intelligent being in general, or even for the good of mankind in general?

26. What is meant by the religion of nature?

27. If the light of nature be sufficient to enable us to judge rightly, in matters of religion, whence is it, that the deists differ so widely in their religious principles?

28. Is it a true maxim that what concerns all, must be knowable by all?

29. Did not the unerring wisdom of God employ the most suitable means for human happiness? If so, is not the light of nature the most suitable mean to that end?

30. Does God ever prescribe services to man, which are in themselves, matters of indifference?

31. If there be new things required of us in revelation, which are not prescribed to us by the law of nature, does this imply a change in God?

32. Is the diversity of sentiments among Christians, a stronger argument against the truth of Christianity than the diversity of sentiments among the deists is against the truth of the law of nature?

33. If we knew the nature and tendency of all moral actions, should we not be omniscient in morals?

34. Is it tyranny in God to require some things of us merely to try us?

35. How do you prove that the Scriptures are a revelation from God?

36. What is the internal proof of the truth of the Scriptures?

37. What is the external proof of the truth and divine original of the Scriptures?

38. Are miracles impossible?

39. Are miracles incredible because contrary to our experience?

40. How do you prove that the whole Old Testament is not a forgery?

41. How do you prove that the books of the New Testament were written at the time they claim to have been written and by the men whose names they bear?

42. How does it appear that the apostles were not imposed upon as to the facts which they relate?

43. How does it appear that the apostles were not designing impostors?

44. What remarkable facts of the gospel are attested by profane writers?

45. Are all the prophecies of the Old Testament of the facts of the New, allegorical?

46. Can we have evidence that the Scriptures are a revelation from God, without previous evidence of the moral perfections of God?

47. Was revelation after the fall, necessary in order to any religion?

48. Does the moral and spiritual excellency and glory of the Scriptures prove them not only to be true, but to be given by divine revelation?

49. Is it not inconsistent to argue the truth of a book or system from the manifest truth of the doctrines it contains, and then to argue the truth of those doctrines, from the circumstance that they are contained in that book?

50. In what sense does revealed religion depend on the reason of things?

51. Are we not to act reasonably in all things; and so follow our reason? If so, do we not really, and must we not necessarily set up reason above revelation?

52. Wherever the internal evidences of divine truth are found, are not external evidences needless?

53. Unless we grant the sufficiency of the light of nature, must we not allow that God has not given most men such rules and means as are necessary for their own happiness? And then how will you reconcile this with the moral perfections of God, especially his infinite and impartial goodness?

54. Is the gospel by the changes of tongues, the errors of transcribers, &c. become so obscure, that there is not sufficient evidence of its divine original?

55. Is the Scripture itself sufficient to lead mankind to virtue and happiness? If not, why is the insufficiency of the law of nature to this end, brought as an argument in favor of divine revelation?

56. Are we accountable for any error in opinion concerning moral and religious subjects?

57. How do you prove a future state?

58. How do you prove the immortality of the soul?

59. Is a future state of rewards and punishments taught in the Old Testament?

60. Is a future state of rewards and punishments taught in the writings of Moses?

61. How do you prove the divine mission of Jesus Christ?

62. How do you prove the divinity of Christ?

63. If Christ were a creature could he atone for the sins of men?

64. Is Christ the Son of God in any other sense than Adam was?

65. Did Christ first become a son by his birth of the Virgin Mary?

66. Does the Sonship of Christ consist in his appointment to the work of Redemption?

67. Was Christ a Son from eternity?

68. Was Christ necessarily or voluntarily begotten of the Father?

69. Is there more absurdity in supposing that Christ was eternally begotten, than that he was eternally the second person in the Trinity?

70. Was the human soul of Christ created before his conception by the Virgin?

71. How do you prove the personality of the Holy Ghost?

72. How do you prove that the three persons of the Trinity are one God?

73. Was the tripartite distinction of the Deity from eternity?

74. Was the subordination of the three persons in the Trinity, as first, second and third, from eternity?

75. How do you disprove the doctrine that those three persons are three distinct characters only?

76. Is it not a plain contradiction, that God should be one God and yet three persons?

77. What is the Arian scheme of the Trinity?

78. What is the Socinian scheme of the Trinity?

79. Whence arose the Manichean notion of two Gods? And how is it confuted?

80. Whence arose the polytheism of the pagans? And how is it confuted?

81. The internal faculties and external advantages of mankind being sufficient, why are they not in all ages united in true sentiments concerning the one true God?

82. Were the moral character of God and moral law understood and loved, would there be any objection against revealed religion?

83. What is the true idea of God's decrees?

84. Are God's acts or volitions successive? or do they successively take place in the divine mind?

85. Did God decree the existence of sin?

86. For what end did God decree the existence of sin?

87. In what sense is sin agreeable to the will of God?

88. Is the present system of the universe the best possible?

89. What is the difference between the secret and revealed will of God?

90. In what sense and in what manner did God introduce sin into the world?

91. How do you answer the objection, that this makes God the author of sin?

92. If the influence of God destroy the creature's free agency, can that influence produce sin in the creature?

93. If the divine influence do not destroy the creature's free agency, in what sense, liable to objection, is God the author of sin?

94. What is necessary to constitute a moral agent?

95. What is that liberty, which is necessary to moral agency?

96. Do we always act from motive? or what do you mean by motive?

97. Is a capacity to know our duty, necessary to moral agency?

98. Is self determination necessary to moral agency?

99. Are we conscious that our volitions are not effected by any cause without ourselves?

100. Must our volitions be self determinate in order that they may be our own?

101. Are men moral agents?

102. What is the difference between natural and moral necessity and ability?

103. How can absolute moral necessity and inability be consistent with free agency?

104. How can the doctrine of universal absolute decrees be consistent with free agency in man?

105. Is it consistent with human liberty that God should efficiently produce volition in the human heart?

106. Is it equally consistent with human liberty, that God should efficiently produce in the human heart an evil volition as a good one?

107. If God were to produce an evil volition in the human heart, would it prove that God were a sinner, or that he loves sin?

108. If moral necessity be inconsistent with liberty, can God be the author of sin?

109. How do you make it appear that men may be accountable, though they be not the efficient causes of their own volitions?

110. If all the volitions of men be decreed, how are they in a state of probation?

111. How do you prove a particular, special providence in every event?

112. What is meant by the covenant of redemption?

113. Which of the person in the Trinity created and governs the world?

114. What is the last end of creation?

115. Was the display of the divine glory the end of the happiness of the creation? Or the happiness of the creation the end of the display of the divine glory?

116. Did God create the world for his own happiness in display of the divine glory?

117. Are God's own happiness and glory, and the happiness of the creation, two distinct ends of creation?

118. How do you make it appear, that God's own glory or happiness and the happiness of creation are one?

119. If man was created in original righteousness, how was that consistent with moral agency, as it is said that necessary holiness is no holiness?

120. What was the constitution under which man in innocence was placed?

121. What is sin?

122. Is a mere want of love to God sin?

123. What was Adam's first sin?

124. If Adam had broken any precept of the moral law, would he have been liable to the death threatened?

125. What was the death threatened in Genesis 2.17?

126. In what sense, consistent with truth, was the sentence of death executed on Adam, in as much as he did not die the same day?

127. Had Adam before the fall any more freedom of will than we have?

128. Was Adam under the same necessity of falling that we are of sinning?

129. Are all intelligences, sinners and devils, bound to love God supremely?

130. Is the law of God, holy, just, and good? And how do you prove it?

131. Is a damning God the proper object of love?

132. How great is the demerit of sin?

133. How do you prove the endless duration of hell torments?

134. How do you reconcile the endless duration of hell torments with the perfect justice and infinite goodness of God?

135. How do you reconcile the endless duration of hell torments with those tests, which say, Christ died for all men-God will have all men to be saved?

136. Has God made any man to be damned?

137. Is God obliged by veracity to execute the threatening of his law?

138. Are the rewards and punishments of the gospel inconsistent with disinterested affection? Or do they prove Christianity to be a selfish scheme?

139. How does it appear that human nature is originally depraved?

140. Whence comes the original depravity of human nature?

141. What do you mean by total depravity?

142. How do you prove human nature to be totally depraved? What arguments from Scripture? from reason, or experience and observation?

143. How do you prove that Adam was the federal head of his posterity?

144. In what sense is Adam's sin imputed to his posterity?

145. Is Adam's sin thus imputed by a judicial or sovereign act of God?

146. In what sense are Adam and his posterity one?

147. In what sense are mankind punished for Adam's sin?

148. Is it a punishment to the posterity of Adam that they come into the world in a depraved state?

149. Does God bring any evil on mankind, which he might not, consistently with justice have brought upon them, if Adam had not been their federal head?

150. What is the covenant of grace?

151. Why was a satisfaction, or atonement, necessary to the dispensation of pardon?

152. Are the divine law and gospel consistent with each other?

153. Why was a satisfaction, or atonement, so great as that of Christ, necessary to the dispensation of pardon?

154. In what consisted the essence of the atonement of Christ? In his obedience, or suffering, or both?

155. In what sense did he satisfy divine justice by his sacrifice?

156. Was God under an obligation of justice to provide an atonement for sinners?

157. Does the appointment of a Mediator prove that God is already reconciled to men?

158. Did Christ redeem all men alike, the elect and non-elect?

159. In what sense does God love the elect, while unregenerate, different from what he loves the non-elect?

160. Is there evidence from Scripture, or from history and observation, that any of the heathen are saved?

161. Is there evidence that none of the heathen are saved?

162. What are the reasons assigned in favor of the idea of the salvation of heathens?

163. Are a precise number of mankind elected to eternal life and the rest reprobated?

164. Did God from eternity foreknow all future events?

165. Is this foreknowledge founded on his decrees or his decrees on his foreknowledge?

166. What do you mean by absolute and what by conditional election?

167. Is election absolute, or conditional, and founded on the foresight of the repentance and faith of the elect?

168. Does election extend to individuals, or to communities only?

169. Can the offers of the gospel be made with sincerity to the non-elect?

170. What chance of salvation have the non-elect, more than if Christ had never died?

171. Did Christ suffer in the stead, as well as for the benefit of his people?

172. Could he have made an atonement without suffering instead of his people?

173. Did Christ pay the debt for the elect, so that they can claim salvation on the foot of justice?

174. Were the sufferings of Christ to the supporting of the divine law, equivalent to the endless torments of the sinner?

175. Do the sufferings and obedience of Christ prove the divine law to be a just law?

176. How is redemption applied to the elect?

177. What is the office of the Holy Ghost in the work of our salvation?

178. What is regeneration?

179. What is the difference between regeneration and conversion?

180. What is the native blindness of mankind?

181. Is the native blindness of mankind entirely criminal?

182. What is divine illumination?

183. Are spiritual beauty and glory seen by pure intellect?

184. Is the sight of beauty distinct from the love of beauty?

185. Is it a matter of duty to all men to see the spiritual glory of divine objects?

186. Does regeneration immediately affect any faculty of the mind beside the will?

187. Is regeneration effected by light?

188. What do you mean by the physical operation of the spirit in regeneration?

189. Is the subject of regeneration active or passive in it?

190. Whence arises the necessity of regeneration?

191. Is not the physical operation of the spirit, and the passivity of the subject under the operation of regeneration, inconsistent with the moral agency of the subject?

192. What is true love to God? And what is the primary foundation of it?

193. What is true benevolence to man?

194. What is repentance unto life? And how distinguished from legal repentance?

195. Does true repentance imply that we are sorry that we have committed those sins, which we have committed?

196. What is saving faith? And how distinguished from historical and doctrinal faith and the faith of miracles?

197. Have all a warrant to exercise an appropriating faith?

198. Is an appropriating faith a saving faith?

199. Is there a specific difference between common grace and special grace?

200. What is pardon of sin?

201. What is justification?

202. Is justification from eternity?

203. What is the meritorious cause of justification?

204. What is the influence of faith to justification?

205. In what sense is the believer one with Christ?

206. Is the believer, in justification, received and considered as one with Christ, and really thought by God to be one with him?

207. What is the true idea of the imputation of the righteousness of Christ to the believer?

208. Is the believer considered by God as possessed of the righteousness of Christ or does he think that he possesses that righteousness?

209. Is justification a declaration that the believer stands right with respect to the divine law?

210. Is free pardon included in justification as an essential part of it?

211. Is the justification of the believer a judicial and legal act, or an act of sovereign grace?

212. Has the believer on account of the righteousness of Christ, a right to demand justification as justly and legally due to him?

213. Is the believer even after he is justified by faith, condemned by the divine law?

214. In what sense then is the believer free from the law?

215. How are full satisfaction and free pardon consistent?

216. Is the sinner forgiven before he repents?

217. Is forgiveness granted on account of the sinner's repentance?

218. Does forgiveness extend to future sins?

219. Is the sinner forgiven by God's absolute goodness, or grace, without satisfaction?

220. If the sinner had of his own accord repented and become perfectly holy, could he have been forgiven, without the satisfaction of Christ?

221. Is the faith by which the believer is justified, a mere speculative assent?

222. If faith imply love, which is a moral exercise, or a work, is not the believer justified by works? Yet he is justified without the deeds of the law.

223. In what sense is the believer justified by works?

224. How do you reconcile James' account of justification, with Paul's?

225. Exhibit your proofs that James means justification in the sight of God?

226. Will not this scheme of justification derogate from the grace of God in act?

227. Is sanctifying grace, at all needful to any man, unless it be with respect to that which is his duty, and in respect to which he is without excuse?

228. What is the sum of man's duty, and what the effect produced by the sanctifying influence of the Spirit?

229. Can that holy volition in us, which is wholly the effect of divine power, be wholly our act, and our duty?

230. How can it be made to appear that unbelief is a sin and that all error, in moral matters, are of a criminal nature?

231. Will the wicked, the heathen, Jews, Infidels, and errorists of every kind, be without excuse in the day of judgment?

232. What is the essence of true virtue or holiness?

233. Is there no virtue in the exercises of natural conscience, the moral sense, natural compassions, natural generosity or natural affections?

234. What do you mean by self love?

235. What do you say concerning this definition of self love?

236. Is not self love the root of all virtue?

237. Are the voluntary exercises of self love positively sinful?

238. Does self love proceed from an original, and peculiar bias, or principle?

239. As distinguished from selfishness, can self love be subordinate to the general good?

240. Does a sinner love himself, more than a saint loves himself?

241. Is the enmity of the sinner against God disinterested?

242. What do you mean by disinterested love?

243. Is God to be loved disinterestedly?

244. If a man love God directly, and disinterestedly at all, will he not love him supremely?

245. Are the voluntary exercises of natural compassion, natural generosity, natural affection, and all voluntary exercises in the unregenerate, positively sinful?

246. What do you mean by moral obligation?

247. What is the primary foundation of moral obligation?

248. Is the knowledge of the will of God, necessary to moral obligation?

249. Is the will of God itself or his moral perfections the primary foundation of moral obligations?

250. Is the knowledge of the existence of God, necessary to moral obligation?

251. Is the existence of God itself, necessary to moral obligation?

252. Is God himself free from moral obligations?

253. If the tendency of an action to happiness, be the primary foundation of moral obligation, will it not follow, that natural good is more valuable and important than moral good?

254. What other foundations of moral obligation, have been invented and published?

255. In what sense do the unregenerate desire to be regenerated? And in what sense can they pray for regenerating grace?

256. Is it the duty of the unregenerate to pray for regenerating grace?

257. Do the unregenerate desire the happiness of heaven?

258. What is the utmost which the unregenerate do in the use of the means of grace?

259. Is any real duty done by the unregenerate in the use of the means of grace?

260. Are all the voluntary external actions of the unregenerate, positively sinful?

261. Do the unregenerate grow better in the use of means?

262. What is the immediate duty of the unregenerate? And to what are they to be exhorted?

263. What is the real advantage, of an assiduous use of means, to the unregenerate?

264. To whom are the promises of the gospel made? to the regenerate or unregenerate?

265. Are there no encouragements given to the unregenerate? And what are they?

266. How do you prove the saints perseverance?

267. Can you make it appear that the promises of the gospel mean more, than that those who persevere shall be saved?

268. Is assurance attainable by saints in this life?

269. Is assurance essential to faith?

270. By what means is assurance to be obtained?

271. What is the witness of the Spirit? And is it mediate or immediate?

272. What is the seal of the Spirit?

273. Do all real Christians know the time of their conversion?

274. Do all real Christians certainly know that they are converted at all?

275. Are great awakenings and convictions of conscience, followed with great joys and comforts, and attended with texts of Scripture, extraordinarily suggested to the mind, proofs of real conversion?

276. Is the state of the righteous and the wicked, between death and the resurrection, a state of sensibility? And how do you prove it?

277. How do you prove the resurrection of the body, and the general judgment?

278. How do you prove the immortality of the soul?

279. Will the secret sins of the righteous be made public at the day of judgment?

280. Do the saints in heaven know any thing that is done on earth?

281. How do you prove that the institution of the Sabbath is of perpetual obligation?

282. How do [you] prove that the Sabbath is changed from the seventh to the first day of the week?

283. How do you prove that public worship ought to be attended on the Sabbath?

284. Which evening is to be kept as a part of the Sabbath?

285. What is the foundation of the duty of prayer, since God is immutable?

286. How do you prove that family prayer is a duty?

287. Ought we to pray for perfection in this life?

288. What is the nature of a Christian church?

289. Who are fit subjects for communion in the church?

290. Ought we to have universal charity for all professing Christians?

291. Ought we to think that all sects of Christians are right?

292. What is the nature and import of baptism?

293. How do you prove baptism?

294. Does infant baptism alone give a title to all privileges of the church?

295. What is the nature and import of the Lord's supper?

296. Are the same qualifications necessary for an attendance on both sacraments?

297. What are the rules, and what the end of church discipline?

298. What is just matter of discipline and excommunication?

299. Is heresy a just matter of excommunication?

300. Is Universalism a just matter of excommunication?

301. Is marriage a sacrament?

302. In what case may a divorce take place?

303. May a man marry his wife's sister?

304. May an uncle marry his niece?

305. Is polygamy lawful?

306. What is the character of a good minister of Jesus Christ?

307. Have you reason to think that you are possessed of the spiritual part of the character of a good minister of Jesus Christ?

308. To whom does the performance of ordination belong?

309. May a man preach as a candidate before he is ordained?

310. If we hold that ordination belongs to the elders, must we also maintain that the line of ordination has never been broken?

311. In what does the happiness of heaven consist?

312. Why is holiness necessary to the enjoyment of happiness of heaven?

313. What are the essential or fundamental doctrines of Christianity?

Questions and Answers 1–313

Question 1 [2]. How does it appear that something existed from eternity?

Answer 1. Had nothing existed from eternity nothing would have existed to eternity. It is impossible in the nature of things, that something should bring itself into existence: otherwise, were it to bring itself into existence it must act, put forth an exertion of power, before it had a being. But there can be no power where there is no existence: neither can there be an exertion of power where there is no power: consequently there can be no exertion of power where there is no existence. For a creature to bring itself into existence, it must be and not be at the same time: it must be both the cause and effect of the same action. No effect can take place without some cause. It is perfectly inconceivable, how a thing should start into existence without some ground or cause of its existence or how any effect should take place without some antecedent cause. Since then there are existences they must be effects of some cause or causes. Creatures evidently are not capable of creating each other. They are not possessed of power sufficient. Nor does there appear to be that regular gradation and subordination between the several species and individuals which there must be in case they created each other. There must therefore be at least one being whose existence has no cause without or beyond itself, who is unproduced, uncreated, and consequently from eternity.

Question 2 [3]. How does it appear that this earth and visible system are not from eternity?

Answer 2. This earth and visible system evidently consist of matter, sluggish and inactive, incapable of beginning motion in itself or of communicating it to anything else. That, whose ground or reason of existence is within itself, must be possessed of some power within itself. But matter, evidently, has no power but what is communicated. There cannot then, be any ground or

74

reason of its existence within, but it must be without itself. Its existence must be derived and dependent. If so, this earth and visible system, which consists of matter are the effect of some cause. They were brought into existence by some power superior to themselves. The existence of an effect produced by some cause presupposes the exertion of power. No power can be exerted for this purpose without beginning to be exerted and consequently no effect can be produced without being begun to be produced and that which once began is not from eternity.

Besides, the most authentic histories can extend the antiquity of the world back to but a few thousand years. Every appearance favors the idea that its duration has been but short. Those parts which most probably were never inhabited appeared to be but a little superior to that which has been produced by cultivation. Every part bears evident marks of decay and ruin. But were it from eternity, its existence must be from some ground or reason within itself: it must be underived and independent and consequently might continue to exist to eternity.

Question 3 [5]. How does it appear that the existence of man is derived and dependent?

Answer 3. Man's existence is evidently recent and of short duration. He could not have brought himself into existence because it is absurd and inconsistent to suppose him to act before he had being: to be both the cause and effect of the same action. Nor was there any ground or reason for his existence in his nature originally. Otherwise, he would've been from, and might continue to eternity. Since he did not bring himself into being, his existence most evidently is derived: and since he cannot, agreeably to his own wishes, continue himself in existence it is equally evident, he is dependent, for his continuance in existence.

Question 4 [6]. How do you prove the natural perfections of God; intelligence, omnipotence, omniscience, immutability, omnipresence, and unity?

Answer 4. All being is divided into matter and mind, or intelligence. Matter appears to be dispossessed of every power which might render it capable of creating or producing any effects independently. It is impossible, indeed, to conceive how an unintelligent substance should produce intelligence: how a lifeless lump should produce life and activity; or how one being should communicate a greater perfection and excellence then itself possesses. The greatest argument, however, in favor of God's intelligence, is the evident marks of design and skill which appear in every work of his hands. More particularly, the nature, construction, and situation of this Earth, the variety of its inhabitants, their curious frames, and the means of their support, the proportion kept up, between the sexes; above all, the human constitution, the union of soul and body, and the great and enlarging powers and faculties of the soul are all decisive demonstrations that he who created things and especially human intelligence must himself be possessed of this perfection in the highest degree.

Since all creatures are dependent upon God for their being, continuance in existence, and for all the powers they possess, it is evident, none can resist him and prosper, none can thwart and frustrate his designs. That power then, which created the present system of creatures, might still go on to create systems of creatures, *ad infinitum*. Nor can anything be conceived to be beyond the limits of his power, which implies no contradiction; which is all that is required to be omnipotent.

From similar considerations the omniscience of God appears equally clear. As he gave two creatures their powers and faculties, he is surely acquainted with the extent of these powers; for the meanest workman is acquainted with the work he performs. He is perfectly acquainted with what he has done, can or will do. Since he gave to his creatures all their powers and faculties and since they are constantly dependent upon, and act, in subservience to him it is necessary he should know all things they do otherwise they might counteract and defeat his purposes and introduce confusion and disorder. If then, he is acquainted with all things respecting himself and creatures he is omniscient with respect to all real existences and from what he has done and what we know of his knowledge, we may infer his knowledge of all possible existences.

The ground or reason of his existence speaking in his very nature he must be necessarily existent. The necessity of his existence must be antecedent to, in the order of nature, and independent of his will. And being beyond the reach of change from any other being this necessity of his existence must remain so long as his nature remains. Since then he's not subject to change from his own will or that of any other being he is immutable.

He is over and above all and therefore can be limited by none. Necessity of existence must be unlimited: for as nothing can be conceived of to bound or limit it; so that which is the ground or reason of it must be uniformly the same everywhere. If we might suppose one degree of possible existence unnecessary we might another and consequently every degree. No place therefore can be mentioned where God's existence is not necessary, and consequently where it is not. Besides, not only is God from his very nature necessarily existent everywhere, but he must be in all places to support, uphold and govern all things.

If God be self existent or necessarily existent and consequently infinite, it would be absurd to suppose two gods. If we supposed two beings, self existent and necessarily existent, the ground or reason of their existence must be in their very nature and must be uniformly the same: consequently the beings must be both alike in every respect. If so, then they are not two but one. If they be different one must have what the other has not: and therefore one at least must be imperfect. It is absurd to suppose two infinities in every respect. There can be only one infinite in power or knowledge and consequently but one God.[1]

Question 5 [10]. How do you prove the moral perfections of God; that he is a friend to virtue, absolutely holy, just, good, and true?

Answer 5. Judging from the present appearance of things we should not perhaps be led to determine what is the true moral character of God. From the mixture of good and evil which take place in the world, and the indiscriminate and similar treatment of the virtuous and vicious, we should be at a loss or perhaps suppose him to be of a mixed character. But reasoning from his natural perfections we might rather conclude him to be a friend to virtue; holy, just, good, and true.

Being omniscient and omnipotent we cannot suppose him subject to disappointment. His all sufficiency would place him beyond the reach of want or weakness. In creatures these appear to be sources of depravity and weakness, in part, at least; and since these do not affect him, we should not on account of them suppose him to be evil.

From his giving his creatures capacities of distinguishing between good and evil and morally good and evil character, we might be led to conclude he must himself be good. For were he not so, he must certainly know all his virtuous creatures would hate and detest him, and we should naturally suppose it would be directly repugnant to the feelings and wishes of the supreme being to suffer this from those of his creatures. We might then be led to conclude he must himself be a friend to virtue. He who in heart is a

1. Supplement, p. 376; *Answer 4*. Were God an evil being he could create a holy and good being. In this respect then, he might on this supposition communicate a perfection he has not. Among second causes also we find the effect to be more excellent, frequently than this cause. Thus a son may be possessed of qualities his father had not; and on the whole be more excellent. Since all things are created by God and nothing can come into existence without the exertion of his almighty power it is evident he must be acquainted with all possible existences. We cannot conceive of the universal presence of a spirit, but his knowing all things, and doing all things. God is present in this or other place as he knows those things which are done in them. He is present in places, by his power where he effects anything. Locality, however, is not in the same sense, predicable of a spirit as of God.

friend to virtue is himself virtuous or holy. Once supposing him holy and a friend to virtue, he must be equally an enemy to vice and wickedness.

It does not appear to be consistent with the holy character to suffer virtue to go unrewarded or vice unpunished. The latter is evidently an injury to the system of God's moral government, and must remain so until reparation be made. Repentance and reformation, however great and sincere cannot atone for past offenses or repair the injury already done. Justice therefore will require something further than mere repentance and reformation; and also, the general good must require the damage be repaired. Benevolence, which is but another term for holiness will excite God to do that which is right and fit, and which is calculated to promote the general good. Besides the existence of the moral sense or conscience that sense of fit and unfit, of right and wrong which God has implanted in his creatures is perhaps a strong indication of the justice of his own character: otherwise we might naturally inquire why he gave them such feelings and dread of justice unless he were really possessed of that perfection himself.

Goodness also is but another name for holiness. For what is a virtuous character but a good character? And what is virtue or holiness but the communication of goodness and happiness.

Holiness, justice and goodness cannot be supposed to exist in any character, in an infinite degree, where truth is not. The want of truth is evidently a blemish in any character, in which it is found. It is evidently a mark of depravity of heart. God therefore who is infinite in holiness is also a God of truth. Beside, if he is not only holy but omniscient, omnipotent and all sufficient, he must be beyond all conceivable temptation to falsehood.

It must however on the whole be allowed that the moral perfections of God are not so clearly demonstrable by mere unassisted reason, as his natural perfections. The latter are fully demonstrable, without the aid of revelation; though by this, light is evidently thrown upon them: but for the proof of the former, we must depend upon the declaration he has made of himself, and from a real acquaintance with the exhibition he makes of his character to his creatures.

Question 6 [13]. What do you understand by the light of nature?

Answer 6. In answering this question it may not be improper to explain what we mean by mankind's being in a state of nature, and what by the word "light." Mankind may be said to be in a state of nature, 1) with reference to the state of their hearts. When they are totally depraved in their hearts and corrupt in their lives, when they are alienated from God and his service, then they are with propriety, said to be in the state of nature. 2) they are so, when they have no express intimations of God's will; when they are left to the exertions of mere human reason unassisted by divine revelation, to obtain a knowledge of God, his will, his works, his creatures, of themselves and their situation and duty, then they may be said to be in a state of nature: and in this sense we shall consider them in answering this question.

The word light is undoubtedly used here in a sense different from its original meaning. It is evidently used metaphorically and applied to the understanding. We frequently say, light is let into the mind and the mind is enlightened, when we mean the understanding is informed. So a man is said to throw light upon a subject when he gives a clear and more full understanding of it.

Taking these explanations, the light of nature can be nothing more than that knowledge especially the religious kind, which mankind may or do attain to, by the exertions of mere human reason unassisted by divine revelation.

Question 7 [15]. For what purposes is a revelation necessary?

Answer 7. Mankind unassisted by divine revelation might possibly obtain some knowledge of God and of themselves as sinners. But though they might become sensible in part of their situation as sinners and exposure to divine wrath on account of their wickedness, yet they never could attain to any certainty with respect to the measure and extent of God's wrath; whether he would pour forth the full vials of it, without mercy, or whether he would admit some atonement and become reconcilable on certain conditions. This is evidently a subject to mankind the most important and interesting: and on this, the light of nature is totally deficient. Revelation therefore it is necessary to teach mankind what atonement God requires, what is the method of reconciliation which he has instituted and what will be the situation of those who do not fall in with the terms of reconciliation and obtain his favor and forgiveness. Revelation is also necessary to teach mankind, what would be the situation of those who should make their peace with God or what would be the happiness of the friends of God in a future state. Indeed, the knowledge of mankind unaided by revelation would attain with respect to a future state if they should attain any at all, must be extremely indeterminate and uncertain.

In short without revelation the knowledge of mankind on almost every religious subject must be very obscure and feeble. They might have some knowledge of the natural perfections of God: but his moral perfections would appear clouded, with doubt and uncertainty. The extent of creation, the moral government of God, the requirements and sanctions of his law, as has in part been already intimated could never be fully understood but by the declarations of his word.

> Question 8 [17]. Is not the light of nature sufficient to direct mankind to their duty and happiness?

Answer 8. In answer to the preceding question it was intimated that most probably the light of nature might direct mankind to some knowledge of God, in their own situation as sinners. If the light of nature would inform them that they are sinners and in what respect they are so, it would also teach them at the same time some kinds of wickedness at least which they ought to avoid. For those instances in which mankind see themselves to be sinners must give them a sense of the obligation they are under to live free from vices which make them such.

Possibly the light of nature might direct mankind not only to the knowledge of negative duties, but also to the knowledge of some of the positive kind. But since as was observed before it does not teach them the means of reconciliation and acceptance with God; it does not teach them that duty with which their future happiness is connected and consequently it is not sufficient to direct them to happiness.

> Question 9 [18]. In what sense is the light of nature sufficient to direct men to the knowledge of their duty?

Answer 9. The light of nature might direct mankind to the knowledge of many things they ought to avoid. In teaching them that there is a God and the relation they sustain with respect to him and his creatures, it might direct them some of the relative duties they owe to him and their fellow creatures. It might teach them to fear, revere, love and worship him. But since they must be extremely deficient in the knowledge of God's moral character and government, it is not probable that their notions or practice would arise any higher then the principle of selfishness. Because he is a great and powerful being, they would fear and reverence him. So far as he should do them good they might feel themselves obligated to love him and to avoid his frowns, and conciliate his favor, they might be led to worship him.

In like manner, they might be led to treat their fellow creatures. Those who should be their friends and promote their interest, they might love and respect: but most probably they would esteem it a virtue to hate and destroy their enemies. The light of nature therefore, would never teach mankind universal benevolence, to practice self-denial, to subject all their interests and pursuits to the honor of God. It would not teach them to forgive their enemies, pray for them and treat them with kindness. Nor is it probable it would teach them in what religion principally consists, and that it ought to be seated in the heart. They must be ignorant of the doctrine of total depravity, of regeneration, of the means of reconciliation with God and all those duties with which salvation is immediately connected. In short since the light of nature does not direct mankind to a proper temper heart and affections, it teaches no duty as it ought to be taught.[2]

Question 10 [20]. Is the light of nature so plain to every man, that it is impossible to be rendered more plain by revelation?

Answer 10. If the meaning of the question be whether the knowledge which every man has by the light of nature, is not so perfect, that no additions could be made to it, the answer is easy. It is evident that many, even under the light of revelation, are essentially deficient in the most important doctrines, and ignorant of their own duty in a thousand instances. But if by it be meant whether mankind by the light of nature might not obtain all that knowledge which is necessary and possess it so clearly and accurately that no improvement could be made upon it, the answer is in part, already anticipated.

It is been said by one of the greatest advocates for natural religion that it consists in "belief of the existence of a God and the sense and practice of those duties which result from the knowledge we, by our reason, have of him and his perfections; and of the relation we stand in to him and our fellow creatures."[3] But this author has never clearly described and demonstrated those doctrines of natural religion by reason alone. It is evident he is beholden to revelation for all the accurate and real knowledge he has upon either of these subjects. Notwithstanding all he has written however with the aid of revelation mankind must remain greatly in the dark with respect to the knowledge of God in their own duty. He has never yet demonstrated the moral perfections of God by the light of nature. Nor has he ever proved that God will except of repentance and reformation as an atonement for past transgressions. He has not also demonstrated by the light of nature a future state of retribution.

Natural religion, according to him, takes in everything founded upon the reason and nature of things: and it differs from a revealed religion

2. Supplement, pp. 376–77; Answer 9. Mankind most probably, were they disposed to know and do their duty, without the aid of revelation, might obtain very considerable knowledge of their duty in a number of respects. Adam, in a state of innocence, might have attained to very considerable knowledge without the aid of revelation. It is prejudice and depravity of heart which blinds the mind. While these remain, they would not obtain a knowledge of their duty, by the light of nature.

3. Tindal, *Christianity as Old as Creation*.

only in the manner of its being communicated. But the main object of his whole book appears to have been to prove that there never was any external revelation or at least, that we can have no more than a probable argument in proof of it. He labors hard to prove that God will support true religion at any rate, in every country and age of the world. But there evidently have been a great many religions in the world which were directly opposed to each other. Either, therefore, God has not supported the true religion in every country and age of the world or the true religion must have been directly and totally contrary to itself, in a thousand instances. He says, "God requires nothing of men, but what is founded upon the nature of things and the mutual relations they bear to each other." In this passage, he seems to admit it is absolutely our duty to act agreeably to the nature of things and the mutual relations they bear to each other. Yet he supposes it is lawful to use deception and to lie in certain cases. But surely this is not consistent with the nature of things and the mutual relations they bear to each other unless iniquity is: for according to himself iniquity is the same thing in action as falsity is in theory. Changing the order now falsity in theory is the same with iniquity in action. Consequently, in teaching falsity in theory he teaches iniquity in action. God, he says cannot dispose with the law of nature: yet he himself it seems finds no deficiency in doing so. He proceeds to tell us that the spring of the creature's action is their own good; that the happiness of all beings consists in the perfections of their nature; and that a man's happiness and duties consist in the same things: consequently his duty must be to act agreeably to his own nature, and the spring of that is his own good. This he intimates, also, in a number of other places, where he says, God can require nothing of us but what makes for our happiness, and forbid us nothing but what tends to our hurt—that no one is obliged to do anything that does not some way or another contribute to his happiness—and that whoever so regulates his natural appetites, as will conduce most to the exercise of his reason, the health of his body, and the pleasure of the senses, may be certain, he can never offend his maker. Again he says that the actions of God flow from disinterested love: and in the words of a favorite writer that "in all our inquiries what is pleasing to God our last appeal must be to his nature, which is the great standard of good and evil, by which, we are to measure what is pleasing and displeasing to him."[4] He also says that as long as men believe the good of the society is the supreme law, they will think it their duty to be governed by that law, and believing God requires nothing of them than what is for the good of mankind will place the whole of their

4. Tindal, *Christianity as Old as Creation*.

religion in benevolent actions and to the utmost of their abilities copy after the divine original. Here, according to the descriptions of that duty which natural religion teaches mankind are to act agreeably to their own nature and conformably to the nature of God: they are to act from a principal of self-love or from a regard to their own private good and happiness and they are to act from disinterested love or a regard to the public good, and as he elsewhere observes this benevolence will lead them to applaud a brave and generous action, though they should suffer by it. According to this, no man is obliged to do anything that does not some way or another contribute to his happiness. Yet it seems by the latter representation as though mankind ought to place the whole of their religion in benevolent actions. To complete the whole he says, that the only innate principal in man is the desire of his own happiness; and that the goodness of God requires no more than a right cultivating this principle, and yet somehow, we must conjecture by the rule of contraries, it consists, in preferring a general or public to a particular or private good. Thus, according to this author, that religion which the light of nature or reason dictates, teaches a heap of inconsistencies. Surely then it is possible for a revelation to render the light of nature more plain and consistent.

> Question 11 [25]. Provided the light of nature were sufficient to direct mankind to their duty and happiness, if they would attend to it, may not a revelation be useful and therefore worth while?

Answer 11. Doubtless a revelation might be useful to illustrate, explain and confirm the duty of mankind. It might direct to the knowledge of many new and useful truths, with which their duty would not be so intimately connected, as for their happiness to depend on them, though the knowledge of them might contribute to their happiness. A revelation might also bring to view the reasons and grounds of God's proceedings with his creatures. It might bring to view the history of mankind with respect to past ages and predict or clearly point out the future state of mankind. It might give a more extensive view of God's moral government together with his own character. It might, also, be useful, to support mankind in a more cheerful performance of their duty. A revelation would be useful to direct to the most happy mode of worship. By means of this, God might give mankind more clear and confirmed notions with respect to a future state. On these accounts it would not only be useful but proper to be made.

Question 12 [26]. Provided sinners should become ever so well disposed to receive and obey the truth, would the light of nature teach them the way to pardon?

Answer 12. The light of nature never could teach mankind the way to pardon, which is instituted in the gospel. This method of pardon and salvation would be devised by God alone. Without a revelation from him therefore, it never could be known. The light of nature never could teach with certainty any other way. For no other way could be conceived that would be likely to procure pardon, but repentance and reformation. But since these never could atone for past offenses, mankind could have no well grounded hope for this quarter. Mankind, however, cannot become sincerely disposed to receive and obey the truth until they are experimentally taught the true way to pardon.

Question 13 [27]. If a revelation be necessary, must it not be given to all mankind in all ages?

Answer 13. Though a revelation be useful and necessary, yet God is under no obligation to make one to any of his creatures. Before man fell there was nothing, which could lay God under obligation to reveal himself in any respect. Nor since the fall can it be said, that any had reason to expect it, aside from the goodness and sovereign mercy of God. Had he pleased, he doubtless might have left the whole human race without giving the least express intimation of his will, by means of a revelation. If so, then most clearly, he might make a revelation in what age of the world he pleased; and make it known to whom he pleased, without doing injury to any. Nor is it any more of a mark of partiality or of being a respecter of persons than his furnishing some with greater or different powers and faculties of body or mind than others. He is no more obliged to make revelation universally known than to make the means of grace where they are possessed to become universally efficacious. Indeed he is no more obliged to do this than he is to make the principles of natural religion equally clear to all mankind and in all ages of the world; or to hold up truth of any kind in a light equally clear to every individual.

These observations will appear still more evident if we consider that it is only wholly to the depravity and wickedness of mankind that revelation is not universally known. Had they been sincerely disposed to receive and obey the truth, doubtless it might have been retained in every age and nation of the world, from the time it was first given.

Question 14 [29]. How is it consistent that a revelation should contain mysteries as it is said that a mystery is no revelation at all?

Answer 14. Mystery, when used agreeably to its proper meaning is a word, which stands for something strange, wonderful, or beyond our reason, fully to comprehend. That which is contrary to reason, strictly speaking, is no mystery at all: at least it is no true and proper mystery. Nor is this consistent with a revelation from God that which is contrary to reason, is likewise, contrary to truth; and therefore not worthy to be revealed.

If then, a mystery is consistent with truth, nothing but a capacity sufficiently extensive is wanting, to comprehend it and make it like other truths clear and easy. That therefore, which to one may be a mystery, to another of a more enlarged and capacious understanding, may be clearly and fully unfolded. Thus, to an ignorant and unskillful countrymen, a watch, the spring and movements of it, may be as really mysterious as the greatest mystery in nature, is to mankind in general. Yet, if this countryman had a friend whose truth and honesty he for many years had proved to be inviolable, and this friend should tell him, he fully understood the nature of a watch that the spring of its movements arose from such a cause, doubtless he would act from great disingenuity and want of friendship, if he should disbelieve his friend on this instance; merely because he did not understand these things himself. But to disbelieve a revelation from God because it contains mysteries is far more disingenuous and infinitely more criminal.

God may then declare mysteries to his creatures and with propriety require their belief. Indeed, it is difficult to conceive how a revelation should be made and be anyway complete, which did not contain mysteries. Even in the natural world we are surrounded with a thousand things, which are mysterious and in the disbelieving of which we should show the greatest folly. Thus the doctrines of vegetation, electricity, gravitation, magnetism, the union of soul and body, and the action of mind upon matter are all far beyond the reach of human capacity, fully to comprehend. But a revelation from God, which treats upon subjects infinitely more sublime must of course contain mysteries proportionally greater.[5]

Question 15 [31]. Are we to give up our reason in receiving a revelation, which is inconsistent with reason?

Answer 15. If it were possible to believe a thing to be true, which we knew to be inconsistent with reason we doubtless should give up our reason in

---

5. Supplement, p. 377; *Answer 14*. We do not attend that a revelation undertakes to explain a mystery and tell how it is but only that there is one.

this case; for we should act without reason or common sense. If we should
believe a thing to be true inconsistent with reason, which really was not but
inconsistent with reason we should not properly give up our reason, but it
would be greatly imposed upon and wrongly applied. If therefore a revelation were given, which was inconsistent with reason we should be under no
obligation to give up our reason, to receive it.[6]

> Question 16 [32]. If we are to receive no doctrines under the pretence
> of revelation, which are inconsistent with reason, do we make the dic-
> tates of reason the test of a true revelation? And if so what advantage is
> there in a revelation since we are to try that [it], by the test of reason?

Answer 16. Doubtless we are to exercise our reason in examining and
judging of the evidence offered in support of a revelation and also of its
doctrines. So far then we make reason the test of a true revelation. Yet
a revelation may be highly necessary and advantageous. There may be
many truths no way inconsistent with reason, which yet are above and by
it alone, would never be discovered.

In the common affairs of life, there are some truths, which to some
persons might remain forever unknown unless they were brought to view
by a person of superior understanding. But when once offered to view they
are to use their reason in examining the grounds of evidence on which
they are offered. So some superior creative intelligence may be acquainted
with truths with which we are totally unacquainted: and should an angel
from heaven undertake to reveal any unknown truth we might use our
reason with respect to it, and should be under obligation to receive nothing which is contrary [to] its dictates.

Much more may we suppose that God possesses an infinite number of
truths with which we are unacquainted; and which are in no way inconsistent with reason. Now to suppose that a revelation from God could be of no
advantage to mankind because they were to try it by the test of that reason,
which he had given them, is to suppose either that they know all truth before or that God could not render them capable of perceiving new truths, or
that acquisition of new truths could be no way advantageous.

Besides the truths of a religious kind which the light of nature discov-
ers are so obscure and feeble that a revelation might be useful in enlarging,
illustrating, and confirming them. The case is similar in the common affairs

6. Supplement, p. 377; *Answer 15*. We do not pretend we are to give up our reason
in belief of revelation. It is not necessary, we should investigate everything, which is
told us and see whether it is consistent with reason before we believe it. We are to use
our reason in examining the evidence that is from God, and if we have full proof of his
veracity, that is sufficient to command our belief.

of life. When a man gets but partially hold of a subject he may receive great advantage from the assistance of another, who is more thoroughly acquainted with it but in either case is reason to be laid aside in examining the truth.

Question 17 [34]. Is not the law of nature perfect? If so what need of a revelation?

Answer 17. If by the law of nature we mean what some have supposed it to be in that which requires nothing of us but what makes for our own happiness and forbid us nothing but what tends to our hurt; and which allows self love to be the spring of all actions, doubtless it is, like human nature which dictates it, extremely imperfect and corrupt. But if by the law of nature be meant those which are dictated by pure, unprejudiced reason, is perfect or rather true, so far as it extends; but it is by no means complete. A revelation therefore is still necessary to make additions to the dictates of reason and improvements upon those truths, which it may discover without a revelation.[7]

Question 18 [35]. What according to the light of nature was the end of the creation of man?

Answer 18. Considering the present state of mankind and the prejudices they naturally have against the truth, it is not likely that they would by the light of nature attain to a true notion with respect to the end of man's creation. It is very doubtful whether they would come to a true knowledge of God's moral character, and without this they clearly never could find out the other truth. But this is not owing so much to the want of evidence, as the want of a sincere disposition to understand and receive it. Were they possessed of this disposition and a knowledge of God's moral character, they most probably might arrive to a good degree of truth with respect to the end God has in all his works.

 In considering this subject without the aid of revelation we cannot reasonably suppose that the end of man's creation was that he might communicate something to God of which he was not originally possessed: for God is independent and all-sufficient. Nor has the creature anything, which he did not receive from God. Man, therefore, was not created that he might administer to the happiness of his creator as that servant does to the pleasure in happiness of his master. The end of creating man could not be that God might ostentatiously exhibit his several attributes to excite the astonishment

---

7. Supplement, p. 377; *Answer 17*. It does not follow, because the law of nature or reason is perfect, so far as it goes or teaches nothing but truth, that it would teach everything. It never would teach the doctrine of a resurrection.

and admiration of his creatures this would be a mark of weakness and vanity which are [in] no way consistent with the character of God.

As God is possessed of an infinite fullness of excellence and happiness, and as he [is] infinite in benevolence, the grand end of all his actions and especially of creation must be prompted by benevolence, and therefore excite to the communication of happiness. The end of goodness is doubtless the communication of good. Indeed it is difficult to conceive of the former without connecting the latter. But this will not lead us to suppose that happiness of each individual will be consulted any further then it is consistent with the general happiness. The goodness of God will not suffer him to sacrifice a greater to a less good. The creation of man and his happiness are therefore doubtless rendered subservient to the general happiness of the system.

> Question 19 [37]. If the end of the creation of man were his own happiness, whence so much misery in the world?

Answer 19. The end of man's creation was not his happiness, separately considered, and independently of the general happiness, but that was designed no farther then it should be consistent with this. Upon the supposition, that the end of God's creating man was the happiness of each individual, it is impossible to account for the misery, which takes place in the world. In this case we must either suppose that he was unable to prevent the misery or that he had changed his purpose. It is inconsistent with both goodness and truth to bring evil and misery on a creature, under pretence of communicating good or happiness, and that only: for good and evil, happiness and misery are directly opposed.

> Question 20 [38]. On the supposition of no future state what rational account can be given of the creation of man and of this world?

Answer 20. The mixture of good and evil, the indiscriminate treatment of virtuous and vicious, and above all the greater miseries and afflictions of the virtuous, then the vicious which in a variety of instances take place would leave us without any rational account, respecting the creation of man in this world, on the supposition [that] there was no future state of rewards and punishments. Happiness solely would not be supposed to be the end aimed at, because misery takes place in innumerable instances. For could misery alone be supposed to be the end because happiness in part is enjoyed by almost everyone?[8]

Question 21 [39]. What do you say to the maxim that all who are equally sincere in their religion are equally acceptable to God?

Answer 21. All who are sincere on the gospel plan of sincerity are doubtless equally acceptable or rather, one is as really acceptable as another. One may be more sincere, then another, and may therefore be more abundantly rewarded. But if by sincerity we mean being hearty or cordially and earnestly engaged without reference to the nature of the disposition or cause in which the heart is engaged it will not follow that all are equally acceptable. In this sense a man may be heartily and sincerely engaged, in the greatest wickedness. Indeed, the more wicked he is, the greater is his sincerity. The grossest and most stupid religions in the world are consistent with this kind of sincerity. And the greatest enormities in religion, which ever were committed arose from such sincerity as this. But all this may proceed from a heart totally opposed to God and his law. Surely then we cannot suppose, he will except of such sincerity. But that, and that alone, which proceeds from a disposition to know and do his will in all cases is acceptable.[9]

Question 22 [40]. Is it a matter of indifference what religious belief a man entertains provided he be moral?

Answer 22. A man's religious character is not determined by his outward conduct or speculative opinions, but by the state of his heart. However civil and regular his deportment may be, and however true he may be, in his speculative opinions, yet if his heart is not right his religion is vain. Still however it is not a matter of indifference what religious belief a man entertains. If he be ignorant of those objects and truths upon which the nature of religion is founded, it is impossible his exercises should be right. And since there can be only one set of objects and truths which can be the foundation of a true religion it is evidently necessary, a man's religious belief should be founded upon these. If religion consisted in external conduct, nothing more than morality would be absolutely necessary. But since it consists in a proper exercise of the affections, those things which are the proper objects

8. Supplement, p. 377–78; *Answer 20.* We cannot conceive how it would be consistent with the moral perfections of God to suffer evil and misery to take place unless there were a future state.

9. Supplement, p. 378; *Answer 21.* Upon the supposition that equal sincerity renders the subject of it equally acceptable, the worshippers of dagon, or the worshipers of the devil would be so, for they may have a kind of sincerity.

of these affections must first be known. It is not pretended however, that a man is not a proper subject of salvation until his religious belief is in every respect agreeable to truth. A man's understanding may be misguided in a variety of instances and yet his heart be right and disposed to receive the truth. For instance the man ignorant of the true doctrine of the decrees, but something he supposes it to be. But let him understand the doctrine in every respect and see it in its fullest extent and then if his heart is opposed to it, it is difficult to conceive how it should be right or how salvation can be consistent with such an opposition of heart to the truth. It is therefore, a matter of the greatest importance that a religious belief be founded on those truths which immediately respect salvation and the heart be sincerely disposed to receive the truth.

Question 23 [42]. Will bear repentance and subsequent observance of the law of nature secure pardon to the sinner?

Answer 23. Sin is evidently an injury to community: otherwise it is no sin. That which in its nature and tendency is no way injurious is not sinful. When therefore a sin is committed, community suffers an injury and the general good requires that this injury be repaired. Unless this be done, the happiness of community must remain so far diminished. Repentance evidently contains nothing in the nature of it, which can make up this loss and restore the community to its former state. Nor can a future obedience, however sincere and perfect, for the whole of that is nothing more than what is due to the community independently of this injury. Neither can an edition be made to it over and above what is due. If, therefore, the good of the community required reparation before this it still requires the same. But if it, after these only have taken place require no reparation, but admit the pardon of the sinner, then it never required a reparation of consequences, then it never was injured and if never injured, then there was no sin in the case and consequently no need of pardon. If however there be a sin committed against God's moral law and government, the good of his government or the general good requires that reparation be made. But since repentance and future observance of the law will not affect this, something further is necessary, in order to pardon.

Question 24 [45]. Can God make positive institutions, which are not founded in reason and the nature of things?

Answer 24. Doubtless, God neither can nor does require anything, which is not infinitely reasonable and fit, and best calculated to answer the purposes of universal benevolence. Still however he may establish many institutions,

which would never be binding upon mankind, without an express intimation of his will. Nay, he may command things which otherwise would be infinitely wrong. For instance it is in the reason and nature of things, infinitely
fit and right, that God should be worshiped. Yet, without some intimation
of God's will, they would not be under any greater obligation to keep one
day in seven, then one day in six. God however may establish one day in
seven, or one day in five, for the express purpose of his worship. It would
doubtless be wrong for people to cut and torment themselves and their sons,
by circumcision, unless they were commanded by God: Yet his institution
may make it right and wholly wrong to omit it. In like manner it would
be infinitely wrong for one nation, without provocation to make war upon
another and utterly destroy them. But, God who gives life to all creatures,
who upholds them in life, may surely make it perfectly right and those who
should refuse to comply would be infinitely to blame.

Nothing, however, which is instituted by God is inconsistent with the
best happiness of his moral kingdom. If this be what is meant by the reason
and nature of things, doubtless, benevolence cannot make any positive institution inconsistent with it. Indeed, were it possible, for a creature to take
a comprehensive view of things, in their nature and tendency, with respect
to the whole of God's moral kingdom, those things which ever were or shall
be the subject of his institutions would be as really binding without and
express command as with one. The positive institutions of God, therefore,
may require things of us which to are limited capacities, do not appear to be
founded in the reason or nature of things, or whose nature and tendency to
promote the general good, we never could have discovered.

Question 25 [45]. Is the light of nature sufficient to enable us to judge,
in all cases, what is subservient to the good of intelligent being in general or even of mankind in general?

Answer 25. The light of nature must fail in a thousand instances in determining what would be best calculated to promote the general good either
of the whole of intelligent being or of mankind only. In the common affairs
of life where only a small part of mankind is immediately concerned it is
difficult in a variety of instances to determine what would be for the good
of this small part or community. Even the general good of a family, though
consisting of but a few members or in short of an individual alone cannot
always be determined by the utmost stretch of human foresight. How much
less then would the light of nature enable one to judge what would be for
the good of mankind in general? How much farther still might the light of

nature lead one astray in judging what be for the good of intelligent being in general; which is infinitely greater and more important?

The light of nature never would lead mankind to determine that existence of sin and the innumerable evils and calamities of life; that the sweeping destruction of fire, sword, famine and pestilence; that the death of an important and valuable member of society in the midst of his days and usefulness; or that an indiscriminate treatment of the virtuous and vicious in this world should take place. Yet doubtless all these are for the general good; otherwise we may be sure a being of infinite wisdom and goodness would never permit them.

Question 26 [47]. What is meant by the religion of nature?

Answer 26. By the religion of nature, I suppose to be generally meant that system of doctrines, mode of worship and manner of life, to the belief and practice of which the light of nature might or does lead mankind, unaided by divine revelation. Under this head is included a belief in the existence of God, his attributes, a reverence, fear, love and worship of him; together with a proper treatment of our fellow creatures. Those, however, who plead for this kind of religion do not pretend, that every religion in the world which is not derived from revelation is that they would support. For then, they must plead for religions which are contradictory and totally inconsistent with their own. They however can intend their arms of charity to all and admit of sincerity, according to their ideas of sincerity as a substitute for the truth.

All religions in the world, which are not founded upon and supported by revelation are in a sense the religion of nature. They are dictated by human nature and hence it is, they are so corrupt. But it is doubtful, whether there be such a religion in the world, as natural religion is supposed to be, by its advocates, those who write in favor of it, derive their ideas principally; at least those which are founded in truth from revelation: and those who receive no benefit from it would probably never attain to such a system.

Question 27 [48]. If the light of nature be sufficient to enable us to judge rightly in matters of religion, whence is it that the deists differ so widely in their religious principles?

Answer 27. If the light of nature were sufficient to enable us to judge rightly in matters of religion, it would be difficult to conceive why the deists, who profess to be so great admirers of it, and to adhere to it, so strictly, should differ so much with respect to its dictates. If they all write agreeably to the principles the light of nature dictates then, it dictates principles which are repugnant to each other: and therefore, not to be followed. But if the light of nature dictates no principles but who are true, uniform and harmonious, then the deists have never yet been able to discover them. We muse then, either suppose that the light of nature is insufficient or that the advocates have never yet been able to arrive to its true principles and consequently, that notwithstanding their exertion, a revelation may still be necessary.

The truth of the matter is, were the deists sincerely disposed to receive and obey the truth, the light of nature would teach the truth, so far as it reaches; but would not teach everything necessary to be known. It is not however, owing to this deficiency in the light of nature that the deists differ, among themselves. It is owing, rather to the blindness of their minds and the alienation of their hearts from the truth. They have various prejudices, partialities, desires and interests to be indulged; and as these vary one way or the other, so they fix their principles. The pride of opinion, of appearing singular and new, in sentiment, is another very considerable reason of their difference.[10]

Question 28 [50]. Is it a true maxim that what concerns all must be knowable by all?

Answer 28. God is under no more obligation to make the true religion known to all mankind than he was at first to give revelation of it. Nor in either case is he under any more obligation than he was to make mankind in every respect alike: to endow them with the faculties of body and mind, perfectly alike; and to make truth of every kind appear equally clear to every man.

If what concerns all must be knowable by all, and if the deistic principles be right, then they must have been knowable by all mankind from the first ages of the world, and must also be knowable by all who are now living. If so, whence is it that the greatest part have been and still are so ignorant of these principles? It is but lately that they have been brought to so much perfection in deism and now but a small part of mankind are acquainted either with them or the names of their authors.[11]

---

10. Supplement, p. 378; *Answer 27*. No two of the deists think in every respect alike. Surely they who are so fond of the light of nature must think alike if it be sufficient.

11. Supplement, pp. 378–79; *Answer 28*. Surely the sciences concern all, but they are not known by all. The best mode of living, of getting rich, of carrying on trade and manufactures to the best advantage concern all, but they are not known by all. There is not one in a hundred who knows how conduct in the best manner. If Deism be so important, why do not all Deists equally understand? Why are not the principles of natural religion equally known by all?

Question 29 [51]. Did not the unerring wisdom of God employ the most suitable means for human happiness? If so, is not the light of nature the most suitable mean[s] to that end?

Answer 29. Unerring wisdom always has and will make use of those means, which are calculated to promote the highest happiness of his creatures. God does not, however, consult the happiness of mankind exclusively of the other parts of his creation. The happiness of mankind is no farther promoted than it is consistent with the general happiness of the system.

But to determine that the light of nature is the most suitable mean[s] to promote the end God aims at in his treatment of mankind, we must either, by reasoning *a priori*, prove this or else prove that God never has made use of any other means. The former, it is presumed, never can be done by the limited capacities of man. Nor has the latter supposition ever yet been supported.

Besides, if we judge from observation, we cannot from this suppose the light of nature [is] the most suitable mean[s]. Those who are left to that alone are generally buried in ignorance, idolatry and the greatest wickedness. They are ignorant, many of them, at least not only of that religion which is calculated to make them happy, but of the best mode of living and procuring subsistence.

If the light of nature were the most suitable mean[s] to promote human happiness, then we should suppose the deists who are so great advocates for it, would teach us that religion and those modes of living, which would actually answer this purpose. But this they never have done.

Question 30 [52]. Does God ever prescribe services to men, which are in themselves matters of indifference?

Answer 30. God, who is infinite in wisdom and goodness, never does or can require anything, which is not best calculated to answer the purposes of benevolence and promote the highest happiness of intelligence in general. Nothing then, which he prescribes, is a matter of indifference. If on the whole, it be better calculated to promote the general good than anything else, then surely it cannot be a matter of indifference, whether it be prescribed or not. To us, indeed, whose capacities are so limited, some things may appear indifferent and of no importance: but if prescribed by God, we may be sure, they are both necessary and useful.[12]

12. Supplement, p. 379; *Answer 30*. God does not prescribe devices arbitrarily and without benevolent motives merely because he wills them, and not because they are calculated to promote good and wise ends.

Question 31 [53]. If there be now things required of us, in revelation, which are not prescribed by the law of nature, does this imply a change in God?

Answer 31. To require new things of us not prescribed by the law of nature, no more implies a change in God, than his bringing new things to pass in the natural world. One is as much the effect of his purpose as the other. It no more implies a change, in this case, than his bringing some up in a land of greater light than he does others: or than his giving to some deists greater degrees of knowledge than others. Nor does it anymore than his requiring those new duties, which result from the new and different situations of a man's life. The new things being externally made known by revelation, no more implies change in God than the bringing to pass any phenomenon, in the natural world, which never before appeared.

If it could be proved that these were not determined from eternity, than it would imply change. But if determined from eternity to require these things, by means of a revelation, then his doing this, no way implies a change; because the law of nature does not require the same.[13]

Question 32 [54]. Is the diversity of sentiments among Christians a stronger argument against the truth of Christianity than the diversity of sentiments, among the deists, is against the truth of the law of nature?

Answer 32. If the diversity of sentiment among Christians be any argument against Christianity then the same objection will at least equally hold against deism. No reason can be conceived why it should not in the latter, if it does in the former case. If the truth of any system is to be determined by the reception it meets with, and the uniformity of sentiment among its professors, then Christianity evidently has a very great advantage over deism. The professors of the former are not only more numerous but in proportion to their number, far more uniform in sentiment than the advocates for the latter. But the truth of any system of doctrines is not to be determined by the uniformity of sentiment among its professors, but by the source, whence they are derived and their nature and tendency.

Question 33 [55]. If we knew the nature of tendency of all moral actions, should we not be omniscient in morals?

---

13. Supplement, p. 379; *Answer 31.* Surely the late Deists will not pretend it implies a change in God, because Deism was not brought to so great perfection of thousand years ago.

Answer 33. With respect to any moral action, to determine of what kind it is, all that is necessary is the nature and tendency. And if under the tendency of an action, is considered the consequences, the reward or punishment which attends it, then by knowing the nature and tendency we shall know everything necessary to be known. And by knowing this, with respect to all actions, we shall so far, be omniscient. Indeed, to all who are disposed to know and do their duty, the nature and tendency of an action, aside from the reward or punishment, is all that is necessary to be known.[14]

Question 34 [55]. Is it tyranny in God to require some things of us, merely to try us?

Answer 34. It is no more tyranny in God, to try his creatures, than it is for a parent to try the fidelity and dutifulness of his child, and some will suppose the latter would be tyranny. The latter case however, approaches nearest to it, than the former: for it is impossible, the creature should act upon such high motives as God. Tyranny is but another term for cruelty. It is that conduct of a sovereign in which he has not good and wise ends in view. But surely if a parent can be justified in making trial of his child, then God may have ends in view in the trial of us which are wise and good; and therefore far more important. By this means, he may give us an opportunity to know the state of our own hearts and other views may be connected with the trial, which are calculated to promote valuable and important ends. Though the trial should not terminate finally to our advantage, yet if it is calculated to promote the general good, it is no proof of tyranny.

Question 35 [56]. How do you prove, that the Scriptures are a revelation from God?

Answer 35. The proof that the Scriptures are revelation from God, arises from a variety of sources. These are ranked under two general heads: that of internal and of external evidence. The latter however, is that upon which the greatest dependence is placed.

It is not pretended that the evidence is intuitive or that any are required implicitly to believe, without full and conclusive evidence. But the facts, on which the whole of revelation is founded, depend on human testimony; and

---

14. Supplement, p. 379; *Answer 33*. If the light of nature dictates everything necessary to be known then we should suppose it teaches the nature and tendency of moral actions. If so that mankind must have known this in all ages and countries. Why then has not deism then brought up to its present perfection before? And what need is there of writing to make it more evident?

the credibility of this established, in the same way, and on the same principles, as in all other cases which are similar.[15]

Question 36 [57]. What is the internal proof of the truth of the Scriptures?

Answer 36. The internal proof of the truth of the Scriptures consists of a number of arguments, drawn principally from the Spirit and modes of diction, their general nature and tendency. 1. The Scriptures possess a majesty and dignity of style, which appears in some respects to be beyond the style of human compositions. It is allowed that some writers, besides the sacred penmen, have arrived to a very considerable degree of excellence in this accomplishment. Yet the sublime and majestic language of the deity is thought with propriety to exceed any language of the kind, we find, either in the writings of heathen authors or of those who have derived advantages from the Scriptures, and had opportunities to make improvements if possible. The language is dignified and suitable to the subject in every part. This is also an excellence, which perhaps, no human composition of the same extent and of so great a variety of subjects possesses.

The consistency and harmony add greatly to the dignity and importance of the Scriptures as a piece of composition; and distinguish them in this respect, from other performances of men. In human compositions where the subjects are various and full, we seldom find an author consistent with himself throughout. But in the Scriptures, this is a particular property. One great and extensive plan seems to be set up and preserved entire, throughout the whole. 2. The nature and excellence of the doctrines is another argument, which still confirms the truth of the Scriptures. There is no doctrine but what appears to be pure and unexceptionable; altogether worthy of a God of purity. Some of the doctrines are of such a nature, that it is very doubtful, whether the human mind ever could have invented them, without the aid of revelation. It is difficult to conceive how mankind should have ever conceived of the existence of three persons in unity of the divine essence, or of the union of the human and divine nature. It is very doubtful whether they could have arrived to that knowledge of the divine character and government, which we find in the Scriptures. Nor is it probable considering the corruption of human nature that they would have attainted

---

15. Supplement, p. 379; *Answer 35*. The internal evidence is calculated to prove the truth of the system: that the doctrines are true and good. Indeed, the mysteries, the consistency of the Scriptures and the effects are strongly in favor of there being from God.

to such a system of morals, which are so directly contrary to the natural feelings and sentiments of mankind.

The knowledge they contain of the human heart is far beyond that to which anyone of mankind possesses or even any number of men, however large. Here the human heart is laid open in all its turnings and windings. Here the secret springs of action are all unfolded. 3. The tendency and scope of the whole is a strong proof of the truth of the Scriptures. The design of the whole seems to be, to promote the glory of God and best happiness of his creatures. The methods it proposes for this purpose, considering the present state of the human heart, are disgusting and so mortifying to it, that we should suppose they never could have been invented by mankind.

The tendency of its doctrines is directly different from those, which are most agreeable to the natural feelings of human nature. The tendency of the Scriptures may be known by the effects which attend them in the dispensation and when obeyed and practiced. It is indeed impossible that any composition of itself, could produce such effects, without the energy of some invisible agent. But we cannot suppose that God would accompany the dispensation of it with such striking effects upon the mind, unless the cause were favorable to virtue and immediately from him. The change which attends the Scriptures not only in the heart but life, is also a strong confirmation of their truth. No other system of doctrines ever produced so general and so lasting a reformation of life as the Scriptures. The best systems of deism and natural religion never, perhaps, produced a single instance of the kind.

Question 37 [61]. What is the external proof of the truth and divine origin of the Scriptures?

Answer 37. The external proof that the Scriptures are of divine origin arises from two kinds of divine operation, which seem to be designed immediately for their confirmation. These are miracles and prophecies. Indeed prophecies are a species of miracles and might properly enough be ranked under that head. They do not appear to be calculated directly to prove that the Scriptures are true, but that they are a revelation from God. Then, the truth of their doctrines depends upon the word and character of their author, so far as it is derived from this source.

If then we can prove that God has wrought miracles and given prophecies in favor of this system, we have every reason to suppose, that it is a system of his own, and agreeable to his will. He might, it is true, permit his creatures to perform either of these, especially miracles, in favor of one of a very different nature; even of systems directly opposed to each other, yet I think we have not the least reason to suppose he would suffer that to prevail which was contrary to his wishes and views. Even were he an evil being, but possessed of infinite knowledge and power, we have every reason to suppose, he would support that system, which was best calculated to promote the ends of his moral government. And as the Scriptures have the greatest and indeed, the only rational claim to a divine origin, if the reality of the miracles and prophecies, to which they make pretences can be proved, then their divinity will also be proved.

When we have once proved that the system is from God, then the truth of the doctrines will depend in part upon the internal evidence; but more especially, as was before suggested, on the moral character of God. If then we never have found him to deviate from the truth; but he has acted and spoken on all occasions agreeably to the strictest truth, we have every reason to put confidence in his word. This is a principle on which we act, in judging with respect to the veracity of all characters, with which we are acquainted. If my neighbor has for many years conducted in every respect consistently with truth, I must act the most unfriendly, disingenuous and whimsical part, without the least foundation to suspect his veracity. Much more would this be the case if I should suspect the veracity of God; who is infinitely farther from those temptations to falsehood to which his creatures are subject.

Question 38 [63]. Are miracles impossible?

Answer 38. To come more readily to a full and decisive answer to this question, it may not be improper to give a definition of a miracle. It appears in general to be understood to mean a wonderful and surprising effect, produced by the immediate agency of God, in a manner above or contrary to the common and stated laws of nature. But to understand this fully, we must also understand what is meant by the "laws of nature." Nothing more is meant, than the usual methods of God's operation, in the course and works of providence. It is not pretended by this however, that there is a certain and fixed code of laws superior to him, and by which he is bound in all cases whatever; as a subject is bound by the good and wholesome laws of the state. All things which exist were created by him, and are subject to the disposal of his providence. He is therefore above and independent of these things. When he had produced creation, he was under no more obligation to conduct things in one manner rather than another, but only as seemed to him best.

A miracle then, may be more clearly and precisely defined to be a new and singular effect, different from any which has ever taken place, or at least from those which have generally taken place and produced in a manner different from other effects.

Keeping this in view, the answer is easy and clear. Doubtless, God, who at first created the waters, could as easily turn them into blood as to produce it in any other way. He could as easily turn a rod into a serpent as produce it in any other way. The same may be said with respect to all the miracles, which Moses performed. Doubtless also, it is as easy for him to heal a disorder, cure a lameness, or remove an infirmity instantaneously and without the use of secondary means, as with them. And doubtless, he who gave to man life at first, and upholds him in life, can as easily preserve his body from putrefaction, when dead, as when alive; and restore him to life after what number of days he pleases, as easily as he would give him life at first and afterwards uphold him in life. It implies no more of a contradiction or impossibility, to act one way than it does the other. And if he can produce a miracle by his immediate agency, doubtless he can furnish his creatures with powers, capable of performing at least some kinds of miracles, likewise, but in subservience to him and under the direction of providence.

Question 39 [65]. Are miracles incredible because [they are] contrary to our experience?

Answer 39. Since a miracle is not impossible but as easy to be produced as any other effect, we have no more reason to suspect the credibility of it than any other fact supported by like testimony. It is no more incredible that Christ arose from the dead than that a comet appeared in the year 1532, providing the testimony in both cases be equally strong. It is no more incredible than that there are such places as London and Paris. We have not experienced that there are such places as these, nor have we experienced the comet of 1532 and supposing we had experienced no comet at all, we should act a very irrational part to doubt of their existence merely on this account. But it is said, "When a fact attested is such, as has seldom fallen under our observation, here is a contest of two opposite experiences; and one destroys the other."[16] My neighbor who is a man of the strictest integrity comes in this morning and informs me he was afflicted last night with a most severe turn of the colic. This is a disorder I have never experienced in my life. His experience is positive, mine is negative, it is nothing, a mere cipher. Now according to Mr. Hume's arithmetic, my cipher is equal to his unit. Subtract the former from the latter; and nothing remains.

Suppose in my return from a long journey, I successively meet with a number of honest friends who passed my home at different times; and all to

16. Hume, *An Inquiry Concerning Human Understanding.*

the number of fifty inform me they called at my house; my family were well and all things appeared to be right. But soon after this I meet one who was a day after the last of the others. He is more unknown to me. His character however appears to be unexceptionable. I can conceive no motive, which would induce him to deceive me. But he informs me the night before he passed through the place, my house caught on fire was consumed and two of my children were destroyed in the flames. Shall I now doubt this man's veracity? Is it incredible; because neither of my friends knew any thing of the matter? Or will the negative experience of fifty in this case, amount to one that is positive? It is for my interest and happiness that the information should not be true, but shall this render it incredible?

Question 40 [68]. How do you prove that the whole Old Testament is not a forgery?

Answer 40. It seems to be impossible that the Old Testament could be forged and palmed upon the world, and especially upon the Jews. No period of the world can be fixed upon when any were capable of forging the books it contains and the body of the people incapable of detecting the impostor. The facts are of such a kind that everyone must have known whether they had taken place or not. Everyone must have known whether he had seen anything of the kind. And he must have known whether he had heard of such books and such transactions taking place at a period before his time. The learned especially who were acquainted with the books extant in their time, must have known whether these books were a new addition or whether they had been extant for years before. And when we consider the Jews were peculiarly cautious and incredulous in receiving any books not well authenticated; we cannot reasonably suppose they would ever receive these, were their authority in the least doubtful. They had almost every inducement to prove them a forgery, were they really so. No historian ever gave so unfavorable representations of his countrymen as these books do of the Jews. They are represented as stupid, ungrateful and rebellious beyond measure.

Besides, the religious rites imposed upon them were so expensive and burdensome, that it seems no nation would ever have submitted to them unless enjoined evidently by the highest authority.

These books contain every mark of authenticity we can suppose any books to possess and they are destitute of every conceivable mark of impostor and forgery. The burden of proof however is upon those who dispute their authenticity. It is their business to point out the time when these books were forged and by whom; what was the situation of the world and how they were obtruded upon mankind.

The authenticity of the books may be argued from the prophecies they contain and the fulfillment of these prophecies. No one argument which bears the least probability has yet been instituted to prove the prophecies were written since the facts took place. And if we suppose them to have existed before the facts we may with equal propriety suppose them to have been written at the time they are said to have been written. The prophecies respecting our Savior, were evidently in every particular fulfilled. Those respecting the four monarchies were so clearly fulfilled and the facts are so fully established that the deists themselves cannot doubt of their existence. And one prophecy is daily fulfilling before our eyes. This respects the dispersion, state and contempt of the Jews. The fact is so surprising and so unaccountable on any other principles, than those mentioned in these books, that nothing but a spirit of prophecy could ever have foretold the event.[17]

> Question 41 [71]. How do you prove, that the books of the New Testament were written at the time they claim to have been written; and by the men whose names they bear?

Answer 41. The same may be said, in part, with respect to the books of the New Testament, that was with respect to those of the Old. If they were not written at the time and by the persons they are said to have been, it is impossible with any kind of propriety to conceive when or by whom they were written. Before the dark ages, and since the revival of letters, mankind were possessed of everything necessary to detect an impostor of any kind, and especially one of books pretending to be written before they really were. In the time of the dark ages it is doubtful whether any were capable of forging a book of tolerable merit. And even then we cannot suppose it to be possible to obtrude a book of this kind, though mankind were buried in the greatest ignorance. They were possessed of common sense, and of discernment enough to detect so gross an imposition, as this must have been, if a forgery. They knew surely whether they had heard of those things before; and if they had not, they would naturally be lead to inquire whence these books came and who were the authors. In such a time as that, a man of tolerable abilities must have been more conspicuous than on the greatest at the present day. The number suspected would have been but small and the case of detecting the forgery would of consequence have been proportionally greater.

17. Supplement, pp. 379–80; *Answer 40*. It has been said that the Old Testament was forged, between the time of the Babylonian captivity and the appearing of our Savior. In the time of the captivity the Jews had common sense, and knew whether these were forgeries or not; whether there was any tradition with respect to the transactions of Moses and several books written by him.

The prophecies also of the New Testament are a strong proof of the authenticity of it. They have been and still are fulfilling in a manner equally clear and convincing with those of the Old Testament.[18]

Question 42 [72]. How does it appear that the Apostles were not imposed upon as to the facts which they relate?

Answer 42. With respect to the facts, which the Apostles relate, nothing more is necessary to enable a person to judge of them, and to detect an impostor than the senses and understanding common to mankind. If they could see, hear, and feel, and [possess] their reason in full exercise, they were as far removed from the danger of imposition as the greatest philosopher. Indeed in some respects a man of common abilities is more capable perhaps of judging with respect to facts depending upon the senses than a philosopher. The latter is selected from the world and far less acquainted with sensible objects than the former and sense experience accompanied with a common understanding is the best guide, we must conclude a philosopher would not be the best judge.

Now, the Apostles evidently possessed all the qualifications necessary in such case. There is nothing in their character, which can render them suspected of being subject to a weak and incautious credulity. They do not appear to have taken anything up on grounds, which were not well supported with evidence. So far from this they appear to have been remarkably incredulous. [For] instance Thomas, [though] he was told by the other disciples who were his friends and whose veracity he had fully experienced, that they had seen the Lord; yet he would not believe that he was risen unless he should see in his hands the print of the nails and thrust his hand into his side. Indeed, this incredulity seems at that time to have characterized all the disciples. When they were informed by the women that Christ was risen and they had seen him, their words seemed to the disciples like idol tales and they believed them not. Through the whole of these transactions they discovered a resolute and obstinate determination not to believe without the highest and fullest evidence.

Question 43 [75]. How does it appear that the Apostles were not designing impostors?

---

18. Supplement, p. 380; *Answer 41*. The books must have been written before the dark ages, and act or near the time they are said to have been written, for they are quoted by the Fathers and others. Either the latter are forged or the former must have been written at the time of their date.

Answer 43. Designing impostors always have some worldly motives in view, which lead onto the impostor. Considering the present feelings and sentiments of the human heart we cannot conceive it to be otherwise. But nothing of the kind would induce the Apostles to undertake an impostor. They do not appear to have possessed ambition in a moderate degree. The prospects of riches, pleasures or honors could promise them no compensation for the fatigues, distresses, and contempt which they underwent. They did not make use of that artifice, insinuation and address which particularly characterize impostors. All which they did was open and exposed to the inspection of the world.

Besides they evidently did not possess the rare talents of impostors. Their education was so slender as to totally unfit them for so adventurous and hazardous an undertaking. The obscurity of their lives must have proved an effectual bar in a presumption of this kind. They were no courtiers. They had no riches to a lower or no honor to induce and no power to compel others to become their adherents.

Honesty and integrity are never supposed to mark the character of impostors, but these are strikingly we exhibited both in the writings and the lives of the Apostles. Even their own faults and foibles they freely and fully exposed without any palliation. Had they been impostors they must have known that this would be the most direct way to defeat their purposes. It is directly contrary to human nature to expose its own failings and defects. This would seem to be courting infamy and reproach. So far is it from this that it is disposed rather to cover and conceal its turpitude. Human nature must have operated upon them in a manner very different from what it does with mankind in general, or they must have possessed a spirit and temper far superior to what mankind generally experiences and still more above the spirit and temper of impostors.

They both taught and practiced the purest system of morals. Their lives, irreproachable. They did not, like the philosophers, teach one way, and practice another. Nor were they like the imposter Mahomet (Mohammed), addicted to pleasure and sensual gratification. Their whole aim appears to have been to do good; and that disinterestedly. This is a characteristic which it is presumed can never be found in an imposter.[19]

Question 44 [77]. What remarkable facts of the Gospel are attested by profane writers?

19. Supplement, pp. 380–81; *Answer 43*. It is surprising if the apostles were designing impostors, none ever apostatized and discovered the secret. If we suppose the whole of the apostles or even the twelfth were in the secret can hardly suppose all would have adhered to it firmly, especially when the danger, hazard and punishments were so great.

Answer 44. Some of the most remarkable facts of the Gospel are the taxation of Herod, appearance of the star at Christ's birth, his life and the several circumstances of it, his crucifixion and resurrection; together with the life and character of the apostles. These, for the greater and most important part of these facts have been attested by profane writers. Among others may be mentioned Tacitus, Suitonius, Marcobius, Celsus, Porphyry. The two latter were bitter enemies to Christianity; and cannot be supposed to say anything designedly in favor of a cause they so greatly opposed.

Question 45 [78]. Are all the prophecies of the Old Testament of the facts of the [N]ew [Testament] allegorical?

Answer 45. An allegory is a figurative mode of expressing an idea of an important kind when found in Scripture. It is assuming one thing for another to which it bears some resemblance; and keeping the assumed object in view throughout the whole of the representation. Some of the prophecies in the Old Testament contain something of this kind. Yet however, the truth is as really expressed with respect to the foundational objects of the representation as if they were mentioned by name. That which is said of the assumed objects is properly applicable to those for which they are assumed. Some of those which respect the facts of the New Testament are delivered in this manner. It does not however, lessen the dignity or diminish the truth of prophecy; but in some respects renders it more striking and points out the objects of the prophecy more clearly. But many do not appear to contain anything of an allegory. Those especially do not in Genesis 49.10, Deuteronomy 18.15–18, Ezekiel 21.27, Daniel 9.24, 25, Haggai 2.6–9.

Question 46 [79]. Can we have evidence that the Scriptures are a revelation from God without previous evidence of the moral perfection of God?

Answer 46. If we suppose God to be possessed of the natural perfections ascribed to him, we must unavoidably allow [that] he is capable of communicating his mind and will by means of external revelation what ever may be his moral perfections. Even were he an evil being, he would evidently do this and he could produce such evidence as is necessary to produce full conviction of its being from him. The most important and indubitable evidence do in favor of revelation, arises from miracles and prophecies. But doubtless these he can affect whatever his moral character be and to determine whether it be from him, is not necessary to recur to his moral perfections.[20]

20. Supplement, p. 381; *Answer 46.* If we can have evidence that God created the world without a knowledge of his moral perfections, we might also of his affecting a

Question 47 [80]. Was a revelation after the fall necessary in order to any religion?

Answer 47. It does not appear from the history of mankind that after the fall they ever would have attained to any rational system of religion without the aid of revelation. They appear almost immediately to have plunged into the ignorance, idolatry, and superstition. This is the case at the present day with all who are ignorant of revelation. Mankind evidently would never have attained to the true religion that which teaches the way to pardon and happiness. Probably then mankind without revelation would have fallen into some kind of religion; evil of the most absurd and stupid kind. But revelation was necessary to lead them to any rational system and especially to the true religion.

Question 48 [81]. Does the moral and spiritual excellency and glory of the Scriptures prove them not only to be true, but to be given by divine revelation?

Answer 48. The moral and spiritual excellency of the Scriptures are the beauty, dignity and superiority of the doctrines; considered as the system or taken separately. It's a tendency of the doctrines to promote virtue and the support they engage to those who obey them; the encouragements, promises and reps and names of rewards and punishments; and indeed all the prospects they hold up to view, constitute part of this excellence. Under this also is considered the knowledge they possess of God, especially his moral perfections, the knowledge of the human heart, the rational account of creation and of God's works and providence in general. This moral and spiritual excellency and glory taken as an argument alone would not perhaps be efficient to support the divinity of the Scriptures. Creatures might actually do possess sentiments favorable to virtue and compose documents which contain an excellency and glory in themselves considered. In connection with other arguments however, they strengthen and confirm the evidence in support of revelation. But though the system be pure and altogether worthy of God, yet we cannot merely from this arrive in so clear and demonstrative a manner as a certainty of their author by arguing *a posteriori* as we may with respect to the works of creation.[21]

---

miracle, curing the blind, turning water into wine, and raising the dead, etc.

21. Supplement, p. 381; *Answer 48.* The piety, holiness and goodness contained in the Scriptures most probably might be felt and expressed by a holy, pious and good man.

Question 49 [82]. Is it not inconsistent to argue the truth of a book or system from the manifest truth of the doctrines it contains; and then to argue the truth of those doctrines from the circumstance that they are contained in that book?

Answer 49. The argument in support of revelation derived from the manifest truth of the doctrines is a considerable importance. But to go upon the supposition the system is true before it gets proved to be so; and to attempt to prove the truth of the doctrines, merely because they are contained in this system, yet on unproved, would to be sure, be inconsistent. But it is presumed, no friend to this system ever undertook this mode of proof.

When we have established the truth of the system by fear and conclusive reasoning from the manifest truth of the doctrines; then we may come with propriety, appeal to it to decide the controversy respecting the doctor said to be contained in it or get used from it. In this case is not suppose this system is questions. He only object is to prove the doctrine is contained in the system. But if the truth of the doctrine the questioned, whether it be in the system or not, then it must stand on the same ground, each of the doctors in the system did, in proving this system to be true. Or if we can prove this system is from God and not that she is a God truth; then we have asked full evidence that it is a system of truth, at that seafood review it will tell us no lie. See you may then consistently appealed to the system for the truth of any doctrine.[22]

Question 50 [84]. In what sense does revealed religion depends on the reason of things?

Answer 50. If by the reason of things being managed the truth fitness and privacy of things revealed religion depends so far upon it as to be agreeable to it. We should not expect God would reveal anything inconsistent with the reason of things. The reason of things is founded date in the general good. That which is calculated to promote the general good is reasonable and think. Using this thing is the fitness of things in the fitness of things is their capacity to promote the general good. Revelation proceeding from a god of truth and universal benevolence will so far depending upon the reason of things as it is constituted by the general good. But revealed religion does not depend upon what mankind, unassisted, would discover of the reason

---

22. Supplement, p. 381; *Answer 49.* We argue the truth of the Scriptures from the manifest truth of its moral and religious truths, which are comprehended by human capacities. Finding these to be true and from God we may rationally suppose the trinity, incarnation, etc., are so likewise.

of things for this would be depending not on the reason of things but on the capacities of mankind.

> Question 51 [85]. Are we not to act reasonably in all things and so to follow our reason? If so, do we not really and must we not necessarily set upon reason above, revelation?

Answer 51. To act reasonably is to act in subservience to the general good. And in all cases we are to exercise our reason and judging what will best promote this. But if we are unable to determine this some superior being upon whom we may depend will inform us than in this case reason requires us to rely upon his information. Much more if God by revelation points out our duty; we are to use our reason in informing our sentiments and actions agreeably to it and not contrary to revelation. We are not therefore to be led by our reason above or contrary to revelation but to use our reason in examining, changing, and acting agreeably to it.

> Question 52 [86]. Wherever internal evidence of divine truth are found are not external evidences needless?

Answer 52. To a candid mind internal evidence most probably would be convincing and leaves no doubt on the mind. But the external evidence seems to have been designed immediately for a proof of revelation. They are more confounding to gainsayers and are calculated more effectually to silence their cavils and insinuations. They likewise, still more strongly confirm the friends of truth. Besides, in a revelation from God it seems most fit that something should be exhibited expressly for its confirmation. This must be an evidence of the external kind. Internal necessarily belongs to a revelation from God.

> Question 53 [86]. Unless we grant the sufficiency of it, like that nature must mean not allow God has given most men some tools and means as are insufficient for their own happiness? And then how will you reconcile this with the moral perfections of God especially his infinite and impartial goodness?

Answer 53. Doubtless the light of nature is insufficient. And doubtless God has left most men without the means of grace or the knowledge of the way to pardon and reconciliation with him without which there can be no door of hope or prospect of us. This however is no way inconsistent with the perfections of God. He was under no obligation to mankind to give them any express rules and means for their happiness. Since then they had no claim on him, it is no more partial goodness that he does not make the means of happiness universally known and universally efficacious. Besides, it is owing to the fall of mankind alone that the names are so fine and so little known. If the whole of God's dealings in this respect are calculated by infinite goodness to promote the general good it is as really reconcilable with the perfections and impartial goodness of God, as his giving greater capacities and a more extensive knowledge of natural objects to some, than to others.

Question 54 [88]. Is the gospel by the changes of tongues, errors of transcribers, etc., become so obscure that there are not sufficient evidences of its divine original?

Answer 54. If we supposed God is getting a revelation today time we cannot reasonably suppose she would ever suffer to be so far skewered by any means whatever has to be destitute property creative evidence in support of it. Those reasons which at first rendered a certain degree of evidence necessary still exist. It is by no means consistent this character to suppose people requiring them to believe without a sufficient degree of evidence to support his belief. This appears to be the case. The changes of times may have occasion to some small errors yet you cannot have anything very essential with respect to evidence. And the evil of this may be removed by recurring to the original languages in which the books were at first written. Nor is it reasonable to suppose an error has taken place in transcribing which will affect the evidence. In this case also you may be corrected by a faithful application to the original. It is readily allowed, however that some errors may have taken place. The idioms of different languages differ in some instances so far as to render it difficult to translate one into the other and always give precisely the same idea. Such instances, however, do not frequently occur on any subjects and they occur less most probably on religious subjects than any other. Objects of religion are applicable to every age and nation of the world and to all languages. As for transcribers they must have been under the watch installation of their employers and the world in general. This would secured them from any errors that might be go so far as to obscure the evidence and copy most probably were so greatly multiplied from the original as that by comparing one with the other end with the spirit and port of the whole thing might correct every everything of importance even admitting errors have been taking place had taken place yet we find sufficient evidence in support of the gospel from every quarter. There is evidence of every kind which will could be wish were expected. The doctrines are sufficiently clear to everyone who is disposed to see if no big truth. The gospel at the present day has advocates who would strongly

oppose and reprobate every change or interpretation tribulation which in
my dispose today be disposed to me. And doubtless such friends and advocates it has had in every stage of it since its first promulgation.[23]

> Question 55 [90]. Is the Scripture on itself sufficient to lead mankind
> virtue and happiness? If not, why is the insufficiency of the law and
> nature to this end brought as an argument in favor of revelation?

Answer 55. The Scripture unaccompanied by the influences of God's Spirit,
will be ineffectual to lead mankind to virtue and happiness. If is not pretended by the advocates for revelation that the dead letter giveth life. No
means, however, good in themselves, will be able to produce a change in
the heart and life. But the insufficiency of the law of nature is not applied
to its inefficacy or want of power in itself considered. It is deficient in that
knowledge which is necessary to salvation. That light which mankind derive
from the law of nature, evidently does not bear that proportion to the light
of revelation, which the evening twilight does to mid-day.

No doubt, God might if he pleased, inspire mankind without the
means of external revelation, without the means of external revelation, with
a knowledge of all truths necessary in order to salvation. Yet we find he
actually does not do this but leaves a large part of men, in such ignorance,
that unless their knowledge is increased and applied to their hearts, we can
conceive no grounds to expect their happiness. But revelation contains
a system of truth which, without an addition, were they understood and
obeyed, would lead directly to happiness. Here then is the superiority of
revelation. It contains truths which mankind would never obtain by the law
of nature. And God is pleased to make those truths, in many instances, effectual to lead mankind to virtue and happiness.[24]

> Question 56 [92]. Are we accountable for every error in opinion con-
> cerning moral and religious subjects?

Answer 56. The Scriptures are given to us as a rule of our faith. They are
written in so clean and intelligible a manner that none who are disposed
sincerely to receive the truth need err with respect to their doctrines. Some
passages, it is allowed, are the skewer and not easy to be understood. Yet

---

23. Supplement, pp. 381–82; *Answer 54.* Notwithstanding the various readings, the
evidence is not obscured. Whereas to set aside those texts which are questioned the
essential and imparted doctrines would still be supported.

24. Supplement, p. 382; *Answer 55.* Were one regenerated among the heathen
he could have no rational exercise of affections without the knowledge contained in
Scripture.

this does not affect the truth necessary to be known. And most probably, the truth is these passages contain or in some other parts more clearly and fully expressed. If then, we believe not according to these truths, it is because so far at least there is no light in us. If we will not examine the law and the testimony, this willful neglect is doubtless criminal. If we do examine and willfully shut our eyes against the truth, then we are aggravatedly criminal. The reason why mankind under the gospel do not receive an embrace the truth is that in their hearts they are opposed to it. It is because of the blinding of their hearts and because they love darkness rather than light.

With respect to the heathens, who are ignorant of the gospel, they are not on accountable, for not exercising faith in the savior of whom they have never heard. Yet they are accountable for not receiving and obeying these truths which the light of nature of affords.

Question 57 [93]. How do we prove a future state?

Answer 57. The doctrine of a future state, most probably mankind would never have a team to, without the aid of revelation. Is this, which has brought the doctrine of immortality to light. When once suggested, it becomes evident be rational and consistent with the perfections and moral government of God. The future existence of the soul has been concluded from its immateriality, which renders it Compatible with immortality and also from its desire of existence. But the surest and most convincing mode of proving it is derived from Scripture.

The future state appears evident from the probationary status of mankind in this world. They are everywhere considered as under along. This is a rule by which the real characters of those who are under it or measured and determined. With this, or connected promises and threatening's of rewards and punishments. Now, the virtuous and the dishes are treated indiscriminately in this world. The virtuous do not receive those rewards which are promised nor did the dishes set for those punishments which are threatened. We may then rationally conclude that the for filament of Scripture requires a future state.

Mankind are represented as passing at death into a future state of existence. Thus to the thief Christ said, "today shalt thou be with me in paradise." Luke 23.43. In Saint Paul says, "we are confident and willing rather to be absent from the body and to be present with the Lord." 2 Corinthians 5.8. The same appears from the revelation he had when he could not determine whether he was in the body or not, and from his desire at another time to depart and be with Christ. 2 Corinthians 12.2, Philippians 1.23.

They future state appears from what I said of the situation of those who are dead. The parable of the rich man and Lazarus is designed immediately to represent the different situations of mankind, after death according to their different characters while in this world. In Hebrews 12.23, the spirits of the just or spoken of as being made perfect, which doubtless has reference to their future state. And in 2 Corinthians 5.1, It is said, "well we know, that if our earthly house of this tabernacle were dissolved, we would have a building God, the house not made with hands, Eternal in the heavens." And Judas, in Acts 25 is said to go to his own place. In Revelation 5.8, 9, those who were redeemed are represented is falling down before the lamb and saying "thou wast slain and hast redeemed us to God by thy blood, out of every kindred and tongue and people and nation." And in Revelation 6.9, 10, "The souls of them that were slain for the word of God and for the testimony which they held. And they cried with a loud voice, saying, 'How long O Lord, holy and true, dost thou not judge and avenge over blood on them that dwell on the earth.'"

The same truth is evident likewise from the design and the general representation of the resurrection. In John 5.28, 29, the design is intimated. "The hour is coming in which all that are in the graves shall hear his voice. And she'll come forth, they that have done good unto the resurrection of life, and they that have done evil unto the resurrection of damnation." In Luke 14.14 Christ speaks of the recompense which takes place at the resurrection of the just. The apostle, in 1 Thessalonians 4.16, 17 speaks of the dead who are raised first and those who are then alive being caught up together to meet the Lord in the air and to be ever with the Lord.

A future state appears from the general judgment. "Fall we must all appear Before the judgment seat of Christ that everyone may receive the things done in his body, according to that he hath done, whether it be good or bad," 2 Corinthians 5.10. Accordingly, after the representation of Christ gives of the general judgment, in Matthew 25.46, "these shall go away into everlasting punishment," meaning the wicked, "but the righteous into life eternal."

Question 58 [98]. How do you prove the immortality of the soul?

Answer 58. The immortality of the soul is argued from its immateriality, capacity for constant improvement, thirst for immortality and dread of annihilation. But it is by revelation alone, that we can come to any certainty represent this matter. What is said of the happiness of the righteous and the misery of the wicked evidently more especially respects the soul. And as they are said to be everlasting, eternal, etc the soul mist be rendered immortal to enjoy one or suffer the other. See particularly Matthew 19.29, Luke 18.30, Galatians 6.8, Matthew 18.8, 25, 46, 16.9, 2 Thessalonians 1.9, Mark 3.29, Hebrews 9.15, Jude 7, Matthew 25.46, Revelation 20.5.

Question 59 [99]. Is a future state of rewards and punishments taught in the Old Testament?

Answer 59. Thought the Old Testament is not full and explicit, as the New, with respect to a future states, yet a variety of passages evidently contain the doctrine. Job says, "Though after my skin, words destroy this body, yet in my flesh shall I see God," Job 19.26. And in Ecclesiastes 12.7 it is said, "Then shall the dust return to the Earth and it was and the spirit shall return unto God who gave it." These evidently have reference to the existence of life after the death of the body and therefore imply a future state. The resurrection and general judgment are clearly represented in Daniel 12.2 and Ecclesiastes 12.14. "Many of them that sleep in the dust of the earth shall awake, some to everlasting life and some to shame and everlasting contempt." "For God shall bring every work into judgment, with every secret thing whether it be good or whether it be evil." The idea of a future state appears to be supported also by Psalm 116.15, Isaiah 26.19, Job 14.13–15.

Question 60 [101]. Is a future state of rewards and punishments taught in the writings of Moses?

Answer 60. All the important doctrines necessary to salvation our taught in the writings of the Old Testament. Yet perhaps none are so clearly revealed in that as a new. The writings of Moses in particular are not so express and clear. Especially with respect to the doctrine of a future state as the other books of the Old Testament. It is however taught so clearly that those who are not enemies to the truth would have no difficulty in discovering it. They would naturally be led to it by a variety of considerations. The knowledge the writings of Moses afford by means of prophesies, types and institutions of various kinds respecting the atonement with direct them to that salvation which a savior, yet to come, will effect for all who believe in him. And this salvation they must know did not respect this world but a future state. He acceptable sacrifice of Abel and unacceptable sacrifice of Cain would naturally lead them to some notions and expectations of a future state of rewards and punishments where each would be treated according to their real characters. The translation of Enoch has a strong presumptive argument in favor of seeing doctrine else why should a good man be so soon removed? And what should be the meaning of the phrase, "God took him?" The destruction of

Sodom and Gomorrah is a strong presage on future punishments that we should suppose it would hardly escape and notice of the attentive.

It cannot however be disputed by the doctrine of a future state was fully believed. Even those who assert that is not continued in the writings of Moses allow that it was believed by Egyptians and Babylonians. If so, we cannot suppose the Israelites were ignorant of it. Besides we may rationally conclude that Noah, who was a preacher of righteousness, would not have omitted arguments derived from this doctrine especially since they are so important and necessary. Also, what was said to Moses at the appearance of the bush, "I am the God of thy fathers, the God of Abraham, the God of Isaac, and the God of Jacob," was a strong intimation of a future state. For as is said in Matthew 22.32, "God is not the God of the dead but of the living." From what is said to Abraham in Hebrews 11.19. It is evident he believe the resurrection and if so, doubtless he believed the doctrine of a future state. Indeed the greater part of this [eleventh] chapter of Hebrews fully supports the idea that the doctrine was generally believed, especially what he said in verses 13, 14, 15, and 16.

Question 61 [102]. How do you prove the divine mission of Jesus Christ?

Answer 61. The divine mission of Christ maybe proved from a variety of considerations. Indeed his name Christ or Messiah imports his being anointed and sent and if so by whom could he thus delegated unless by God. The greater part of Christians allow him to have been at least the greatest of all creatures. None then could send him but God. Besides he is frequently spoken of as the anointed of the Lord. The prophecies, especially with respect him, thus denominate him. All the prophecies which respect is coming, person, offices, sufferings, etc., are a strong confirmation of his divine mission. Some of the passages which speak with reference to this are Psalm 84.9, 1 Samuel 2.35, Isaiah 61.1, Daniel 9.24, Psalm 115.7, Romans 8.3. The predictions of the angel to Mary in Luke 1.32 and to Joseph in Matthew 1.21 fully establish his mission. If he is called the Son of the highest, if God has given him the throne of David, and if by divine authority he is to save his people from their sins, doubtless his mission is divine.

Question 62 [103]. How do you prove the divinity of Christ?

Answer 62. The Divinity of Christ maybe proved from the name subscribed to him. In Isaiah 40.3, verse three he is called Lord. "The voice of him that crying in the wilderness, prepare ye the way of the Lord, make straight in the desert highway for our God." The word Lord is said to be seen in the original with Jehovah which is an incommunicable name of deity. It is observable also, that the word God evidently refers to the same person with Lord. If it can be proved the passage has reference to Christ, his divinity will also be proved. Now in Matthew 3.3 and Luke 3.4, John Baptist is expressly declared to be the person predicted by Isaiah and said to prepare the way of the Lord. From Luke 1.17 and 3.16–24, John 1.6–18, and Matthew 11.10–20, it is clearly asserted that he was the forerunner of Christ and sent on purpose to prepare his way. It must then of consequence follow that Christ is the Lord and God spoken of by Isaiah. In John 5.20, he is called the true God. In Jeremiah 23.6 and 33.16, he is called, "The Lord, our righteousness." In Matthew 1.23, it is said, "And they shall call his name Emmanuel, which being interpreted is, God with us."

2. The divinity of Christ is proved from attributes of deity which are applied to him equally with God the Father. His eternity is supported by Micah 5.2, "Thou Bethlehem, Ephrathah, though thou little among the thousands of Judah, yet out of the thee shall he come forth unto me that is to be ruler in Israel whose goings have been from an old from everlasting." Now this prophecy in Matthew 2.6 is directly applied to Christ. His eternity is proved, also from Hebrews 13.8.

His omnipotence is equally supportive. Revelation 15.3 represents him as possessed of this attribute. "And they sing the song of Moses the servant of God and the song of the lamb, saying great and marvelous are thy works Lord God Almighty, just and true are thy ways, thou King of saints." It is the lamb who in every part of this book is represented as fighting the battles of the church and on account of some signal victory he is here celebrated in this manner. In Revelation 1.8, he styles himself, "The Almighty." In Isaiah 9.6 he is called the mighty God. Colossians 1.16–17 he is represented as creating and upholding all things which is an actual exercise of his almighty power.

He is represented as omniscient. The treasures of wisdom and knowledge are said to be held in him, Colossians 2.3. He is said to know the thoughts of the Pharisees, Matthew 12.25; to know also what is in man. John 2.25, and to know all things, John 21:17. And he is said to him, "All the churches shall know that I am he which searcheth the reins and hearts." Revelation 2.23. These express his omniscience with a peculiar degree of force, more so, perhaps than if they had declared the matter in a short, explicit, phraseology.

He is also possesses the attribute of immutability. This is wonderful by some 102:25–27. [Verse] 25 years represented as having created the earth and the heavens; 26 there mutability is expressed; and in 27 in direct opposition to this it is said to him, "But thou art the same, and thy years shall have no end." This passage is addressed to Christ is fully clear from the manner of it's being quote and use made of it, in Hebrews 1.10. In Hebrews 13 and he said "the same yesterday and today and forever." 5. His omnipresence, though not so explicitly is as really understood in a number of passages. Matthew 18.20, he says, "where two or three are gathered together there in my name, there am I in the midst of them." And 28:20, "Lo I am with you alway even unto the end of the world." The former of these passages cannot, with any priority be understood as some have understood it; to refer to his being in the midst of them with his authority, for their being gathered together in his name, means by his authority. To suppose authority to be meant in both places we'll make it near tautology. The same may be inferred from what is said in Colossians 1.17, Hebrews 1:3, John 1.18 & 3:13. 3. Another argument in proof of Christ's divinity arises from being the object of religious sonship. "God also hath highly exalted him, and giving him a name which is above every name; "that at the name of Jesus every knee shall bow, of things in heaven and those things in earth; And that every tongue should confess that Jesus Christ is Lord to the glory of God the Father." Philippians 2.9–11. Other passages equally clear might be adduced are not this sufficient. Hebrews 1.6 and John 5.23 equally ascribe worship to him. Besides various acts of religious worship directed to him are particularly expressed. Swearing by his name is an act of worship. Romans 9.1 & Isaiah 45.23. Baptism is instituted in his name, equally with the Father, Matthew 28.19. He is an object of that faith, trust and reliance, which are expressed as acts of worship. 2 Timothy 1.12, John 14.1. Prayer is directed to him. Isaiah 11.10, Matthew 15.22 and 25, Mark 9.24, 2 Corinthians 13.14, 1 Corinthians 16.23, Philemon 25, 1 Timothy 4.22. Under this had me be included doxologies, which are such descriptions of praise, as belong only to God. 2 Peter 3.18, Jude 24, 25, Revelation 1.5–6, 1 Timothy 6.15, 16.

Question 63 [108]. If Christ were creature, could he atone for the sins of mankind?

Answer 63. The infinite evil of sin appears from the dignity and excellency of God against whom it is committed, and also from threatenings against it, and the actual execution of those threatenings. But since justice requires the full punishment due to sin it is evident from the finite capacity of a creature he never could fully pay the demands of justice. Had Christ been only a creature what he did and suffered might have been consistent with a sinless character and perfection of a holy creature. Yet neither his obedience nor his sufferings would have been more than finite. His finite capacity would not have supported an infinite load.

It was necessary then Christ should be more than a creature, that he might support his human nature from sinking under the infinite wrath of God. It was also necessary that he should be a person of infinite worth and dignity, to give importance and value to his atonement. Otherwise, the law which measures transgressions according to truth and which threatens infinite evil as a punishment must have fallen into contempt. For so far as a law is evaded or abated, reflection and dishonor are cast upon the author of that law, his authority and government. To this may be added, it was necessary he should be more than a creature to give dignity and efficacy to his intercession, that he might be able to bestow that gifts of the spirit to his people, that he might possess power to conquer and subdue the enemies of himself and people, that he might be able to bring his people to everlasting salvation, and that he might the object of their supreme delight and highest enjoyment.[25]

Question 64 [110]. Is Christ the Son of God in any other sense than Adam was?

Answer 64. The human nature of Christ was as really created as was Adam's. He possessed the powers, faculties, feelings and sentiments peculiar to human nature; so far as they are not accompanied by moral evil: and these were communicated to him by God. Christ was therefore the son of God in the sense similar to Adam with respect to his human nature. But with respect to his divine nature, he is a Son in a sense totally different from Adam. His divine Sonship is peculiar to himself alone. It is with reference to this generally, if not wholly, that he is called the Son of God. That this is the case is evident in that the highest title and respect are denoted when he is denominated Son. "He shall be great and shall be called the Son of the highest." Luke 1.32. "This is my beloved Son in whom I am well pleased, hear ye him." Matthew 17.5. Hence he is called "the only begotten of the Father," "the only begotten Son," "his own Son," and hence it is said "that all men should honor the Son even as they honor the Father."

That Christ's Sonship respected his divinity is clear from what he said of himself. "My Father worketh hitherto, and I work." John 5.17. In this he fully intimated his works were similar to those of the Father, which were defined. "I and my Father are one." John 10.30. In calling God Father, he evidently expressed his relation to him as Son: and in saying they were one he is clearly expressed his equality to the Father, in this character. This is more strongly confirmed by the reception the Jews gave to what he said.

---

25. Supplement, p. 382; *Answer 63*. The human nature of Christ might have been supported by God under his sufferings though he had been no more than a creature.

They supposed he spoke with reference to his divinity, and on this account expressed the highest indignation against him. Hebrews 1.5.

Question 65 [111]. Did Christ first become a son by his birth of the Virgin Mary?

Answer 65. If the Sonship of Christ respects his divinity as is evident from the above quotations and if he possesses in his divine nature the attributes of duty especially eternity as has likewise been proved then doubtless he was Son even before the existence of the virgin Mary. Besides the phraseology of Scripture would naturally suggest this idea. "God so loved the world that he gave his only begotten Son." John 3.16. "God sent his only begotten Son into the world." 1 John 4.9,10. The most natural construction of this is that he existed as Son before he was sent and consequently before his birth of Mary. "For this purpose, the Son of God was manifested, that he might destroy the works of the devil." 1 John 3.8. "God was manifested in the flesh." 1 Timothy 3.18. These passages are evidently parallel and the "son of God" in the first and "God" in the last referred to the same person. But God is from eternity, consequently the Son of God or Christ with respect to his divinity is also from eternity.

Question 66 [112]. Does the Sonship of Christ consist in his appointment to the work of redemption?

Answer 66. If assumption of Christ consisted in his appointment to the work of redemption without this appointment the distinction into Father and Son would have never existed and then instead of there being three persons, there would have been only one. But the general language of Scripture seems to speak of this distinction as existing independently of redemption. "My Father worketh hitherto and I work." "The Son can do nothing of himself but what he seeth the Father do: for whatsoever things he doth, these also doth the Son likewise." John 5.17,19. Christ fully intimates here that the works which the Father does are equally performed by him in the capacity of Son. But as there are other works besides that of redemption is evident the Sonship of Christ does not respect the merely, and therefore does not depend upon it. The Scripture indeed universally speaks of that distinction into Father and Son, without the least degree of limitation to the work of redemption. Christ is said to be "the only begotten Son, which is in the bosom of the Father." John 1.18. He says himself "I am the Father are one." John 10.30. This fully intimates that the distinction exists without reference to the work of redemption. Hebrew 1.2,3. John 1.49.

Question 67 [114]. Was Christ a Son from eternity?

Answer 67. If the Sonship of Christ does not depend upon the work of redemption and if "Son of God" imports his deity as appears by comparing 1 John 3.8 and 1 Timothy 3.18, then he must have been a Son from eternity. "The Lord hath said unto me Thou are my Son, this day have I begotten thee." Rom 2.7. This is the language of Christ, as is evident from the application of it in Hebrews 1.5. "Unto which of the angels said he, at anytime, Thou art my Son, this day have I begotten thee." On this last passage two things may be remarked. 1. There is a peculiarity in the nature of Christ's Sonship. The angels are in some sense the sons of God, as appears from Job 38.7. But the phrase "my Son," imports some distinction and doubtless means the same with "my beloved Son," "own Son," "only begotten Son." 2. There is some peculiarity with respect to the duration of his Sonship in the phrase "This day." It cannot mean any particular day to which the beginning of a cinch it is referred, nor does it here to have reference to any particular period of time, which marks the distinction. But agreeable to phrases of a similar kind, it must rather be designed to exclude the idea of time and to intimate that his existence, as Son, was without beginning or from eternity.

Question 68 [115]. Was Christ necessarily or voluntarily begotten of the Father?

Answer 68. If the distinction into Father and Son was from eternity, then the distinction is as necessary as the existence of God. His existence is independent of his will, and Christ "In him dwelleth all the fullness of the Godhead bodily," must also, possess an existence as Son independent of his will. Besides to suppose that he was voluntarily begotten, will imply that he began to exist as Son. For God must in this case have willed before the Son's existence.[26]

Question 69 [116]. Is there more absurdity in supposing Christ was eternally begotten, than that he was eternally the second person in the Trinity?

Answer 69. There appears to be no more necessity of priority in point of time between the Father and the Son, then between the first and second persons in the Trinity. Nor is it more absurd, that the Son should proceed

26. Supplement, p. 382; *Answer 68*. This question respects the will of the Father. Te Son was no more voluntarily begotten than light is voluntarily produced by the Son or secondary qualities by the primary. Nor is there any more distinction of time in the former than in the latter case.

from the Father, by eternal generation, than that they should be with respect to each other, first and second. If there is a distinction of first and second, doubtless there is something which constitutes the distinction; and what ever this be it implies no more absurdity to denominate it an eternal generation of the Son then an eternal constitution of the second person. Nor does the former imply priority of time more than the latter. But since Scripture favors the former phrase, rather than the latter, the former is without doubt the least absurd.

The distinction of the Father and Son implies no more inferiority then that of the first and second. If Christ may be second person and not inferior, then he may be Son and not inferior. Among men the relation of second, as really implies inferiority, as that of Son. But there is no relation among men or any creatures by which that of Father and Son in the Trinity may be accurately and fully compared. Nor is there any generation among creatures similar to the eternal generation of the Son. To pretend therefore to compare this with the generation which takes place among mankind and thence drew on absurdity when the comparison will not hold and is unfair and disingenuous.

Question 70 [117]. Was the human soul of Christ created before his conception by the Virgin?

Answer 70. It does not appear from the general representations of Scripture respecting the incarnation and birth of our Savior, that we should ever be led to suppose that his human soul possessed an existence, previous lacks union with the body, unless we had some favorite scheme by means of this doctrine to support. "Unto us a child is born, unto us a son in given." Isaiah 9.6. "Behold, a virgin shall conceive and bear a son." Isaiah 7.14. "Thou shalt conceive in thy womb and bring forth a son." Luke 1. "And knew her not till she had brought forth her first-born son." Matthew 1.25. Now, under the idea of son is included not merely a body but a soul likewise. A body in human appearance without a soul would be another and not a proper child. This evidently is the natural construction of these passages and there is nothing in them which would lead us to conjecture, that the soul preexisted, before its union with the body. "Wherefore in all things it beloved him to be made like unto his brethren." Hebrews 2.17. But if the soul which was united to the human body had a preexistence, he was not made like unto his brethren in all things, but only in his body. "For we have not an high priest which cannot be touched with the feeling of our infirmities, but was in all points tempted like as we are, yet without sin." Hebrews 4.15. But if he existed before his appearance in human flesh and had experienced a trial previous to this than he was not in all points tempted like as we are.

Question 71 [119]. How do you prove the personality of the Holy Ghost?

Answer 71. The distinction of the Trinity is clearly expressed in 1 John 5.7. "There are three that bear record in heaven, the Father, the Word and the Holy Ghost." And in Matthew 26.19, "Baptizing them in the name of the Father, and of the Son, and of the Holy Spirit." These passages clearly hold up the idea of the Holy Ghost, as a person distinct from the Father and Son.

The divinity of the Holy Ghost is proved by his being called Lord or in the original Jehovah. Isaiah 6.6, 9 compared with Acts 26.25, 26; by his being called God, Acts 5.3, 4 and by the various attributes ascribed to him.

In Hebrews 9.14 he is called "The eternal Spirit." The works which require omnipotence to perform are ascribed to him. 1 Corinthians 12.11. His Omnipresence is asserted Psalm 139.7 and implied in Romans 8.28. His omniscience is implied in 1 Corinthians 2.10.

Again worship is directed to him. Matthew 9.38 compared with Acts 13.2 and 20.28, also 2 Thessalonians 3.5. Benedictions are pronounced in baptism is to be administered in his name equally with the other persons. Also doxologies are ascribed to him, all which are particular modes of worship and evince his divinity.

Question 72. How do you prove that the three persons in the Trinity are one God?

Answer 72. The three persons in the Trinity are but one God appears from a number of passages of Scripture. "There are three that bear record in heaven, the Father, the Word, and the Holy Ghost and these three are one." 1 John 5.7. "I and my Father are one." John 10.30. "But when the comforter is come, whom I will send unto you from the Father, even the Spirit of truth, which proceedeth from the Father, he shall testify of me." John 15.26. In the first of these passages, the three persons are expressly said to be one. In the second Christ asserts that he and the Father are one. And in the last the Holy Spirit is said to proceed from the Father. Now that this imports there being one may be argued from what Christ says of himself. In John 8.42, he says, "I proceeded forth and came from God." This doubtless means the same with his being one with the Father as in the passage just quoted. If then Christ's proceeding from the Father implies he is being one with him the procession of the Spirit implies the same.

Besides it is evident each of these persons is possessed of the attributes of deity. Each is omnipotent, omniscient, independent and all sufficient. Now to suppose that they are distinct gods would be absurd and inconsistent, for then each must have all power, all knowledge. Again suppose love and adoration and praise and homage are to be paid to God. But if there are three gods then there must be three Supremes in each of these exercises.[27]

Question 73 [121]. Was the tripartite distinction in the deity from eternity?

Answer 73. It has already been proved that each of the persons is spoken of distinctly, as possessing of the attribute of eternity. If so, then we have every reason to conclude there was from eternity this tripartite distinction. There is no passage of Scripture which would favor a contrary idea, unless forced from its most obvious meaning.

Besides, either we must suppose that this distinction was from eternity or that some change has taken place to produce the distinction, or that this consists only in three different properties or qualities. The latter would render a very considerable part of Scripture which speaks of method deity, futile and absurd. The second would destroy the immutability of God, and the sense of those parts of Scripture on which it is established.

Question 74 [122]. Was the subordination of the three persons in the Trinity as first, second and third, from eternity?

Answer 74. If there has been the distinction of Father, Son, and Holy Ghost, following eternity, as appears from attributes of deity, and especially that of eternity being ascribed to each, or if there has been the tripartite distinction then there has been the subordination of the three persons, as first, second and third. The tripartite distinction consists in the different denominations of Father, Son, and Holy Ghost, or the first, second and third. The former has been proved to have been from eternity. In that consists all that subordination there does in the denomination of first, second and third. Indeed, this depends upon that: and is rather an arbitrary distinction then one derived from Scripture expressions.

Question 75 [123]. How do you disprove the doctrine, that those three persons are three distinct characters only?

27. Supplement, pp. 383–82; *Answer 72*. It will not follow that the persons are one with the Father because they proceed from him. One may proceed from another and not be of the same essence. The same respects they are one, they are not three. The Indian illustrated the Trinity by three branches growing from one stump, St. Patrick by three clover leaves from one stock, and a woman by folding her apron into three parts.

Answer 75. If there can be proved that there are three United, in the Godhead, expressly spoken of as so many distinct persons, the doctrine which supposes these three to be only characters will at the same time be disproved. To say that characters are persons, or persons are characters, would be to confound language and destroy the meaning of words. Character is some quality or property belonging to a person. Without the latter, the former could not exist. It is all owed however that properties or characters are sometimes personified and represented as performing actions which are effected by the person who possesses them. Yet this figure always when properly used bearers such marks as to be easily distinguished from the plain meaning. This is the case with all writers of perspicuity in style and dignity of sentiment: much more should we suppose this would be the case in the Scriptures.

But unless we are to receive those passages which speak of the tripartite distinction in different persons, agreeably to their literal meaning, they will be on meaning and absurd. Now under the attribute of wisdom is included the idea of omniscience. But suppose we should say the omniscience or the wisdom of God is omniscient, omnipotent, omnipresent, unchangeable, holy, just, good, and true it must seem to every acquainted with language like on meaning and frivolous expressions, especially when delivered in a didactic style, and with a direct purpose to inform us, with respect to the deity and his several attributes. It would be still more absurd, to describe worship to the properties of God, to perform baptism and pronounce a benediction in the name of the 3 characters of God; and not expressly in his own personal name.

In short, every mark personality is described to the 3 persons in the Trinity and in such manner as would remove all doubt from our minds unless we were disposed to support some favorite tenet. The three personal pronouns are applied equally to each. "The Lord said unto my Lord, sit thou at my right hand, till I make thine enemies thy footstool." Psalm 110.1. "Thou art my Son, this day have I begotten thee." Psalm 2.7. "When he is come, he will reprove the world of sin, and of righteousness and of judgment." John. 16.8. Each of the persons also is represented without the least appearance of a figure, as acting, sending constituting, and the like.

Question 76 (125). Is it not a plain contradiction that God should be one God and yet three persons?

Answer 76. It implies no more contradiction to suppose that there are three persons in one God, then that three right lines united to form one triangle, or that six shillings make one dollar. To say that three gods constitute one God should be a plain contradiction. Though the Father, Son and Holy Ghost are united in one God, yet they are not three distinct gods. And though the attributes of deity are predicated of each, yet it is with reference to their personal distinction, and not any distinction into deities. When therefore, it is said, that each of these persons is eternal, Almighty, omniscient, yet it is not meant that there are three eternal, Almighty and omniscient beings. Among mankind personality is a distinction of being, but this is not the case, in the deity. There's no illustrating the matter, therefore, by a comparison with any union of persons which takes place among mankind. How the divine persons subsist in one being is beyond human capacity to comprehend or determine but merely because we cannot comprehend it, is no proof of a contradiction. If it were, then the union of soul and body would be a contradiction: for this is as really beyond our comprehension.

Question 77 [127]. What is the Arian schema of the Trinity?

Answer 77. The Arians take their denomination from Arius, who lived in the fourth century. Their peculiar doctrine is that the "son is totally and essentially distinct from the Father" that he is a mere creature; but the noblest and greatest of all creatures that he was created out of nothing, so he is in every respect inferior to the Father that by his subordinate operation the Almighty Father formed the universe and that the Holy Spirit is of a nature different from the Father or Son but was created by the Son.

The dispute rests principally in the divinity of Christ. The Arians suppose Christ has nothing which really is divine, but figuratively they suppose anything very excellent maybe thus called. And that on account of Christ's Excellency or delegated dominion over the system of nature, he may be entitled to the name of God.

Question 78 [127]. What is the Socinian scheme of the Trinity?

Answer 78. The Socinians take their denomination from Socinus, who lived in the sixteenth century. Their peculiar notions respecting the Trinity are that God, by an act of that power which is exerted in the government of all things, produced an extraordinary person of the virgin Mary that this person, called Jesus Christ, God first translated to heaven, by that portion of his power called the Holy Ghost that having given him proper instructions, he sent him to this world to promulgate a new rule of life to mankind more excellent than that they had before, to spread divine truth, by his ministry, to confirm it by his death.

The first propagators of the doctrine supposed Christ had power and dominion bestowed upon him, and that on this account, the title of true

God might be given to him; though originally he was no more than a human creature.

At first worship was paid to Christ: but at the present day both Socinians and Arians agree, that the supreme God alone is the object of prayer.

Question 79 [129]. Whence arose the Manichean notion of two Gods? And how is it confused?

Answer 79. The Manichean doctrine arose from Manes, a Persian by birth, who originally was of the sect of the Magi. But turning from this, he attempted to unite the doctrine of the Magi with the Christian system.

He asserted that there are two principles from which also things proceed. One he supposed to consist of a pure and subtle matter, denominated light, the other of grass and corrupted substance, denominated darkness. He supposed that over the former presides a being called God; and over the latter a being called Hyle or Demon: And each of these he supposes was from eternity.

This doctrine, it is presumed, has no foundation in Scripture but is the product of a wild and ungovernable fancy. Manes supposes, that the prince of darkness, after he had been defeated in a war with the prince of light, produced the first parents of the human race. But the Scriptures represent God as the creator the heavens, earth and of man, particularly be the first parents of the human race.[28] The Scriptures nowhere speak of more than one God. On the contrary, they expressly assert there is but one. Though they speak of three persons yet they declare that these three are one. "Hear, O Israel, the Lord our God is one Lord." Deuteronomy 6.4. "There is none other God be one." 1 Corinthians 8.4. Besides, an eternal being must be self-existent or necessarily existent. And necessity, in this respect being uniformly the same in every possible degree of exist, he must also be infinite. But there can be only one Being who is infinite. The doctrine and, therefore leads to principles which are absurd and inconsistent.

Question 80 [130]. Whence arose the polytheism of pagans? And how is it confuted?

Answer 80. The polytheism of the pagans arose primarily from the corruption of the human heart. Had not mankind been prejudiced against the truth opposed to the real character of God the Father would have been disposed, to deify so many, or to form such contemptible notions of their deities. But under the present depravity and wickedness of the human heart,

28. Gelston excises: If the prince of darkness be eternal, than he is self-existent, infinite, and consequently a God likewise.

left to the guidance of their imaginations, passions and lusts, and assisted by revelation, they were led to deify those who had hereto for given them assistance, and who they supposed were still able to give assistance, though absent by death. Others also whom they feared they were disposed to treat as deities lest they should provoke them by their negligence and that they might conciliate their favor. Probably, some notions were originally derived by tradition, from revelation: yet they were so obscured by inventions and alterations as to be almost lost and destroyed.

This polytheism may be abundantly refuted by Scripture. That not only asserts there is but one God, but ascribes attributes to him very different from those described by the pagans to their deities. In short, they ascribe nothing to their deities which is consistent with the character of deity. They respect them in many respects as inferior to men and possessed of characters which would be degrading to the lowest of men.

Question 81 [132]. The internal faculties an external advantages of mankind being supposed to be sufficient, why are they not in all ages united, in right sentiments concerning the one true God?

Answer 81. The internal faculties in external advantages being supposed to be sufficient to direct mankind to right sentiments, concerning the one true God, if notwithstanding this, they do not pertain to right sentiments, it must be because they are prejudiced against the truth. This prejudiced must arise from some corruption and wickedness of the heart. "Having the understanding darkened, being alienated from the life of God, through the ignorance that is in them, because of the blindness of their heart." Ephesians 4.10. The true character of God is opposed to theirs; and so long as they remain in their present character it is not for their interest to suppose him such a being, as he really is. In proportion then as their character is bad, they will be disposed to level his character to their own wishes. It is not surprising, therefore, that the degrees of blindness, stupidity and prejudice our different, and lead some much farther from the truth than others.

Question 82 [133]. Were the moral character of God and moral law understood that loves would there be any objection against revealed religion?

Answer 82. Did mankind properly understand and sincerely love the moral character and laws of God, they would be so far from being displeased with a revelation from him then they would greatly desire one, and readily receive every intimation of his will. Or were revelation to give such a description of God's moral character and law, as would indulge them in their wickedness and gratify their wishes, there would be no objection to it: but they would become its strongest advocates. But in spite of this, the moral character of God is totally opposed to theirs and his law condemns them from every breach of it, and for every gratification in which they wish to be indulged. This is the reason then, why they hate and oppose God and his law, and why they are opposed to a revelation which gives such representations of these, and of their own characters.

Question 83 [134]. What is the true idea of God's decrees?

Answer 83. The idea of God's decrees is that all things are foreordained, fixed, and determined by him. Nothing cometh to pass beyond his great and extensive designs. Not a sparrow falleth to ground without being noticed by God: the very hairs of our head are all numbered: and even the minutest circumstance which respects any of his creatures, however insignificant to human appearance, is established by his decree.

The decrees of God are so far as we can judge, no more than the energetic acts of his will. In willing the existence of anything, he decrees existence of that thing. Accordingly it is said, he "Worketh all things after the counsel of his own will." Ephesians 1.11.

Question 84 [134]. Are God's acts or volitions successive? Or do they successively take place in the divine mind?

Answer 84. In the divine mind there is no succession of volitions or acts. With God there is no such thing as present, past, or future: but all things are beheld as though they are present. It is not meant however, that he sees things to be in existence, which are not so: but their future it is as certain as if they now were in existence. When things are not in existence, God perfectly knows it. And when they come into existence even at that instant, he knows it. How this can be without an accession of ideas, is to us inconceivable and unaccountable. But that there is no such thing as an accession of new ideas, or recent acts of will in the divine mind, it is clear from the knowledge we have of his attributes. If he has new ideas, he knows something now, he once did not: consequently he was not omniscient. If we suppose the acts of his will to be successive, he now has an act which either it is the same with that he always had, or is different, if the same, then with respect to this there is no succession: if different, then there is a change of his will: and as his will is a part of his nature, there is a change of that: he is therefore not immutable. But this is directly contrary to Scripture. "Every good gift and every perfect gift is from above and cometh down from the Father of lights, with whom is no variableness, neither shadow of turning." James 1.17. "But he is one mind, and who can turn him? And what his soul desireth, even that he doth." Job 23.13. "Declaring the end from the beginning, and from ancient times the things that are not yet done, saying 'My counsel shall stand and I do all my pleasure.'" Isaiah 46.10.

Question 85 [136]. Did God decree the existence of sin?

Answer 85. If the number of hairs in our head and the falling of a sparrow to the ground are objects of God's providence, doubtless sin is; whose consequences are of infinitely greater moment. Now, as God is omniscient, he must have known the future of sin, before it took place. This he must have known either with or without the consent of his will. If he knew the future of sin, with the consent of his will he desired its existence. But if he knew it would take place and with his will was opposed to its existence, but was unable to perform it, this would limit his power and destroyed his omnipotence at once. In short, if sin may take place in the first instance without his consent it may in every possible instance, and in this way his moral system might be defiled and his government in a measure at least, destroyed. To suppose that sin took place contrary to the will of God when he had power to prevent it would be the highest reflection on his wisdom and goodness.

It is not meant however, that decrees of God rest on his foreknowledge. On the contrary in order of nature, foreknowledge depends on the decree. Otherwise, it would be difficult to conceive how a thing should be absolutely foreknown unless he had determined its future existence: or how he would be able to overrule and superintend the actions of his creatures. If foreknowledge precedes the decrees, then it must depend on the actions of the creatures, and then God, in knowledge must be dependent. It is also most agreeable to Scripture phraseology, to place the decree first. "Him, being delivered by the determinant counsel and foreknowledge of God, ye have taken, and by wicked hands have crucified and slain." Acts 2.23.

That sin is the object of God's decree seems evident from the variety of passages, especially those in which God is said to harden the heart, and where the cause is said to be from the Lord, when the effect is sin. One of the greatest crimes which ever was committed, most probably, was the betraying and crucifying of our Savior. Yet it is said, "For of the truth against thy holy child Jesus, whom thou hast appointed, both Herod and Pontius Pilate, with the Gentiles and the people of Israel were gathered together to do whatsoever thy hand and I counsel determined before to be done." Acts 4.27, 28.

Question 86 [138]. For what end did God decree the existence of sin?

Answer 86. The end for which God decreed the existence of sin is the same with that of his other works. All God's works are represented as works of goodness or mercy. "To him who alone doth great wonders; for his mercy endureth forever." Psalm 136.4. "To him by wisdom made the heavens; for his mercy endureth forever." Psalm 136.5. As all the works of God were designed by infinite wisdom, for good and important ends, so doubtless sin was introduced to promote the highest good of the system. How is overruled for good is not for us to determine: but that it is thus overruled, we have every reason to suppose but that it is thus overruled, we have every reason to suppose, both from the knowledge we have of the divine character and the light the Scriptures afford upon the subject. The sin of Joseph's brethren, of Pharaoh, Sihon, of Judas, and others are represented as being decreed and that for wise and good engines. If in these instances it was designed for the greatest good, we may rationally suppose it is in all cases.

Without the existence of sin it is impossible to conceive how God's moral character could have been fully known and enjoyed: at least it never would have been fully manifested. And as the greatest happiness of his creatures consists in the enjoyment of him, the greater knowledge they have of his character, the greater will be [their] in enjoyment and happiness.

Question 87 [139]. In what sense is sin agreeable to the will of God?

Answer 87. Sin is not agreeable to the will of God on account of itself, nearly, or its neutral tendency. It is not agreeable to God that his creatures should hate him, his law, moral government, etc.: Because he delights in these things. But it is agreeable to him, on account of the good he intends to produce from it. If he could not overrule it for the good of his creatures, then it might be disagreeable to him on the count of the consequences which follow it. The sin of betraying and crucifying our Savior is not, on account of itself, agreeable: but taken in its connections and consequences, it was agreeable and pleasing to the will of God.

Question 88 [140]. Is the present system of the universe the best possible?

Answer 88. The present system of the universe is devised by infinite wisdom and goodness. Now to suppose it is not the best possible, would be the greatest reflection on both. If a better system could have been adopted then is already adopted, then either God must have been incapable of discovering it or destitute of that goodness which would be disposed to communicate and promote the greatest good. But this none will assert who are acquainted with the moral perfections of deity.

Question 89 [141]. What is the distinction between the secret and revealed will of God?

Answer 89. The secret will of God is but another name for his decrees; and
it is invariably the same. The revealed will of God respects his outward dispensations, which are various and manifold. But whenever there is a change
in the outward dispensations we may conclude this change arises from his
secret will for all things which take place are decreed by him. The secret
and the revealed will are therefore, distinct and in many instances, different.
Thus the revealed will to Pharaoh was, "Israel is my son, even my firstborn.
And I say unto thee, let my son go, that he may serve me." But the secret will
of God though unknown to Pharaoh was directly the reverse from this. This
God intimated to Moses, when he said, "I am sure that the king of Egypt will
not let you go." And again, he says, "I will harden his heart, that he shall not
let the people go." Exodus 3.19 and 4.21, 23.

The revealed will of God to Abraham was, "take now thy son, thine
only son Isaac, whom lovest, and get thee into the land of Moriah, and offer
him there for a burnt-offering upon one of the mountains which I will tell
thee of." Genesis 22.2. But from the event, it is evident, that God previously
determined, Abraham should not offer his son in actual sacrifice.

The same may be said, with respect to the threatening against Nineveh,
and the reversing of that ruin in consequence of the Ninevites' repentance.[29]

Question 90 [142]. In what sense and in what manner did God introduce sin into the universe?

Answer 90. God introduced sin by decreeing it, by withdrawing the restraining influences of his spirit, by setting motives before his creatures and by
placing them in such a situation, as for the motives actually to prevail. God
is evidently represented in Scripture as having brought about events which
were sinful, and for which the persons active were blamable: particularly the
sin of Joseph's brother in, of Pharaoh, Sihon, Judas and the like.[30]

Question 91 [142]. How do you answer the objection, that this makes
God the author of sin?

29. Supplement, p. 383; *Answer 89*. By the reveal will is mean more properly the
system of divine revelation. The light of nature is not so generally considered as the
revealed will.

30. Supplement, p. 383; *Answer 90*. It is said by some that God introduced sin or
was the cause; either formally, eminently or virtually.

Answer 91. If by bringing it into existence, by means of his power, is being the author of sin then doubtless he is so. But those who make the objection, are generally disposed to connect the idea of guilt with the term author. They make a sinner and author synonymous terms. But surely they would not suppose that God was a sinner, because he hardened Pharaoh's heart; though that hardness of heart was sin. If we inquire, how the first act of sin came into existence, we should be absurd to suppose it to be an effect without a cause. Because of this first sin, could not itself, be the first sin, unless it be both cause and effect to the same act with respect, which none will suppose. The act then, which produces sin is not sinful: nor is the producer. God, therefore, may by his power produce sin; and not be such as those who objects suppose him. He may be the author, the efficient, and not the blamable author or efficient. We cannot determine the nature of a cause simply from them nature of the effect. Because the effect is material, it will not follow the cause is. Because the effect is selfish, it will not follow, that the cause of the effect is selfish.

Question 92 [143]. If the influence of God destroys the creature's free agency, can that influence produce sin in the creature?

Answer 92. If the influence of God operate[s] by constraint, then the person is forced against his will and his free agency is so far destroyed. In this case, there would be no sin. The nature of an action depends upon the exercise of the will. But if a man is forced to an action, contrary to his will, that which constitutes it moral action is out of the question. If however, the will consents to the act the nature of the act is determined by the nature of the volition. If a man freely chooses and freely refuses, whatever the influence, he may in this respect be a free agent; and this act may be sinful or holy, according to the nature of it.

Question 93 [144]. If the divine influence[s] do not destroy the creature's free agency, in what sense liable to objection, is God the author of sin?

Answer 93. If the creature is a free agent, acts freely, without compulsion or restraint, nothing more can be conceived necessary or desirable, to constitute a person a moral agent or subject of praise or blame, reward or punishment. If the divine influence[s] do not destroy this, then God is not the author of sin in any sense liable to objection.

Question 94 [144]. What is necessary to constitute a moral agent?

Answer 94. The answer to this is in part anticipated. Nothing more can be conceived necessary to constitute a moral agent than an understanding capable of distinguishing between right and wrong, a freedom to will, choose or refuse, and a freedom from coercion and restraint.

A mere perception of the understanding, without the power of will, would not constitute a moral agent. But when an exercise of will accompanies the dictates of the understanding, this act of the will is morally good or evil, according to its agreement or disagreement with the rule of right and wrong. When a person is compelled to an action or restrained from one, with respect to this action, he is not properly a moral agent but the acts of his will respecting this action they not withstanding be morally good or evil. The reason of praise or blame, therefore, depends upon the acts of the will. Without the exercise of the will, there is no moral act; and neither praise nor blame. Hence, it is that the Scripture say so much of the will. "Thy people shall be willing, in the day of thy powers." Psalm. 110.3. "If ye be willing and obedient." Isaiah 1.19. "With good will, doing service." Ephesians 6.7. For it is God, which worketh in you, both to will and to do of his own good pleasure." Philippians 2.13. "If any man will come unto me." Matthew 16.24. "Ye will not come to me, that ye might have life." Matthew 5.40. These passages evidently represent the state of the will as the foundation of praise or blame. From them, we may therefore, conclude, it is the will more especially which constitutes a moral agent.

> Question 95 [146]. What is that liberty, which is necessary to moral agency?

Answer 95. A power of choosing or refusing, agreeably to the dictates of the understanding, or according to the motives presented to the mind, a freedom from co-action and restraint is all the liberty necessary to moral agency.

> Question 96 [146]. Do we always act from motives? Or what do you mean by motive?

Answer 96. Volition is an effect, which like all other effects, must have a cause. This seems to be a dictate of common sense. How anything can take place without a cause is perfectly inconceivable. How a volition can start into existence without some ground or reason is equally inconceivable. Surely, when a man wills there is some reason why he wills thus, rather than otherwise. Now that which determines, or produces, an act of the will is the motive. It is that, without which, there would not be this act. For instance, a drunkard chooses to drink a glass of rum. But had this kind of liquor been unknown, he would not have had this volition. Yet, though a knowledge of this liquor be necessary, this alone would not produce the act. For it might have been known and tasted, and the person notwithstanding, have been totally averse to it. Something more still is necessary. And man might revolve in his mind a thousand arguments, in favor or against drinking this liquor, but without a previous bias, it is difficult to conceive how these arguments should become if effectual. In this bias then, the energy of motives and their principal strength consists. This bias lies at the foundation of the whole and is properly the motive, and the strength of motives.

Question 97 [147]. Is a capacity to know our duty necessary to moral agency?

Answer 97. If a person may become a moral agent without a capacity to know his duty then I do not know why beasts might not be without equal propriety, denominated moral agents. The great difference between them and us is, the capacity to become acquainted with religious truth, and to see the obligations resulting from such a knowledge. But no one will suppose they are moral agents, subjects of praise or blame, in a moral view. Were it possible for a will to be put in exercise without a motive, without a knowledge of right or wrong, or why it acts so and thus, rather than otherwise, it does not appear that the action would be any more of a moral nature, then the movements of a watch.[31]

Question 98 [148]. Is self-determination necessary to moral agency?

Answer 98. If by self-determination be meant, a determination of volition, by means of some antecedent act, doubtless it is not necessary. If one act produce another act, as in this case it must, there would be no freedom in the act produced. For if one act produced another, without any consideration of motive, and from a state of indifference, there is no more freedom in it, then in the motion of a wedge, when it is driven by the beetle (once a term for a maul or hammer used with a wedge to split wood). But without freedom, in willing, there can be no moral agency. If however, there be a series of acts, determining each other, the first determining the second and the second the third, none can be free but the first. The question will arise, what determines the first act? Motives cannot determine it, if it be a self-determinate act. Yet it is not a self-determinate act, because it has no antecedent. It must then, start into existence, without any ground or reason, why it is thus, rather than otherwise. But surely, no one will pretend

31. Supplement, p. 383; *Answer 97*. A person might do that which is wrong without knowing the right. Paul thought he was doing God service when he was doing wrong.

this is necessary to moral agency. Is a drunkard no moral agent when from a habitual bias to intemperance, and a consideration of the pleasure it will afford, he drinks his first and his second glass?[32]

Question 99 [149]. Are we conscious that our volitions are not affected by any cause without ourselves?

Answer 99. We feel no impulse from any external cause, no existence or restraint. We are, indeed, has conscious of freedom from an external cause as we could be, if volitions were to start into existence we know not how, or to be self determinate.[33]

Question 100 [149]. Must our volitions be self-determinate in order that they be our own?

Answer 100. If it be ourselves that will, then the volitions of our will are our own, whatever be the cause of them. For one volition to determine another, will not anymore render the one determined, free, than if it were determined by motives, and consequently no more our own.

Question 101 [149]. Are men moral agents?

Answer 101. Men are possessed of all the qualifications necessary to moral agency and are therefore, moral agents. They are capable of distinguishing between good and evil, right and wrong, and of being influenced in their will, by reasons, arguments, or motives.

Question 102 [150]. What is the difference between natural and moral necessity and ability?

Answer 102. Not true necessity arises from some natural cause with respect to the person himself, it depends no way on his will or any of his mental faculties. Where a man is confined by bars, and chains, a natural necessity is laid upon him. When a man is afflicted by pain, he is under a natural necessity of enduring this pain. But moral necessity is of a very different kind. It is a phrase used sometimes to denote the obligation a man is under to perform any particular duty. A man is said sometimes to be under a moral necessity, when his interest or reputation is at stake.

---

32. Supplement, p. 383; *Answer 98*. It would be well to define liberty and consider whether it consists in self-determination.

33. Supplement, p. 383; *Answer 99*. From our feeling we cannot determine with result to an external cause. We only feel our volitions, not motives operating, not any external force.

Sometimes also, moral necessity is used in contradistinction from absolute necessity. This is used with reference to evidence, arising from testimony and the various circumstances attending it. The most important kind of moral necessity however, arises from the infallible connection between the strongest motives and volitions. When any object of choice is presented to the mind, the prevailing or strongest motives produce as real a necessity of volition as cutting the flesh does of pain.

Natural ability is applicable to a person's power to do a thing, when he wishes to. And moral ability is applied to the exercise of the will. The man is morally able when he is willing. On the contrary, natural inability is applicable to the want of power, when a person has a will to do it thing. It is used with reference to constraint, restraint, bodily indisposition, or a defect of the understanding. Moral inability is used, with reference to a want of will. A man is under a moral inability, to love God, when he, in his heart, is opposed to him and his law. A man of religion and virtue, while in the exercise of grace is under a moral inability to steal, rob, and commit murder.

Question 103 [151]. How can absolute moral necessity and inability to be consistent with free agency?

Answer 103. Moral necessity and inability consist in the will. When a man asked agreeably to his will, he is under a moral necessity to that action, and inability to the contrary. But to act voluntarily is to act freely. Free agency, then, consists in this moral necessity and inability. A man is not any less free because he is influenced by reason. If he were, then the greatest freedom would be consent in act unreasonably. He who loves virtue and who chooses it is necessarily virtuous. So he who loves vice and chooses that is necessarily vicious. Yet no one can suppose that these are not free; that they do not act freely. No one, by examining his own exercises, will find any other moral agency or free agency, then what consists in voluntary acts.[34]

Question 104 [152]. How can the doctrine of universal, absolute decrees be consistent with free agency in man?

Answer 104. Free agency consists, in a man's acting voluntarily. But decrees no way infringe this kind of liberty. One man was constituted a moral agent, he, at the same time, was constituted a free agent. When the latter is destroyed, the former ceases. But decrees are so far from destroying these, that they rather establish them. They know more destroy free agency, then foreknowledge. The latter denotes a certainty, or necessity, as the former.

34. Supplement, p. 383; *Answer 103*. Liberty or freedom is a negative term. It implies the absence of something.

Now if decrees be inconsistent with free agency it must be, by fair making the events certain; for they have no more of a come holster re-force on the will and foreknowledge. Yet no one will pretend that this is inconsistent with free agency.

>Question 105 [152]. Is it consistent with human liberty that God should efficaciously produce volition, in the human heart?

Answer 105. If human liberty consists, in voluntary exercises of the mind, in producing volition, God produces that in which liberty is exercised. Motives, reasons and the bias of the mind may be rendered efficacious: but so long as a man has the power of choosing agreeably to these motives, his liberty, so far as it respects accountableness, is secured. He who consults his own feelings, must be sensible that to act voluntarily is the highest kind of freedom, any can possess; and that voluntary exercises are free exercises.[35] If then, God produces an act of volition, he produces a free act; and consequently that which is consistent with human liberty.

>Question 106 [153]. Is it equally consistent with human rarity that God should efficaciously produced in the human heart an evil volition as a good one?

Answer 106. An evil volition is as freely exercised if indicates as much freedom as a good volition. A man who chooses vice is as free in his choice as one who chooses virtue. Now, no reason, it is presumed, can be given why the production of one, by the efficacious influence of God, is not as consistent with liberty as the other. If the exercise of the will is the exercise of freedom, then the production of volition is consistent with freedom, whatever the nature of volition be.

>Question 107 [154]. If God were to produce an evil volition in the human heart, would it prove that God is a sinner or that he loves sin?

Answer 107. It would no more follow that God is a sinner, were he to produce volitions that are evil, then that he is matter, because he produced that, no more then it will prove his own heart was hard, where he hardened Pharaoh's. Sin consists in the nature of the volition and he is a sinner who exercises the volition. To produce a volition and to exercise a volition are things totally distinct. If God should produce a selfish exercise in the heart,

---

35. Gelston excises: without an exercise of the will, the mind is no more free, then the body when confined.

he who experienced this within himself, would be the selfish person, and not God who produced it.

Merely producing an act will not prove that he loves that act on its own account. If he produce it for the purpose of some good beyond the act itself, then that good which he intends to produce, by means of it, is what he loves. The production of moral evil is no greater proof of God's being in love with it, then that of a natural evil. Both are designed for good and to answer the purposes of benevolence.

> Question 108 [154]. If moral necessity be inconsistent with liberty, can God be the author of sin?

Answer 108. If by the author of sin be meant decreeing sin and producing selfish volitions, then God may be the author of sin, whether moral necessity be inconsistent or consistent with liberty. But by the phrase be meant, his being the sinner, or the sinful producer of sin, he cannot then be the author of sin, in either case. If you produce is selfishness, in any of his creatures, he is not the selfish being. He is no more the sinner in this case, then he is the painful sufferer, when he brings misery on his creatures. To determine then, whether he be the author of sin or not, we need not recur to the consistence or inconsistency of moral necessity of liberty.[36]

> Question 109 [155]. How do you make it up here, that demand may be accountable, though they be not the efficient causes of their own volitions?

Answer 109. The capacity of knowing one's duty, of willing and acting accordingly are the only requirements to constitute a moral agent, a subject of praise or blame. If mankind freely chose evil, however this choice be produced, they are accountable for it. This common sense dictates: and this is the dictate of conscience also. Pharaoh doubtless was guilty, though God hardened his heart: and in proportion as his heart was hardened, his guilt was increased.

> Question 110 [156]. If all the actions of men be decreed, how are they in a state of probation?

Answer 110. A probationary state depends partly upon the certainty of events. If they were totally uncertain, if every event took place by chance,

36. Supplement, p. 384; *Answer 108*. The meaning of this question is whether God can be the author or sin in the creature and yet have moral necessity inconsistent with liberty. If moral necessity be not consistent with free-agency then there will be not sin. No sin can be produced in a log or tree.

without design or direction, it is impossible to conceive how they should be accountable for such actions, or how the character of a moral agent could be determined by them. But decrees do no more than make the events certain. At least they know more infringe liberty, then foreknowledge: or the latter makes the event, as certain as to decrees.

To be in a probationary state, nothing more is necessary, then moral agency and a rule of right and wrong. The decrees are consistent with these, as is evident from mankind acting voluntarily, with a sense of right and wrong, of praise and blame it. Joseph's brethren, Pharaoh, Sihon, and Judas were undoubtedly in a probationary state, when they committed to those sins, which were decreed and some of them foretold.[37]

Question 111 [157]. How do you prove a particular, special Providence, in every event?

Answer 111. The particular, special providence of God may be inferred, from the decrees of God, from his being the ruler and governor of all things. If he is a being of infinite goodness, we may be sure he will not suffer any disorder or unhappiness to take place, without his notice. The small circumstance random, without an overruling hand might in its consequences produce the most fatal effects.

Scripture, however, abundantly asserts the providence of God; and speaks of its being directed to the most minute affairs. Thus our hairs are all said to be numbered: a sparrow falls not to the ground without a notice of God. "Known unto God are all his works from the beginning of the world." Acts 15.18. "Whatsoever the Lord pleased, did he in heaven and in earth, in the seas, and all deep places." Psalm 136.6. "The eyes of the Lord are in every place, beholding the evil and the good." Proverbs 15.3. "For in him we live, and move, and have our being." Acts 17.28.

Question 112 [158]. What is meant by the covenant of redemption?

Answer 112. By the covenant of redemption, I understand that natural consent which took place between the several persons in the Trinity, especially the Father and the Son; for the undertaking and accomplishment of the great designs of goodness and mercy towards the following race of mankind. God, for maternity, foresaw the ruin and misery of the human

---

37. Supplement, p. 384; *Answer 110*. To be a probationer a man's character is to be on trial, agreeably to some rule and with reference to some future day of decision. The angels or saints in heaven are not now in a state of probation nor are the devils. But man, who neither know the decision and event of his own character and conduct is in a state of probation.

race: and also from eternity entered into a plan for the recovery of a part of the human race; their restoration to favor and happiness. The Father seems to be represented as proposing and the sun as consenting, to undertake the arduous work of man's redemption. Hence it is said "I, the Lord, have called thee in righteousness, and will hold thine hand, and will keep thee, and give thee for a covenant of the people, for a light of the Gentiles." Isaiah 42.6. "I was set up from everlasting, from the beginning, or ever the earth was." Proverbs 8.23. "Then said I, lo, I come; in the volume of the book it is written of me." Psalm 40.7.

From the execution of this redemption, we may conclude the sun engaged to undertake the offices of profit, Priest and King; and the Holy Spirit to make application of it to the souls of men.

Question 113 [159]. Which of the persons in the Trinity, created and governs the world?[38]

Answer 113. The Son, or second person in the Trinity, is represented as the creator and governor of the world. "All things were made by him; and without him was not anything made that was made." John 1.3. "For by him were all things created that are in heaven, and that are in earth, visible and indivisible, whether they be thrones, or dominions, or principalities, or powers: all things were created by him and for him." Colossians 1.16. In these passages suggests the second person is evidently referred to, and represented as the creator of the world and all things. By some who suppose Christ to be only a creature, he has been said, to have been no more than an instrument. But these passages with many others give no such intimation. They clearly ascribed to work to his own power. Creatures are made use of in producing effects, and are rendered subservient to the introduction of all things into being, which before had no existence. Yet we have no authority to suppose that the power of creating matter or mind has been delegated to any creature; or indeed that any creature can be endowed with this power. Besides, when we consider other arguments in favor of the divinity of Christ and of his being a second person in the Trinity, we have no right to say he acted as an instrument; but as the Son and true God. Though creation be ascribed to him, yet as it is a work of divinity, it is virtually and really performed by the several persons equally. What one performs, as God, the other does: though some works are ascribed to one and some to another.

Christ, as God or the second person, in the Trinity is represented, not only as the creator, but governor of the world. Hence it is said, "Thy throne, O God, is forever and ever: the scepter of thy kingdom is a right scepter."

38. Gelston inserts "-Prove it-" following the question.

Psalm 45.6. And hence, Christ is called "the Prince of the kings of the earth." Revelation 1.5.

Christ is governor of the world, in being the head of the church. In this, he rules as "leader and commander." He not only rules in and reigns over those who are his followers; but he subdues their enemies and his, supports them under trials and sufferings, and overrules all things for his own glory and their good. "Thy people shall be willing in the day of thy power." Psalm 110.3. "For he must reign until he hath put all enemies under his feet." 1 Corinthians 15.25. "Ask of me, and I shall give the this season for thine inheritance, and the uttermost parts of the earth for thy possessions." Psalm 2.8. "In all their afflictions, he was afflicted and the angel of his presence save them: in his love and in his pity he redeemed them, and he bore them, and carried them all the days of old." Isaiah 63.9.

Christ will act, as governor, likewise, at the day of judgment. He is universally represented as the judge, who will a judge mankind according to the deeds done in the body. "And behold, I come quickly, and my reward is with me, to give to every man according as his works shall be." Revelation 2.10. "For we shall all stand before the judgment seat of Christ." Romans 14.10. "For the Father judgeth no man, but hath committed all judgment to the Son." John 5.22.

Question 114 [161]. What is the last end of creation?

Answer 114. Judging from the moral perfections of God, we should naturally suppose the highest and he could have in view, would be the communication of good. He was from eternity, possessed of an infinite fullness of excellence and happiness. We cannot rationally suppose, he would be disposed ostentatiously to exhibit himself, with a view merely to be known, and not enjoyed. This would not be worthy of a God of infinite wisdom and goodness. Nor is it rational to suppose he treated beings, in expectation of receiving something from them, which he originally had not. As he was completely happy in the enjoyment of himself with the future existence of creation, the only happiness and rational and he can be conceived to have had in view, must be the greatest possible increase of happiness, among a system of creatures. In this, his happiness partly at least, consisted. Creation never taken place, we cannot conceive his happiness would have been so great as it now is. For without this, he could not have enjoyed the happiness of communicating happiness, which all created beings, in proportion to their goodness, may or do actually enjoy.

In Scripture, God is represented, as making himself the end of creation. Yet as was observed above, he had no ostentatious or selfish motives.

"For of him and through him and to him are all things." Romans 11.36. "For by him were all things created, that are in heaven, and that are in earth, visible and invisible, whether they be thrones or dominions, principalities and powers, all things were created by him, and for him." Colossians 1.16. "The Lord hath made all things for himself." Proverbs 16.4.

In some places, got his representatives making his glory, name, the knowledge of his perfections and his praise the ultimate end. "For I have created him for my glory." Isaiah 43.7. "Oh Lord, how excellent is thy name in all the earth." Psalm 8.1. "The heavens declare the glory of God, the firmament showeth his handiwork. Day unto day uttereth speech, night unto night showeth forth knowledge." Psalm 19.1,2. "Out of the mouth of babes and sucklings hast thou perfect praise." Matthew 21.16. These things results from the nature, situation, in obligation of God's creatures. To communicate the greatest possible degree of happiness, it is necessary, his name, perfections an essential glory should be known, that he may be fully enjoyed; and that his creatures may render praise to him, for these things.

That the communication of good was the end of creation appears from a variety of passages, which represent this to have been the object aimed at in all his works. "The Lord is merciful and gracious." Psalm 103.8. "God so loved the world that he gave his only begotten Son, that whosoever believe if in him, should not perish, but have everlasting life." John 3.16. "To him that by wisdom made the heavens; for his mercy endureth forever. To him that stretched out the earth above the waters; for his mercy endureth forever." Psalm 136.5-7.

> Question 115 [164]. Was the display of the divine glory the end of the happiness of the creation? Or the happiness of the creation the end of the display of the divine glory?

Answer 115. The display of the divine glory and happiness of the nation are frequently spoken of as distinct; not however, with propriety. Were not the greatest happiness, possible, produced in creation, there would be no display of the present moral perfections of deity; but of attributes opposite to these. But, in producing the greatest possible degree of happiness, a display of the divine glory and perfections is made. But also in making this display, the happiness of creation is produced. When cannot be without the other for they mutually imply each other. One therefore, was not the end of the other: but they are the same.

> Question 116 [165]. Did God create the world for his own happiness, in distinction from the happiness of the creation?

Answer 116. God did not create the world in expectation of deriving happiness from the unhappiness of his creatures. This would be inconsistent with his attribute of infinite goodness.[39] The happiness his creatures experience is not the same which he experiences. It may be the same in kind, though in an infinitely less degree: but not precisely and identically the same, any more than one man's happiness is another's. But God does not take happiness, in his creatures, but by the communication of the greatest degree of happiness. In this communication of happiness, consists his happiness and not in this respect, the one is not distinct from the other.

> Question 117 [165]. Are God's own happiness or glory, and the happiness of the creation, two distinct ends of creation?

Answer 117. It has already been observed, the happiness both God and that of creation are not properly distinct: or at least, that God's happiness consists in the communication of happiness to his creatures. They mutually imply each other. The end of creation, doubtless, was that which is actually obtained. This we find to be one uniform and glorious end. This happiness, however, is applied to different objects; and enjoyed by different beings. In God, it exists in an infinite degree. In the creature, it exists in a finite degree. But the aggregate is a glorious and infinite degree of happiness. In creation, therefore, God did not propose his own happiness as one and distinct from that of the creation and without any view to that. Nor on the other hand, did he propose the happiness of creation, as an end distinct from his own happiness, and without a view to that.

> Question 118 [166]. How do you make it appear that God's glory or happiness, and the happiness of creation are one?

Answer 118. The happiness of God and that of creation are one, inasmuch as one implies the other with respect creation. One does not exist without the other. On the contrary the happiness of God consists in the happiness of creation.

> Question 119 [167]. If man was created in original righteousness, how was that consistent with moral agency, as it is said, that a necessary holiness is no holiness?

Answer 119. The idea that a necessary holiness is no holiness is doubtless a false idea. A necessary holiness is a free and hearty choice of holiness. A

---

39. Gelston excises "On the contrary, his happiness consists, in the communication of grace and happiness."

virtuous man in the exercise of virtue is incapable of the contrary. He is under moral necessity to virtue. But this necessary holiness surely is holiness, if
anything can be conceived to be so. If a hearty and willing choice of virtue is
not virtue, then something must be so, which does not depend upon a choice.
Common sense however, dictates that this kind of necessity is consistent with
virtue. It is also inconsistent with moral agency: for no man, it is presumed is
virtuous, who is not at the same time a moral agent. Besides, the increase of
will is necessary in order to moral agency; and this is supposed in a necessary
holiness. These are therefore, consistent with each other.

Now righteousness is but another term in this case for holiness. It matters not, whether this holiness or righteousness take place, in the first stage
of existence, or at some after. Whenever it does take place, originally or
afterwards, if it be free, voluntary and no way inconsistent with choice, then
it is perfectly consistent with moral agency. The exercise of a holy volition is
the exercise of moral agency. If God can, by regeneration, produce and holy
volition, in a heart before unholy, no reason can be given why he cannot
create a being whose first exercises should be holy.

Besides if a necessary holiness be inconsistent with moral agency, then
God himself is not a moral agent. His holiness is doubtless as necessary as
his existence.

Question 120 [168]. What was the Constitution under which men, in
innocence, was placed?

Answer 120. The Constitution under which man in innocence was placed,
was partly of the nature of a law, and partly of a covenant. As a law, there
was a penalty threatened, in case of disobedience, and of consequence, an
exemption from this necessarily implied, in case of obedience. In the short
description of the transactions, with our 1st parents, we have not a particular
narration of the moral law: but doubtless that was understood, and enforced
obedience to all positive precepts. The sum of this is love. A breach of any
positive precept, would in effect, be a breach of this law of love, a moral law.
And disobedience of either would merit the like punishment.

The precept which seems to be most noticed is that which by an overt
act of wickedness was the 1st broken. This respected a particular tree. "Of
the tree of the knowledge of good and evil, thou shalt not eat of it: for in the
day that thou eatest thereof, thou shalt surely die." Genesis 2.17. Other positive precepts, most probably, were given: and had any other been broken,
instead of this, that rather than this, would then have been mentioned. The
breach of this was as before observed, a breach of the moral law. The penalty of all laws ought to be measured according to the magnitude of crimes.

The magnitude of the crime must be measured according to the dignity and Excellency of the person, against whom it is committed. As God is infinite in every perfection and excellence, the punishment due to every breach of his law must also be infinite, so far as the capacities of offenders will admit.

The penalty annexed to the law and expressed by the word "death" doubtless was the just demerit of sin. We cannot reasonably suppose a God of infinite justice would threaten and execute anything short of this. That death which is said to be the wages of sin is everywhere represented as an infinite evil.

The constitution under which man in innocency, was placed, appears to have partook of the nature of the covenant. A strict obedience to the law would have entitled him to nothing more then the continuation of that life and happiness he then enjoyed. Whatever was promised or from the dispensation of God reasonably expected came not by the law, but was rather, in consequence of a covenant. That there was something of this kind appears from several considerations. The general mode of God's truth is, this is a state trial or, as is. This most probably is this case is. Some, in the course of their trial fell, in consequence of disobedience from a state of happiness, into a state of misery. The others doubtless, who continued faithful and obedient through the time of trial, were confirmed in a state of happiness, whence they now cannot fall.

Judging from the goodness of God, we should suppose this would be the treatment he would give to all his rational creatures. We can hardly suppose he would, always, keep his creatures in suspense. Unless man was placed under such a trial, in the mode of a covenant, he cannot fully account for the positive precept, in which he actually broke. Indeed, the evident design of it seems to be, which was given to him to make trial of his fidelity. But the strongest proof, that there was something of the nature of the covenant transaction arises from what is said of the tree of life. This seems to have been a seal of what, a pledge of that blessing or favor, which should be conferred in consequence of obedience. This blessing was life. Hence, it is called the tree of life. "And now, lest he put forth his hand, and take also of the tree of life, and eat and live forever." Genesis 3.22. And hence, it is alluded to Revelation 2.7 and 22.14 to represent the state of happiness, in which they should be confirmed, who should continue to the end, as faithful followers of Christ.

Question 121 [171]. What is sin?

Answer 121. The existence of sin implies the existence of some rule of law, by which the actions of moral agents are determined: for "where no law is, there is no transgression." Romans 4.15.[40] But where a law is, "the transgression of the law" is sin. Sin is sometimes called iniquity or unrighteousness: because it is withholding that which the law justly requires. It is sometimes called trespass or transgression: because it is an actual violation of the positive precepts and prohibitions. "For it is written, Cursed is everyone that continueth not in all things which are written in the book of the law, to do them." Galatians 3.10. "Whatsoever committeth sin, transgresseth also the law: for sin is the transgression of the law." 1 John 3.4.

Question 122 [172]. Is a mere want of love to God sin?

Answer 122. Were any of God's rational creatures totally ignorant of his being and character, they would not be condemned, most probably, for not loving him. Their sin would be the sin of ignorance. Where possible, for any of his creatures to possess knowledge of his character, without exercising any affection against him, or towards them, and still remain moral agents, this want of affection towards him would be sin, and of the negative kind. This however, is a case which, is presumed, is not to be found among any of his rational creatures: and which seems hardly to be possible, inconsist[ent] with moral agency. Where no love is, there is hatred. If God's character, so far as it is known is not love, it is actually hated. Sin is not, therefore, merely the privatization of good, but the actual existence and exercise of evil. It is not merely negative, but positive.

Question 123 [173]. What was Adam's first sin?

Answer 123. The first actual sin of Adam which is expressly mentioned was the eating of the forbidden fruit. Yet doubtless, there were previous exercises of heart which were positively sinful. Every distrust of God and disposition to listen to what is said contrary to his word evidently carries with it the nature of sin, and indeed it is a sin of the greatest kind. Such was the first sin of Adam. The disposition of Adam to harkin to his wife or the suggestion of the serpent, most probably arose from the want of confidence in the wisdom, veracity or goodness of God: and also was of the nature of inquiry to.

Question 124 [173–74]. If Adam had broken any precept of the moral law, would he have been liable to the death threatened, Genesis 2.17?[41]

40. Gelston inserts "Sin is not imputed where there is no law." Romans 5.13. There is no indication where this is to be inserted.

41. Though relatively brief, the answer that Gelston supplies for question 124 underwent what appears to be several rounds of editing and is thus almost completely

Question 125 [174]. What was the death threatened in Genesis 2.17?

Answer 125. The death threatened (Genesis 2.17) was the wages of sin. It was doubtless the same with that due to a solution any precept of the moral law: at this in effect, this precept was a breach of the moral law. That it was the just demerit of sin, may rationally conclude from the infinite justice of God. Sin, being committed against a being of infinite greatness and excellence, he's an infinite evil and therefore the punishment must be infinite. Accordingly we find the punishments threatened throughout the Scriptures is of this kind. The death, said to be a wages of sin, is uniformly set in opposition to eternal life, the reward of obedience.

Question 126 [175]. In what sense consistent with truth, was the threatening of death executed on Adam, in as much as he did not die on the same day?

Answer 126. On the day in which Adam sinned, he became obnoxious to death. He was as really dead as St. Paul was when sin revived. "When the commandment came, sin revived, and I died." Romans 7.9. The meaning of this dying seems to be that he found himself to be justly exposed to eternal death, and that it might be inflicted at any moment. This was the case with Adam. Death might justly have immediately been inflicted. The design of the threatening, however, "In the day that thou eatest thereof, thou shalt surely die," seems not designed to limit the time to the day, in which she actually transgressed; but to declare the certainty of the punishment, as a consequence of one and the first transgression. "One day is with the Lord as a thousand years, and a thousand years as one day." 2 Peter 3.8. "The righteousness of the righteous shall not deliver him in the day of his transgression. As for the wickedness of the wicked he shall not fall thereby in the day that turneth from his wickedness. Neither shall the righteous be able to live in the day that he sinneth; but for his iniquity that he hath committed, he shall die for it." Ezekiel 33.12–13. The term day evidently in this passage, has no reference to a fixed period, but determines the certainty of the event.

Question 127 [176]. Has Adam, before the fall, any more freedom of will than we have?

Answer 127. It is not possible to conceive, how any moral agent can have a greater freedom of will than we have. We have the power of will from motive, agreeably to the dictates of our understanding and the internal bias of

_____

illegible.

the mind. Adam had no more. Even now, the most virtuous have no more freedom of will than the most vicious.

Question 128 [176]. Was Adam under the same necessity of falling that we are of sinning?

Answer 128. The necessity of falling arose from Adam's being left of God, without a sufficient degree of restraining grace to prevent his falling, and the strength of motives. These are circumstances similar to what we experience.[42] It cannot be conceived that any of Adam's posterity previous to their first actual sin, have any more of necessity or previous disposition to sin than Adam had previous to his first actual sin.

Question 129 [177]. Are all intelligences, sinners and devils, bound to love God supremely?

Answer 129. The foundation of love is the worthiness of an object. The more worth an object, the greater obligation are we under to love that object. Now as God is infinite, in goodness and excellence, he is worthy of a love proportionably great. If we do not love him, when nothing but a disposition is wanting, this want of a disposition can never excuse us. So far is it from excusing us that the opposite disposition is our greatest guilt. All intelligent beings are doubtless possessed of capacities of loving: had they but a heart to exercise this love. This is the case with sinners and devils, as much as with saints and angels. The difference between them is the latter have a disposition to love God; the former have not. But surely, that in which their guilt consists can be no excuse. So long then, as God remains a being of infinite worthiness, all are bound to love him who has capacities; whether they are disposed or not.

Question 130 [178]. Is the law of God holy, just and good? And how do you prove it?

Answer 130. Since God is a being infinitely holy, just and good, we are confident his law must be so. If he were to make a law which was not, it would be strong proof, that he is destitute of those perfections himself. But the declarations of Scripture abundantly prove the law to be, like its author, holy, just and good. "Wherefore the law is holy and the commandment holy, and just, and good." Romans 7.12. "The law of the Lord is perfect." Psalm 19.7. Not all been holy, just and good, it is not reasonable to suppose God would have

42. Gelston excises: The moral necessity of sinning we are under consists in the actual exercise of the will and this was the case with Adam.

sent his only begotten Son to suffer and die, to support the honor of it. So far from this he would at once have destroyed a law which did not possess these proprieties; but was on holy and unjust. The sufferings of Christ in connection with the character of God are the perhaps one of the strongest arguments in favor of God's law.

Question 131 [178]. Is a damning God the proper object of love?

Answer 131. If God took pleasure in damning and making his creatures miserable, merely for the sake of this, and because it was his disposition, this would be a mark of malevolence and a character which instead of being loved onto the hated. But if you're wise and holy purposes, he's pleased to suffer his creatures to sin and then punish them without which there since just deserve, this is no impeachment of his character. Nor ought he to be the less loved. If he brings no misery upon his creatures, but what is justly deserved and open rules all for the greatest good of his creatures in general, he ought the rather to be lost on this account. If damning those of his creatures who have rebelled against him, would exclude him from a right to be loved then bringing into this world to the smallest degree of natural evil on his creatures would in some proportion destroy his loveliness.

Question 132 [179]. How great is the demerit sin?

Answer 132. The demerit of sin is in proportion to the altercation violated. The application is measured by the dignity and excellency of God. As therefore, he is infinite in every perfection and excellence, the obligation is infinite in the violation of it is a sin infinitely criminal. As also, all sin is in effect of this description, the demerit of all sin is infinitely great.

Question 133 [180]. How do you prove the sunless duration of hell-torments?

Answer 133. The restoration of hell-torments may be argued from the nature and emeritus in. That is an infinite evil and as justice requires a punishment adequate to the crime, it requires sin should meet with a punishment equally great. Not only strict justice, but the general good requires this. This evil which sin produces is an injury done to the general good. And unless this injury be paired, the loss must be sustained; and universally felt. Since therefore, the evil produced be infant in the punishment inflicted to repair the loss must also be infinite. And since those who suffer are finite, to inflict the punishment deserved they must undergo a punishment and less in duration.

But the Scriptures fully establish the doctrine of an endless punishment. Thus we are informed, with respect to those who are punished in the future world, "the smoke of their torment ascendeth up forever and ever." Revelation 14.11. "Then shall he say also unto them on the left hand, Depart from me, ye cursed, into everlasting fire, prepared for the devil and his angels." Matthew 25.41. "Any many of them that sleep in the dust of the earth shall awake, some to everlasting life, and some to shame and everlasting contempt." Daniel 12.2. "Who shall be punished with everlasting destruction from the presence of the Lord, and from the glory of his power." 2 Thessalonians 1.9.

Question 134. [181]. How do you reconcile the endless duration of hell-torment with the perfect justice and infinite goodness of God?

Answer 134. Justice is that attribute, which requires the full punishment due to every transgression of the law. Now since sin is an infinite evil justice requires the punishment inflicted to be an infinite evil likewise. This can be accomplished only by and endless duration.

Again, sin is an evil done to the general good. But it is not consistent with the goodness of God that the community should sustain an infinite evil and no separation be made. Infinite goodness requires, therefore, that this loss should be repaired. This, by means of punishment, can be done no way but by and endless duration of punishment.

Question 135 [182]. How will you reconcile the endless duration of hell-torments with those text which say, Christ died for all men, God will have all men to be saved?

Answer 135. Those passages of Scripture which say, Christ died for all men, God will have all men to be saved, and the like, are to be explained doubtless in a manner consistent with other parts, which represent some of mankind as finally missing of salvation and suffering the endless punishment of hell torments. Scripture in all cases is to be its own interpreter. Many passages taken in a detached manner and agreeably to their literal meanings would seem to favor doctrines wholly inconsistent with the general scope of Scripture. This is the case with the texts before us. The Scriptures fully support the doctrine that the atonement of Christ itself is sufficient for all men: that God has made such provision in the gospel, that all who are willing to accept of the offered salvation shall actually obtain it. The terms on which salvation is offered are so easy that nothing but willingness is necessary to produce a cheerful performance. Besides, not only is the provision amply sufficient and the terms easy, but the offer is made to all. "Whosoever will, let him take the water of life freely." Revelation 22.17. This appears to be the import of the passages now under consideration. But this does not imply that all shall eventually be saved. God has not laid himself under any obligation to save all mankind, nor is he willing all should be saved except in the way of the gospel.

Question 136 [183]. Has God made any man to be damned?

Answer 136. God has not made any man to bring any evil upon him, merely on account of the evil or of any pleasure he takes in inflicting it. God does not bring misery on any of his creatures because he delights in misery, but because he delights in the good and happiness resulting from it by means of his providence. But if God may make a man for a small degree of evil and misery, he may for a greater, and even for the greatest. Now he expressly says to Pharaoh, "and in very deed for this cause. Have I raised the up, for to shew in thee, my power, and that my name may be declared throughout all the earth." Exodus 9.16. In a similar sense, finally, impenitent sinners are raised up to be damned. They are represented, Romans 9.21. As being in the same manner made to dishonor as those who are saved or to honor. And in the next verse. They are said to be "Vessels of wrath fitted to destruction."

Question 137 [184]. Is God obliged by veracity to execute the threatening of his law?

Answer 137. If the owner of the law and the divine government can be supported without an execution of the threatened penalty. It is not conceived that God's veracity would oblige him to execute it. It does not appear that the veracity of God, or of any legislation, is pledged or the execution of threatening of his law. The law was designed for the support of government and at the same time to exhibit the moral character of God and his opposition to send. This rather belongs to the attributes of justice and goodness. And if this can be accomplished without the actual execution of the threatening, then the purposes for which a law was instituted are answered. If the execution of the threatening would be attended with evil consequences of a tendency more injurious to community, than a suspension of the threatening, then that which at first required the establishment of the law now requires a suspension of its penalty. Surely God never engaged to do anything which would be inconsistent with the general good.

Question 138 [185]. Our rewards and punishments of the gospel inconsistent with this interested affection? Or do they prove Christianity to be a selfish scheme?

Answer 138. The rewards and punishments of the gospel. Suppose mankind professed of a desire for happiness and an aversion to misery. But this is as really consistent with a disinterested as a selfish disposition. Disinterested affection is the noblest exercise of this principle of nature. So far from its extinguishing it, therefore, it presupposes the existence of such a principle.

Now the rewards promised in the gospel are calculated to promote the genuine exercise of this principle. Disinterested affection seeks the greatest good. So do the rewards in the gospel. They are not promised to individuals exclusively. But they are to be dispensed in a consistency with the general good. So far, therefore, they agree in their tendency with disinterested affection. A man may be influenced by them. On this account. He may be influenced by the rewards because they will place him in a situation to render the highest praises to God and to add to the general some of happiness. On the same principle, he may be influenced by the punishments threatened in the gospel. He may wish to avoid them because they would put it out of his power to exercise those disinterested affections which are calculated to promote the general happiness.

Question 139 [186]. How does it appear that human nature is originally depraved?

Answer 139. Observation proves that mankind, as soon as they have moral exercises, are sinful. The first appearances of their depravity are the first expressions of their heart. Children, at a very early period, evidently discover those expressions, evidently discover those expressions and feelings which result from a corrupt heart. These are as clear by and fully to be discovered, as are the marks of rationality. But the Scripture puts the matter beyond doubt. "That which is born of the flesh, is flesh." John 3.6. "Behold, I was shapen in iniquity, and in sin did my mother conceive me." Psalm 51.5. "The wicked are estranged from the womb, they go astray as soon as they are born, speaking lies." Psalm 58.3.

Question 140 [187]. Whence came the original the gravity of human nature?

Answer 140. The original depravity of human nature comes in, in consequence of Adam's breaking that covenant which God made with him in innocence. The effects of the fulfillment on breach of it were evidently to extend to his posterity. The nature of it was such that if Adam fell, his posterity were to be born into the world in such a situation as that they would inevitably sin. Hence it is that mankind, in consequence of Adam's apostasy, are brought into the world with the nature which, without restraining grace, leads them on a immediately to sin. This is a nature created with them; and no more derived from Adam, then anything else corporeal or mental.[43]

Question 141 [188]. What do you mean by total depravity?

Answer 141. By total depravity I mean that corruption of nature which mankind originally possess and which indisposes them to all good, and disposes them to evil, only evil, and that continually until they are regenerated by the grace of God. Every moral exercise they have, while in this state, is an exercise of this depravity and is infinitely criminal.

Question 142. How do you prove human nature to be totally depraved? What arguments from Scripture, from reason, or experience and observation?

Answer 142. The total depravity of human nature is abundantly asserted in Scripture. "And God saw that the wickedness of man was great in the earth, and that every imagination of the thoughts of his heart was only evil continually." Genesis 8.21. "The heart is deceitful above all things, and desperately wicked, who can know it." Jeremiah 17.9. "Unto the pure all things are pure, but unto them that are defiled, and unbelieving, is nothing pure, but even their mind and conscience is defiled." Titus 1.15. "What is man, that he should be clean? And he which is born of a woman, that he should be righteous?" Job 15.14. "The carnal mind is enmity against God: for it is not subject to the law of God, neither indeed can be." Romans 8.7. No language, it is presumed, could more completely represent the total depravity of human nature than those now quoted. Besides, this doctrine is evident from the necessity of regeneration. If mankind be not totally corrupt, what necessity would there be of a new heart, a new spirit, and of being born again. If they were only partially corrupt, then an improvement upon the remaining good principles would be sufficient. But this is not the representation of Scripture. "Except a man be born again, he cannot see the kingdom of God." John 3.3. "And you hath he quickened who were dead in trespasses and sins. Wherein in time past ye walked according to the course of this world, according to the prince of the power of the air, the spirit that now worketh in the children of disobedience. Among whom also we all had our conversation in times past, fulfilling the desires of the flesh, and of the mind; and were by nature the children of wrath, even as others. But God, who is rich in mercy, for his great love wherewith he loved us. Even when we were dead in sins, hath quickened us together with Christ." Ephesians 2.1–5.

43. The final sentence of paragraph is illegible and is crossed out with annotation.

Again, selfishness is a principal directly contrary to that which the gospel requires area and so far as it prevails, a man is depraved: for it is everywhere represented as a mark of depravity. Hints, it is said of the last days, "men shall be lovers of their own selves, lovers of pleasures more than lovers of God." 2 Timothy 3.2, 4. Not only the Scripture represent mankind as being wholly influenced by selfishness, but universal experience and observation evince this. Whatever stands as competition with the selfish views and objects of a natural man, he uniformly opposes it. Experience and observation evince, also, that mankind by nature are totally opposed [to] those holy duties which the gospel requires. No one holy duty, it is presumed, could be mentioned, which is agreeable to the carnal heart. "Because the carnal mind is enmity against God: for it is not subject to the law of God, neither indeed can be. So then they that are in the flesh cannot please God." Romans 8.7, 8.

Mankind, in all ages and countries of the world, have universally acknowledged themselves to be sinners so depraved. Hence it is, that heathen nations have been disposed to make use of sacrifices to expiate those offenses of which they are conscious they are guilty. That have acknowledged themselves to be actuated by principles which, in the light of the gospel, are evidently known to be the result of depravity and wickedness.

Question 143 [191]. How do you prove that Adam was the federal head of his posterity?

Answer 143. By being the federal head I understand Adam's being constituted so far, the representative of his posterity, as that they were to be made like him in nature, capacity, and appearance. That they were to possess the like power over the inferior parts of creation. And, above all, that if he continued through the time of his trial faithful and obedient, his posterity should share in the happy effects: but if he became unfaithful and disobedient. His posterity should share in the unhappy effects. His posterity were to be brought into the world in a situation similar to that in which the results of his trial as a federal head placed him.

With respect to the former part of this, Adam appears to have been constituted that natural ad of his posterity. "And God said, let us make man, and let them have dominion over the fish of the sea, and over the fowl of the air, and over the cattle, and over all the earth, and over every creeping thing that creepeth upon the earth." Genesis 1.26. By the plural pronoun them, doubtless, mankind in general are referred to. It is evident from the fact that mankind are made like to Adam, with the like faculties, and with power over the inferior parts of creation, at least equal to what he possessed after his apostasy.

That Adam was constituted the federal head of his posterity in a moral capacity appears evident from the real effects, which mankind actually experienced in consequence of his apostasy. But the Scriptures abundantly support the doctrine. "And hath made of one blood, all nations of men, for to dwell on all the face of the earth, and hath determined that times before appointed, and the bounds of their habitation." Acts 17.26. "Wherefore, as by one man sin entered into the world, and death by sin; and so death passed upon all men, for that all have sinned." Romans 5.12. It is also said, "if through the offense of one many the dead. And not as it was by one that sinned, if by one man's offense, death reigned by one. Therefore, as by the offense of one judgment came upon all men the condemnation for as by one man's disobedience many were made sinners." Romans 5.15–19. "For as in Adam all die, even so in Christ shall all be made alive." 1 Corinthians 15.22. "The first man is of the earth, earthy. As is the earthy, such are they also that our earthy, and as we have borne the image of the earthy, we shall also bear the image of the heavenly." 1 Corinthians 15.47–49.

Question 144 [193]. In what sense is Adam's sin imputed to his posterity?

Answer 144. By divine constitution, our standing or falling was suspended upon the conduct of Adam. If he remained faithful and obedient to his posterity were, in consequence of this, to be made righteous and happy. They were to be treated as if they had personally fulfilled the law. On the contrary, if he broke the law and fell from that state in which he was originally placed his posterity were to become depraved and to be treated in all respects as if they had personally been guilty. God, doubtless has the same right to suffer his creatures as soon as they begin to act as moral agents, to involve themselves in guilt and misery, as he had to suffer Adam to sin and fall from a state of holiness and happiness.

Now we are brought into the world and left in a state different from that in which we should have been had Adam never sinned. We experience in memorable evils and calamities of life, which we should never have experienced. As soon as we begin to act as moral agents. We exhibit the like corrupt and depraved feelings which he experienced. As soon as we begin to act as moral agents we exhibit the like corrupt and depraved feelings which he experienced after his apostasy.

His sin, however, is not so imputed to us as that it becomes ours in the same sense any act we personally commit is ours. Nor is it transferred to us and made really and virtually ours; any more than any of the after acts of his life. In the effects or consequences, it is imputed. Or we suffer the same consequences as really as if it were our personal act.

Question 145 [194]. Is Adam's sin thus imputed by a judicial or sovereign act of God?

Answer 145. A judicial act is where a subject is treated agreeably to his own personal conduct. Thus Adam, by a judicial act was condemned and exposed to the punishment of the threatened death in consequence of his actually and personally transgressing the law. But a sovereign act is that which is not regulated by the laws of strict distributive justice, but depends [upon] the will of the sovereign. The sovereign acts of God, are regulated by infinite wisdom, but do not depend upon the existence of the law. They are rather above and beyond the reach of his law.

Such was that act of God, which placed Adam as a federal head of all mankind, and which established such a constitution that if he sinned his posterity should share in the evil effects. In consequence of the sin of Adam, agreeably to the will of God, and for wise and important ends, his posterity actually experience the evil effects of it as mentioned above. But this is not done in a judicial manner. All the evils they experienced in consequence of Adam's sin are in a sovereign manner inflicted. Were they considered and viewed as actually guilty of the same sin, it would rather be a judicial act: for then these evils would arise in consequence of their own personal sin. But this would be inconsistent with truth.

Question 146 [195]. In what sense are Adam and his posterity one?

Answer 146. Adam and his posterity are one nominally, rather than really. They are treated with respect to the consequences of the fall as if they were really one. As Adam suffered the evil effects of his apostasy, so in like manner do his posterity. As he fell into the depraved, calamitous state; in a similar state are they. As he became habitually and totally depraved, so are they. As he was subjected to pain, disease, accidents, misfortune and death, so are they. And as he was to eat his bread in the sweat of his brow, the like is the case with his posterity. They suffer as really and as fully as if they had been actually engaged with him in his apostasy.

Often, men, trading in company, depute one of their body to transact the whole of their business abroad, for certain. What ever he does in this capacity is, with respect to the consequences, as really though, as if they had conducted the business as a body. Still, however, the act. He performs, what ever it be, is not really, but nominally theirs. If he conduct with prudence and become successful, the profits will be equally shared. But if with one impudent and rush stroke. He sinks the whole of their property, they as really become bankrupts as if they had actually done this themselves. Yet this one man was not those ten men. Nor were those ten men, this one man. Nor also was this act their personal act. But the consequences felt equally upon all. So far, they were one.

In a similar manner. Adam and his posterity were one. They did not personally act with Adam. Nor were they present to give their consent to his act. Much less did they act in him. But the consequences fall alike upon him, and upon them.

Question 147 [197]. In what sense are mankind punished for Adam's sin?

Answer 147. Mankind are not punished for Adam's sin unless it be by suffering the evil consequences as mentioned above. By consequences of his sin, they become sinners and are exposed to the various evils to which he was exposed. [Editor note: text is not clear]. Still, however, what mankind suffer as punishment for sin is for their own sin. In the day of judgment. The sentence pronounced upon sinners will be for and according to their own personal sins.

Question 148. Is it a punishment of the posterity of Adam that they come into the world in a depraved state?

Answer 148. Strictly speaking, the bringing of mankind into the world in a depraved state does not appear to be a punishment. The idea of punishment rather supposes previous guilt and a judicial act of condemnation. But mankind were not guilty before they were born. Nor was a judicial sentence passed upon them before they were guilty. It was more properly, as before observed, a sovereign act of God. To be brought into the world in a depraved and sinful state is a calamity and a great evil, but it does not appear to be any more of the real and proper punishment to mankind, than is a punishment to the beasts to be brought into the world in a calamitous state, and to suffer the evils they experienced in consequence of the fall.

Question 149 [198]. Does God bring any evil on mankind, which he might not consistently with justice have brought upon them, if Adam had not been their federal head?

Answer 149. The imputation of Adam's sin, or the bringing of mankind into the world in such a depraved and calamitous state is, as been already observed, a sovereign act, rather than a judicial act, or an act of justice. Had

God pleased, he might have brought mankind into the world in the same situation in which they now are, had Adam never fallen, or had he not been their federal head. It would have been no more injustice or injury to them than the present constitution, or than it was to Adam to suffer him to fall. Now, when they once become sinners. There is no evil, they experience, either in this world or the future, which day do not deserve; and which, therefore, is not perfectly consistent with justice.

Question 150. What is the covenant of grace?

Answer 150. The covenant of grace, taken in the most large and extensive sins, includes all the transactions respecting the redemption and final salvation of mankind. But taken separately from the transactions. Between the several persons of the Trinity called the covenant of redemption, the covenant of grace respects that which takes place between God and the believer. It is generally used in contradistinction to the covenant or law of works. This covenant is proposed to all mankind, and the blessings of it are offered on certain conditions. The conditions are faith, repentance, love, new obedience. Faith more immediately has Christ for its object, and is more particularly insisted upon: but all are equally important and necessary. The believer at once becomes a party in the covenant, and by virtue of God's promise is entitled to the blessings. These are the blessings which Christ has procured and which are offered in the gospel. "But now hath he obtained a more excellent ministry, by how much. Also he is the mediator of a better covenant, which was established upon better promises." "Behold, the days come (saith the Lord.) When I will make a new covenant with the house of Israel, and with the house of Judah." "This is the covenant that I will make with the house of Israel after those days saith the Lord; I will put my laws into their minds and write them in their hearts: and I will be to them by God, and they shall be to me of people." Hebrews 8.6, 8, 10.

Question 151 [200]. Are the divine law and gospel inconsistent with each other?

Answer 151. The sum of the duty which the divine law requires his love. "Thou shalt love the Lord thy God with all thy heart, and with all thy soul, and with all my mind. This is the first and the great commandment. And the second is like unto it, thou shall love thy neighbor as thyself. On these two commandments hang all the law and the prophets." Matthew 37, 40. "Love is the fulfilling of the law." Romans 13.10. Love is also represented as the sum of the duty which the gospel requires. Hence, it is said, "love is of God and everyone that love is, is born of God, and know if God." 1 John 4:7. "God is love, and he that dwelleth in love, dwelleth in God, and God in him." 1 John 4:16. The law and the gospel, therefore, perfectly harmonize. Besides, the law is a transcript of God's moral perfections. He then, who is conformed to the character of God according to the gospel, will in heart, he pleased and delighted with the law. It is therefore said of the man who walketh not in the counsel of the ungodly, nor standeth in the way of sinners, nor sitteth in the seat of the sinful, that "his delight is in the law of the Lord, and in law doth he meditates day and night." Psalm 1:1, 2. Indeed, there is not a single precept in the law, which is not equally binding under the gospel.

> Question 152 [201]. Why was a satisfaction or atonement necessary to the dispensation of pardon?

Answer 152. In order to the dispensation of pardon and atonement or satisfaction is necessary: because without this the law and the moral government of God must fall into content. If a law be made, and the penalty be not executed when broken, it is of no more consequence than if no penalty had been annexed. Indeed, the law is of no more importance than mere advice. In the view of all rational beings. It would be more contemptible than advice: four. It pretends to something which is not supported. Not only the law, but the character of the lawgiver must fall equally into content. This is the case in human governments, and this would be the case in the divine. If the honor of the law be not supported by a proper execution of its threatenings, the moral government of God would be subject to constant disorder and confusion. In this case, the rebellious may go on with impunity and with increasing wickedness. Nor would there be anything to deter others from the like. In this way, infinite mischief may be produced and be forever experienced without any diminution or relief.

Either, therefore, the full penalty of the law must be executed or some atonement must be made which, in support of the divine law and government, will answer the like purposes with an infliction of the punishment. No pardon of consequences can be obtained without an atonement or satisfaction which is equivalent to the full demands of the law.

> Question 153 [202]. Why was a satisfaction or atonement so great as that of Christ necessary to the dispensation of pardon?

Answer 153. The evil of sin is infinite, and in its nature and consequences tends to produce infinite mischief in the moral government of God. No atonement, therefore, could wipe off this evil, but that which is also infinite. The sinner would make no atonement by repentance and reformation, for they are already do. He cannot suffer a punishment of the temporary kind which will be adequate to the crime; for it would be but finite. Nor could any creature, however great, a tone: because what ever he should suffer would still be finite. It is allowed, however, that a creature more excellent than man might have made an atonement proportionably greater. But to render an atonement completely adequate, the person must be infinite in dignity and excellence, or suffer and infinite evil fully equal to the sins of those for whom he makes atonement. Hence, it was that an atonement so great as that of Christ was necessary.

> Question 154 [203]. In what consisted the essence of the atonement of Christ? In his obedience, or his sufferings, or in both?[44]

> Question 155 [204]. In what sense did. He satisfied divine justice by his sacrifice?

Answer 155. Christ so completely answered the demands of the law as that, the believer may be saved from the curse of it, and yet the honor of the law and the dignity and authority of the divine government be fully supported. The penalty of the law. However, may still be executed to the full extent upon the finally impenitent. Justice therefore, has received no satisfaction with respect to them. And indeed, the believer, were it not for the constitution and promises of God might, notwithstanding all Christ has done and suffered, experience the full punishment due to his sins. The believer, therefore, would not demand a release from punishment, as a debtor might demand a release from his debt when a third person had paid for him the full demand of his creditor. Justice, therefore, is not satisfied with respect to the believer as it is with respect to the debtor. God was under no obligation from justice to accept the atonement which Christ has made: and if he actually does except of it, it must be from sovereign mercy and free grace.[45]

> Question 156 [205]. Was God under an obligation of justice to provide an atonement for sinners?

Answer 156. If God had been under an obligation of justice to provide an atonement for sinners. It must be on account of the injustice of his law: four. Surely if the law of the holy, just and good, so far from requiring God to provide an atonement, strict, distributive justice requires the actual punishment due to the violation of the law. Since, therefore, the law is thus holy, just and good, as is evident from the nature of it, and the declarations of

---

44. Answer 154 is missing from Gelston's manuscript.

45. Supplement, p. 384; *Answer 155.* If by justice be meant public justice or the general good that was satisfied.

God's word, if an atonement be made for the violation of it, it must proceed not from justice, but the goodness, mercy and grace of God.[46]

Question 157 [205]. Does the appointment of Mediator prove that God is already reconciled to men?

Answer 157. If the appointment of Mediator prove that God is already reconciled to men, then it will prove that he is so without the execution of the office as Mediator. If so, then, there was no necessity of Mediator. But surely a God of infinite goodness and compassion would never require any thing of this kind, unless absolutely necessary. The design of Mediator is to lay a foundation, so that he may become reconciled to mankind in a consistency with his law and moral government. But to say that reconciliation takes place. Previous to the undertaking and accomplishment of the Mediator's work is to place the effect before the cause.

Besides, none are interested in the benefits of the atonement until they are possessed of those qualifications which are made the necessary prerequisites. Nor are any sinners reconciled to God until they are interested in the benefits of this atonement.

Question 158 [207]. Did Christ redeemed all men alike, elect and non-elect?

Answer 158. The atonement of Christ is sufficient for all mankind would day, but accept of it upon the terms proposed. The invitation of the gospel is in universal terms, "whosoever will, let him take the water of life freely." Revelation 22.17. So far, the elect and non-elect are alike. But the application of this redemption will be made to the elect alone. Nor was it the design of God. From eternity that any but the elect should actually accept of the proposed atonement and enjoyed the happiness of the redeemed. It is the elect who are chosen of God in Christ before the foundation of the world. Ephesians 1.14. It is the elect who are "Justified by his grace freely through the redemption that is in Jesus Christ." Romans 3.24. It is the elect who are redeemed from the curse of the law. Galatians 3.13. And it is the elect who "seen a new song, saying, Thou art worthy to take the book, and to open the seals thereof: for thou wast slain, and hast redeemed us to God by thy blood." Revelation 5.9.

Redemption, when used with reference to Christ, seems to mean the application of the benefits and blessings which he has procured to believers

---

46. Supplement, p. 384; *Answer 156.* If God were under obligation from justice to provide an atonement, it would destroy free grace.

in this world, and the actual introduction of them to happiness in the world to come. But this is a happiness which none but the elect experience.

Have the atonement of Christ been designed to be extinguished. The guilds of a certain number of sins, as a man liquidates a debt of a certain fixed and determinant sum of money, he doubtless would have had the sins of the elect in view, and would have extinguished the guilt of these, but this does not appear to have been the object of the atonement. Strictly speaking, the atonement has extinguished. Neither the seems of the elect nor of the non-elect. But it has laid a foundation so that the punishment due to the sins of those who are interested in it, may as completely be removed as if they never had been guilty. Here, then, lies, the distinction: the elect will experience this. But the non-elect, in consequences of their neglect, will not experience it.

Question 159 [209]. In what sense does God love the elect, while unregenerate, different from that in which he loves the non-elect?

Answer 159. While unregenerate, God takes no more complacency in the character of the elect, then of the non-elect. The term love is used in a variety of sentences according to the different objects and acts of God, to which it is applied. Electing love is the making choice of those who are the objects of it, in Christ, to a holy life, and to a final and complete happiness. It is a mark of infinite goodness and benevolence that God was pleased to make choice of any to eternal life. Now it is the elect who are the objects of this expression of benevolence, and while in a state of being regenerate. It is this, therefore, which distinguishes them from the non-elect while in this state.

Question 160 [210]. Is there evidence from Scripture, or from history and observation, that any of the heathens are saved?

Answer 160. There does not appear to be any real evidence from Scripture that any of the heathens who never hear of the gospel will be saved. Those passages which at first might appear to be in their favor. Become, the less so, the more thoroughly. They are examined. Peter, in consequence of what took place with respect to Cornelius, who had been. He then, observed, "of the truth, I perceive that God is no respect or of persons, but in every nation, he that feareth him and work at the righteousness is accepted with him." Acts 10:34, 35. The observation seems to have been made in opposition to a prejudice which he and others of the Jewish nation had possessed against the Gentiles. He now saw that God had provided the gospel for the latter, as well as the former: and that the Jews in this respect were not the only favorites of heaven. There is nothing which intimates that a man may and does actually work righteousness without her knowledge of the Savior, but only that those who embrace the Savior, whether Jew, Gentile, or of what ever nation or description before, he will be accepted of God. But we should admit that Cornelius was excepted with God before he saw Peter, still it would prove nothing in favor of those who do not hear of a Savior. Cornelius, most probably, was appointed with the Jewish religion, had heard of Christ, and was a proselyte of the gate.

Another passage, which might seem to be in favor of the heathen is this: "For when the Gentiles, which have not the law, do by nature the things contained in the law, these having not the law, are a law unto themselves: Which shew the work of the law written in their hearts, their conscience also bearing witness, and their thoughts the meanwhile, accusing, or else excusing one another." Job 2.14, 15. On this may be observed that the apostle does not positively say that the Gentiles actually do perform the things contained in the law: But intimates, that on supposition they should do this, it would evince the law to be written on their hearts. It might also evince, for matter of what he says, that they have heard of a Savior. Or if he had reference to something which actually takes place, it will not prove that the heathen will be saved. They may, as many under the gospel actually do, perform things externally agreeable to the law. And this they may do, from convictions of conscience: but the existence of conscience and its various exercises, whether accusing or excusing, will not determine the salvation of anyone.

Again, neither history nor observation affords any data by which we can determine the salvation of the heathen. The greater part are evidently sunk into the greatest wickedness and corruption. There is nothing in their lives, which indicates a real repentance and sincerity of heart. Even the best of those with whose characters history acquaints us were evidently guilty of many vices, even some directly contrary to the doctrines they taught. No one, perhaps, was without some favorite vice. Indeed, those who taught the purest system of morals generally gave him diligence to some kind of wickedness, and encouraged those things which, if followed, would be inconsistent with purity of heart.

Some have supposed that the principle of regeneration will take place in some while in this world, and that as soon as the Savior is presented in the world to come, they will cheerfully and readily embrace him. This, however, is mere conjecture. Doubtless is in the power of God to affect this, but that he actually will do it, we have no authority from Scripture to assert.

Question 161 [214]. Is there evidence that none of the heathen are saved?

Answer 161. A variety of passages might be adduced, which are evidently against the idea of the salvation of the heathens who are ignorant of the Savior. "And we know that we are of God, and the whole world lieth in wickedness." 1 John 5.19. The Apostle here, evidently makes a distinction between those referred to by the pronoun "we" and the other parts of the world, both those who are acquainted with the gospel and the heathens. Without discrimination, all who were not like him, in Christ were in the state of wickedness, and consequently exposed to the divine wrath.

Again, "And this is life eternal, that they might know thee, the only true God, and Jesus Christ whom thou hast sent." John 17.3. "He that believeth and is baptized, shall be saved; but he that believeth not shall be damned." Luke 16.16. "Neither is there salvation in any other: for there is none other name under heaven given among men, whereby we must be saved." Acts 4.12. "And how shall they believe in him of whom I have not heard." Romans 10.14. On these passages several things may be remarked. 1. Not only the knowledge of God, but of Jesus Christ is necessary to inherit eternal life. 2. That not only a speculative knowledge of Jesus Christ, but a knowledge which implies a faith in him is necessary in order to salvation. Or unless a man believed on Christ, he cannot be saved. 3. Salvation is not to be obtained by any other way. There is no name by which any can be saved, who do not believe on this Savior whom God has provided. 4. That none can believe in the Lord Jesus Christ who have never heard of him. 5. It will of consequence follow that what ever the external reformation be, and what ever repentance any sinner may have which does not imply faith on Christ, he can have no title to pardon and salvation.

Now the supposition is that they heathen are ignorant of the Savior, have no faith in him, and have no means of becoming acquainted with him, and consequently, they have no repentance which implies faith in him. Nor can they be reconciled to God, for no mention is made of any other means of reconciliation; but evidence has already been adduced to the contrary. "To wit, that God was in Christ, reconciling the world unto himself." 2 Corinthians 5.19.

Question 162 [217]. What are the reasons assigned in favor of the idea of the salvation of the heathens?

Answer 162. Some have asserted that it is inconsistent with the goodness of God to confine salvation to those who have heard of Christ and believe in him. These, by their reasoning, would entirely set aside the necessity of an atonement. Others suppose that the atonement of Christ placed all mankind in such a situation, that if they live agreeably to the light of nature, they shall be saved, whether they believe in him or not. But this is abundantly refuted by what has already been adduced. Others again suppose the heathens have some glimmering light, by means of tradition, which is sufficient to direct them to the Savior. If this knowledge be sufficient to lead them to a proper a point since with the character, offices, atonement and mediation of Christ, then they are not heathens in the sense of the question. But if it be not sufficient for this, then an obscure and indeterminate glimmering will not lead to salvation. The texts already introduced will still exclude salvation from these dark traditional notions. Others, again, suppose God will buy some secret and unknown method reveal Christ before they go out of the world: or else, that he will regenerate them in this world, and reveal Christ in the future. This is, however, but an imaginary idea and unsupported by Scripture.

Question 163 [218]. Are a precise number of mankind elected to eternal life, and the rest reprobated? Prove it.

Answer 163. That God has elected some of mankind to eternal life may be inferred from his actually bringing them to it. If he did not first choose them, it is evident from the temper and disposition of their hearts, they would not choose him, and the way to eternal life. The hearts of sinners are naturally opposed to the eternal life offered in the gospel, and would forever be so were not God to change their hearts. Now, since he does not bring all mankind to eternal life, those whom he does, he must necessarily have chosen or elected, unless we supposed him to act at random and without design, which would be the highest reflection on his wisdom.

Once supposing that he has elected a certain number, we must suppose also that he has left a certain number to go on to remediless destruction.

He knows the number of his creatures, and he knows whom he has chosen, and whom he has left. The number with him, therefore, both of the elect and non-elect, is precise and determinate. With all this, the Scriptures appear fully to accord.

A certain number are repeatedly represented as being given to the Son by the Father. This fully implies that some are selected and chosen by God, to answer his designs in the work of redemption. The elect and the election are frequently spoken of in a manner which fully establishes this doctrine. "But for the elect's sake, whom he hath chosen." Mark 13.20. "For false Christ's, and false prophets shall arise, and shall shew signs and wonders, to seduce, if it were possible, even the elect." Verse 22. "And then shall he send his angels, and shall gather together his elect." Verse 27. "There is a remnant, according to the election of grace." Romans 11.5. "But we are bound to give thanks all way to God, for you, brethren, but loved of the Lord, because God hath from the beginning chosen you to salvation, through sanctification of the spirit, and believe of the truth." 2 Thessalonians 2.13. "Having predestinated us unto the adoption of children by Jesus Christ to himself, according to the good pleasure of his will." Ephesians 1.5. These passages, and a great variety of others, fully prove, it is presumed the doctrine of election. "All have sinned, and come short of the glory of God." Therefore, hath he mercy on whom he will have mercy, and whom he will, he hardneth." Romans 3.23 and 9.18. This last passage not only supports the doctrine of election, but reprobation, likewise. If not merely suffering a sinner to go on in his sinful course, but hardening him, that he may go on to heap up wrath against the day of wrath do not imply reprobation, it is difficult to conceive what does. Besides, passages clearly support the idea. "What if God willing to show his wrath, and make his power known, endured with much long-suffering the vessels of wrath fitted to destruction." Romans 9.22. "But these, as natural brute beasts, made to be taken and destroyed, speak evil of the things that they understand not, and shall utterly perish in their own destruction." 2 Peter 2.12. "The Lord hath made all things for himself: yea, even the wicked for the day of evil." Proverbs 16.4.

Question 164 [221]. Did God from eternity for know all future events?

Answer 164. The foreknowledge of God will necessarily follow from his decrees. It has already been proved that he decreed all things from eternity. Now if he decreed, he surely knew what he decreed, and his knowledge was coexistent with the decree.

The foreknowledge of God will also follow from his omniscience. If he did not know all things from eternity, he wants was not omniscient. This would undeify him at once, and is contrary to what has already been proven.

"Known unto God are all his works from the beginning of the world." Acts 15:18. The original evidently is designed to express the eternity of his knowledge. "Him being delivered by the determinate counsel and foreknowledge of God." Acts 2.23. Here foreknowledge is ranked equally with the decree. "According to the eternal purpose, which he purposed in Christ Jesus our Lord." Ephesians 3.11.

Question 165 [222]. Is this foreknowledge founded on his decrees, or his decrees on his foreknowledge?

Answer 165. If God for new the events which take place to be certain, independent of his decree, and previous to it, then there would be no necessity of the decree. It would seem as though he were forced to consent, for in this case, it would be out of his power to prevent their actual existence. But if the decree of God fixes the certainty of an event, the certainty could not be known without the existence of that act, which establishes the certainty. The foreknowledge, therefore, must necessarily, in order of nature stand after the decree. Hence, the decree in Scripture is placed first. "Him being delivered by the determinate counsel and foreknowledge of God." Acts 2:23.

Question 166 [223]. What do you mean by absolute, and what by conditional election?

Answer 166. By absolute election I mean the same as by absolute decrees. God has absolutely and frustrably chosen some to everlasting life; not, however, without providing the means necessary, and actually fitting them for it. This election was not on account of any good quality. He foresaw in the elect, as the Apostle says, "who hath saved us and called us with an holy calling, not according to our works, but according to his own purpose and grace, which was given us in Christ Jesus, before the world began." 2 Timothy 1.9.

They who hold to conditional election, I believe, generally suppose that God has chosen mankind in such a sense, as will place the whole matter in the power of his creatures. They suppose the gospel offer is universal, and that God cannot efficaciously produce a willingness to accept of it without destroying free agency. He wishes all mankind to be saved, but whether they will be saved or not, must depend upon them, and of consequence. His choice must be determined by their conduct. They ground their opinion, principally on 1 Timothy 2.14 and 2 Peter 3.9. "Who will have all men to be saved, and come to the knowledge of the truth." "The Lord is not willing that any should perish, but that all should come to repentance." If any suppose this election was from eternity, they must suppose God for new how his creatures would conduct, what their choice would be, and determined his choice accordingly.

Question 167 [225]. Is election absolute or conditional, and founded on the foresight of the repentance and faith of the elect?

Answer 167. The election of God is represented in Scripture as absolute, and not in the least founded on the foresight of the repentance and faith of the elect. "Who hath saved us, and called us with an holy calling, not according to our works, but according to his own purpose and grace, which was given to us in Christ Jesus, before the world began." 2 Timothy 1.9. Here it is expressly asserted that God did not in this matter proceed on the previous ground of good works. "According as he has chosen us in him, before the foundation of the world, that we should be holy and without blame before him love. Having predestinated us unto the adoption of children by Christ Jesus to himself, according to the good pleasure of his will." Ephesians 1.4, 5. In this passage, it is not asserted that the election referred to was for or on account of holiness already supposed in them, but that they might be holy. They were chosen according to the good pleasure of his will to be made holy. "For the children being not yet born, neither having done any good or evil, that the purpose of God, according to election, might stand, not of works, but of him that calleth." Romans 9:11. Here again, the election is said to be not of works. Hence, it is also said, "I will have mercy on whom I will have mercy, and I will have compassion on whom I will have compassion." Romans 9.15. But if election be conditional, according to the ideas of some, this might not certainly be true. God might be disappointed in his wishes. "Even so, then at this present time also, there is a remnant according to the election of grace. And if by grace, then it is no more of works: Otherwise, grace is no more grace. But if it be of works, then it is no more grace: Otherwise work is no more work." Romans 11.5, 6.

Question 168 [227]. Does election extend to individuals, or to communities only?

Answer 168. Election evidently extends to individuals, and it is not communities merely: Otherwise, the numbers of the elect who should be saved must be altogether indeterminate. Indeed, it would not be certain merely from this that any would be saved: for the election would then be conditional, which however, is contrary to what has already been proved. This is manifest from the single consideration, that all of no one nation, in community will be saved. God, therefore, has not chosen anyone community that they shall universally be saved. But of the election extended only to communities, it is evident from this circumstance that it must have been only a conditional election. But Scripture is sufficiently explicit upon this head. "All that the Father gives me, shall come to me; and him that comes to me, I will in no wise cast out." John 6.37. From this it is manifest that the elect shall all accept of Christ and be saved. But no one community will all be saved: at least, there will be some saved of communities; whence, others are lost. They were not, therefore, elected agreeably to this passage. Hence, Christ adds, "this is the Father's will, which hath sent me, that of all which he hath given me, I should lose nothing." Verse 39. "I speak not of you all; I know whom I have chosen." John 13.18. "For the children being not yet born, neither having done any good or evil that the purpose of God according to the election might stand, not of works, but that him that calleth. As it is written, Jacob, I have loved, but Esau I have hated." Romans 9.11, 13. If we consider this as spoken respecting Jacob and Esau. Personally, then the election could not have extended to a community: for even it did not reach the whole of this family. Or if we suppose it to refer to their posterity, the like observation will still hold. All the posterity of Jacob evidently were not saved, but only a part. Nor did they all belong to the election of grace. This is evident from the history of their lives, and from what the Apostle says. "Even so, then at this present time. Also, there is a remnant according to the election of grace." Romans 11.5. And it seems that in the time of Esaius, only a remnant was saved. Romans 9.27.[47]

> Question 169 [229]. Can the offers of the gospel be made with sincerity to the non-elect?

Answer 169. If my sincerity be meant a real and hearty desire that the non-elect should be saved, the offers of the gospel could not be made with such a kind of sincerity. It evidently is not the will of God that they should be saved. But this does not appear to be the proper meaning of sincerity in the present case.

Sometimes sincerity is designed to denote true religion. Sometimes, it is designed to denote the reality of will and endeavor. Thus, a man is said to be sincere and a cause when he is hardly engaged in it, without any reference to its nature, whether it be a good or bad cause. In this sense, a man under strong convictions of conscience may sincerely desire and endeavor, so far as a natural man can use endeavors to escape hell. Sincerity is also, sometimes, applied to the will alone to denote merely a real desire with respect to some particular object. Thus, a man may say he is sincerely wishes for such a thing, or desire that such and such things might take place. But there is another sense still in which sincerity is used. It is sometimes applied to the nature of a proposal or offer. In this case, it seems to be designed to represent the reality of intention to adhere strictly to every engagement in the offer, when the terms are freely and fully acceded to. When the offer is unreservedly accepted it is supposed the integrity and uprightness of the person proposing will not suffer him to fail, but that he will completely fulfill all his promises and engagements. This does not necessarily imply that the person offering really wishes that the offer should be accepted. So far from necessarily implying this, this kind of sincerity may exist consistently with a desire that the offer might not be accepted. For instance, a king may

---

47. Supplement, p. 385; *Answer 168*. The Arminians suppose that election extends to communities and the election is to the enjoyment of external means. It is no more a real mark of partiality to elect to the enjoyment of salvation than the enjoyment of means.

propose to a number of rebellious and refractory subjects to return to their allegiance, and offer to place them on condition of their return in a situation far more eligible than they possessed before. This he may do with the sincerity, which implies a determination to fulfill his promise in case of their acceptance, and yet at the same time for certain reasons of state, he may secretly wish they would not actually accept of the author.

In a similar manner, the offers proposed in the gospel to the non-elect are consistent with sincerity. God has furnished them with such means that if they were heartily willing to accept of the offer no real obstacle would lie in the way. Except giving them a willingness, he has done everything he could be expected to do. Were he ever so desirous they would accept. But he is under no obligation to give them a willingness: Nor is this necessary to constitute sincerity in him. If however, they should accept of the offers. He proposes in the gospel, he would stand ready faithfully and completely to fulfill all his promises and engagements. In this sense, sincerity is consistent with the offers of the gospel. And this is all the sincerity, in the present case, which we have a right to expect. Whatever may be the secret will of God, if we are unwilling to accept of the offer, he proposes we have no right to complain.[48]

Question 170 [232]. What chance of salvation, have the non-elect more, than if Christ had never died?

Answer 170. If Christ had never died. None would have had any chance for salvation. The full penalty of the law would have been fully executed. But since Christ has died, not only the elect, but the non-elect have an offer of salvation proposed to them, and if they are willing to accept as it upon the terms proposed, they will actually and completely be saved. The chance of salvation would have been nothing at all had not Christ died, whatever there will might be. But now, if they have, but a proper disposition of will, the chance is everything. They will actually enjoy salvation. But notwithstanding this, the non-elect will as effectually miss of salvation as if no provision had ever been made in the gospel. And the reason will be because they are not pleased with the offer, but reject and despise it.[49]

Question 171 [233]. Did Christ suffer and die in the stead as well as for the benefit of his people?

48. Supplement, p. 385; *Answer 169*. A sincere offer is a true and real offer.

49. Supplement, p. 385; *Answer 170*. If by chance be meant certainty, there is no certainty that [the] non-elect will be saved, nor is it doubtful. If by it be meant opportunity, there is a chance. The non-elect have an opportunity if they would be embrace it.

Answer 171. Christ suffered a punishment which would fully support the honor of the divine law and the dignity of the divine government, though his people be released from the punishment they personally deserve. Indeed, the object of his atonement was that they might thus be released. Still, however, it does not appear that they can demand this release as a debtor might insist upon a discharge when a third person had fully paid the demand of his creditor. Christ, therefore, did not suffer and die in the stead of his people so as to lay God under obligation to accept of the atonement, whether he chose or not. He, however, suffered and died so far in their stead. That day will not actually experience that punishment, which otherwise, they would have experienced. By his sufferings and death. He completely atoned for the sins of his people. They will not, therefore, be required to undergo any farther punishment.

Question 172 [234]. Could he have made atonement without suffering in stead of his people?

Answer 172. It is not conceived that any thing without suffering would have constituted an atonement. Nothing but this could have shown the awful and tremendous consequences of sin. Nor could anything else have shown the incident evil and instructive tendency of sin. Nothing else would properly have been a penalty of the law. Obedience was already due from every creature, and could, in no sense be considered as a penalty. It does not appear, therefore, that the honor of the divine law or the dignity of the divine government could have been supported except by suffering, either personally, or having a substitute. This substitute must, to make an atonement which would be complete and satisfactory, suffer instead of his people, so far as mentioned above.

Question 173 [235]. Did Christ pay the debt for the elect, so that they can claim salvation on the foot of justice?

Answer 173. When one man pays a debt for another, where a sum of money is due, this other on the principles of strict commutative justice may justly demand a release from his creditor. The reason is, because the creditor has received his full demand, and justice in no case demands more than the law points out, as due. But in matters of distributive justice. The law does not point out the punishment of one man as due for the crime of another. It has no right to demand this. And the one man should consent to suffer for another, the executive authority is not obliged to accept of the substitute. It is against the breaker of the law that it is threatenings are leveled, and it is to him alone that the law looks for satisfaction. Originally, therefore, it knows of no substitute. If then, one man actually suffers the punishment due to another, the demand of the law, according to strict distributive justice, still remains in full force. If the sovereign accept of this punishment as a substitute, it is not because this kind of justice requires his acceptance.

Similar is the case of the elect. This kind of distributive justice will never support any claim for salvation. To a [Editor note: text is unclear] matter of this, the punishment might still be executed.

The general good or general justice, however, admits of their salvation, and by virtue of God's promise, on the ground of this, they have a right to expect it.

Question 174 [236]. Where the sufferings of Christ to the purpose of supporting the divine law equivalent to the endless torments of the sinner?

Answer 174. The sufferings of Christ were not infinite in duration. Nor were they incident in quantity or degree, for it was his human nature, which suffered, and that was capable of only a finite degree of suffering. The infinite dignity of his person, however, gave value to his sufferings, which was fully equivalent to the endless torments of the sinner. Reason teaches us that the sufferings of a king's son, especially if he possess every amiable quality of a man, are of more value and importance than the sufferings of one of his lowest subjects. And in proportion, as the sun is more elevated in station and character, his sufferings will be of proportionably more value in every respect, but especially to the support of the law and the dignity of the government.

We may be sure that the sufferings of Christ are equivalent to the endless torments of the sinner, from God's actually accepting it as such. He would not accept of that which does not answer the demand of the law. This he fully intimates, when he says, "And ye brought that which was torn, and the lame, and the sick; though [Editor note: text is unclear] ye brought an offering: should I accept this of your hands? saith the Lord." Malachi 1.13. That the sufferings of Christ were accepted as an equivalent is evident from what is abundantly asserted. "Who his own self bare our sins in his own body on the tree." 1 Peter 2.24. "As Christ also hath loved us, and hath given himself for us, and offering and a sacrifice to God for a sweet smelling savour." Ephesians 5.2. "For he hath made him to be sin for us, who knew no sin." 2 Corinthians 5.21. "Who gave himself a ransom for all." 1 Timothy 2.6. "For by one offering he hath perfected forever them that are sanctified." Hebrews 10.14.

Question 175 [238]. Do the sufferings and obedience of Christ proved to the divine law to be a just law?

Answer 175. It does not appear that the nature of the law is, in any instance, to be determined merely by its sanctions. The will or character of the lawgiver, the tendency of the law, and the nature of the trends rations against which its penalties are leveled, more properly give complexion to the law. Whenever, therefore, the justice of a law is questioned, the character of the lawgiver is equally questioned. And though he should execute the full extent of the threatening, this would not achieve the difficulty with respect to his law or character, for we know that an unjust and rigorous sovereign may commit the greatest injustice in this way, and be at proportionably greater distance from rectitude of heart. Something more than merely suffering the threatening of the law is necessary to vindicate its justice. Nor Woodmere obedience alone determined the law to be just. One of the contrary nature may be as punctually obeyed as if perfectly just, and it is injustice remain undiminished.

But if we take into consideration the true character of God and of Christ, we have the fullest assurance is law is holy, just and good. Without this, what ever be the sufferings in support of it, or however punctually obeyed, we would have no certainty of its justice.

Question 176 [240]. How is redemption applied to the elect?

Answer 176. Redemption contains a variety of blessings which Christ obtained for his true disciples and followers. These do not consist merely in and exemption from that punishment they justly deserved. But there are positive communications. The actual conferring of the blessings, then, is the application of redemption. This is done in regeneration, conversion, progressive sanctification, and final salvation.

In regeneration the believer is united to Christ and they become one in a certain sense, as Christ and the Father are one. "That they all may be one, as thou, Father, art in me, and I in thee; that they also may be one in us. And the glory which thou gavest me, I have given unto them, that they may be one, even as we are one. I in them, and thou in me, that they may be made perfect in one. That the love wherewith thou has loved me, may be in them, and I in them." John 17:21–26. This oneness consists in a union of affections,

And also a union of interest. The love they possess is reciprocal. That which is calculated to promote the interest of Christ's kingdom is calculated to promote the interest of those united to him. They are in many respects treated as if they were one with Christ.

Question 177 [241]. What is the office of the Holy Ghost in the work of our salvation?

Answer 177. The Holy Ghost is represented as making application of the Redemption which Christ has obtained. He not only effectually applies it, but produces awakenings and convictions in the mind, which do not always terminate in real conversion. "And when he is come, he will reprove the world of sin, and of righteousness, and of judgment." John 16.8. "For it is impossible for those who were once enlightened, and have tasted of the heavenly gift, and were made partakers of the Holy Ghost. And have tasted the good word of God, and the powers of the world to come; If they shall fall away, to renew them again unto repentance." Hebrews 6.4–6.

The convictions which the Spirit produces on the minds of the unregenerate are not properly the application of Redemption, though they generally precede this.

In the actual application of Redemption, the operations of the Holy Ghost are represented variously, according to the effects he produces. He is represented as the author of regeneration. John 3.5, 6; 2 Corinthians 3.10. He is represented as the author of justification and sanctification, and indeed, the various exercises of grace. 1 Corinthians 6.11; Galatians 5.22–25. He is represented as leading to the knowledge of the truth. John 16:13. He is represented bearing witness to the reality of his operations and the happiness to which they will finally lead. Romans 8.16. Ephesians 1.13, 14 and 4.30. He is also represented as helping our infirmities and assisting in prayer. Romans 8.20. Indeed, every gracious exercise is ascribed to him, and it is he who applies the redemption Christ has wrought out while in this world by actually fitting the elect for the enjoyment of happiness in the future.

Question 178 [243]. What is Regeneration?

Answer 178. Regeneration is an effect produced by the operation of the Holy Ghost in which there is an effectual change of the temper and disposition of the heart. In consequence of this, a foundation is laid for the exercise of holy and gracious affections, such as the subject of this change never before experienced. Before, the heart was unclean, deceitful above all things, and desperately wicked; enmity against God, dead in trespasses and sins, etc. But now there is a new heart given, a pure heart, and a heart of flesh, a new spirit, etc. Hence, it is called regeneration, being born again, etc.[50]

50. There are several indecipherable markers that appear in this answer.

Question 179 [243]. What is the difference between regeneration and conversion?

Answer 179. Regeneration is an effect which is applied to the Holy Ghost alone. It is never applied as an act of him who is the subject of it, but conversion is. Regeneration is the actual implantation of a principal. Conversion is the exercise and flowing out of the principle into various acts, and these acts are ascribed to him who is the subject of them. Regeneration is but one act, and produced but once in life. Conversion consists of a great variety of acts, and continues through life. It is actually turning from sin to God, the exercise of the various graces, and the whole progressive work of sanctification.

Question 180 [244]. What is the native blindness of mankind?

Answer 180. The native blindness of mankind consists in the depravity of their hearts and the habits of wickedness they have actually acquired.

This blindness is represented as seated in the heart. It evidently does not consist in the ignorance and darkness of understanding, for it is not always the case that it diminishes with the increase of knowledge, but frequently increases in a proportionable degree. Besides, regeneration, which removes this blindness is everywhere represented as a change of heart and affections. Hence, hatred is said to proceed from blindness. 1 John 2.11. And blinding the eyes and hardening the heart seem to be of the same import. John 12.40.

Question 181 [245]. Is the native blindness of mankind entirely criminal?

Answer 181. The native blindness of mankind, as before observed, is seeded in the heart. This blindness is frequently represented as criminal, and indeed, is that which properly is the only criminality. "Four out of the heart proceed evil thoughts, murders, adulteries, fornication's, fast, false witness, blasphemies." Matthew 15.19. "For the imagination of man's heart is evil from his use." Genesis 8.21.

Question 182 [245]. What is divine illumination?

Answer 182. Darkness and light are frequently applied to the heart, and are designed to convey to you very different ideas. "Ye were once darkness, but now are ye light in the Lord." Ephesians 5.8.

Mankind, while in a state of nature, denominated wicked and enemies to God are said to be in darkness. "The way of the wicked is as darkness."

Proverbs 4.19. "If our gospel be heated, it is hit to them that are lost, in whom the god of this world has blinded the minds of them which believe not, lest the light of the glorious gospel of Christ, who is the image of God, should shine unto them." 2 Corinthians 4.3, 4.

On the contrary, when converted and reconciled to God, they are represented as having their eyes opened, and being turned from darkness to light. Acts 26:10. "Who has delivered us from the power of darkness." Colossians 1.12. "Who have called you out of darkness into his marvelous light." 1 Peter 2.9.

This illumination is not anything which takes place in the intellect merely. It is no new truth conveyed to the understanding. It is evidently represented as applied to the heart, and takes place in that faculty of the lines on the nature of which praise or blame is founded. "I will give them a hard to know me." Jeremiah 24:7. "This is life eternal, that they might know thee, the only true God, and Jesus Christ whom thou hast sent." John 12.3. "And have put on the new man, which is renewed in knowledge after the image of him that created." Colossians 3.10. "God, who commanded the light to shine out of the darkness hath shined in our hearts to give the light of the knowledge of the glory of God in the face of Jesus Christ." 2 Corinthians 4.6. From these passages, and others which might be introduced, it is evident, illumination must be something which takes place at regeneration and affects the heart. That this is the case appears also from knowledge and love being used with the same meaning. "Everyone that loveth is born of God, and knoweth God. He that loveth not, knoweth, not God." 1 John 4.7, 8. On the contrary, hatred, the opposite to love, is used with the same meaning; as darkness, the opposite to light, knowledge in illumination. "He that hateth his brother is in darkness, and walketh in darkness even until now. But he that loveth of his brother abideth in the light." 1 John 2.9, 10.

Question 183 [247]. Is spiritual beauty and glory seen by pure intellect?

Answer 183. To see spiritual beauty is evidently peculiar to the Christian, to him who is spiritual. Hence, it is said, "the natural man receiveth not the things of the Spirit of God, for they are foolishness unto him: neither can he know them because they are spiritually discerned. But he that is spiritual judgeth all things." 1 Corinthians 2.14, 15. Now it is equally evident that the natural man who does not in the least see this spiritual beauty and glory has the powers of intellect to as high a degree, frequently, as one who does see them. Indeed, in many cases, we find that many wicked men possess an understanding, or pure intellect, far superior to some of the most eminent Christians. A man may reason accurately, and have a clear and extensive speculative knowledge of divine truths without having the least pays or relish for them. Something more than this, therefore, must be implied in seeing spiritual beauty and glory. "If any man love God, the same is known of him." 1 Corinthians 8.3. To know God here must mean, to see the spiritual beauty and glory of his character. But this is implied in loving God. It must therefore relate more especially to the affections. If a sight of spiritual beauty and glory consisted in the discernment of the intellect merely, surely it would not be proper to say, without distinction that knowledge puffeth up. This, however, the Apostle says. "Knowledge puffeth up, the charity at edifieth." 1 Corinthians 8.1.

Question 184 [249]. Is the sight of beauty distinct from the love of beauty?

Answer 184. The sight of beauty is not the exercise of the understanding, merely, but is the perception of peculiar to some other faculty of the mind. From a passage quoted above, it is evident, to know God and to love him are of the same import. The sight of beauty and the love of it are frequently spoken of as distinct. With respect to moral beauty, however, it seems necessarily to implied the other. Indeed, it is difficult to point out the real difference in the exercises of the mind. He who spiritually sees the beauty and excellency of divine things will also love and the light in them. And he who loves them, if a real distinction can be made, must in order of nature previously see them.

Seeing the beauty of divine things evidently, as before observed, is not attainable by the natural understanding. It is peculiar to the exercise of the will. It is an object of taste, rather than speculation. If an exercise of the will or the taste of the mind, it is, perhaps, not easy to determine wherein it differs from the exercise of action.

Question 185 [250]. Is it a matter of duty to all men to see the spiritual glory of divine objects?

Answer 185. To see the spiritual glory of divine objects implies a taste or relish for it, and this implies inclination or bias of heart towards it. To have a taste and inclination for holiness, or spiritual glory, must presuppose the existence of a holy principle. This evidently, it is the duty of everyone to pose as. All moral beings are under obligation to be holy, and consequently to exercise a holy principle. "And be renewed in the spirit of your mind, and that ye put on the new man, which after God is created in righteousness and true holiness." Ephesians 4.23, 24.

Question 186 [251]. Does regeneration and immediately affect any faculty of the mind beside the will?

Answer 186. Moral depravity the lies in the heart. And as this renders regeneration necessary, it is evident that it must affect the heart only. If regeneration affected the understanding, or any faculty of the mind, except the will, we should find those who are regenerated possessed of powers beyond the unregenerate. But this evidently does not take place. The will is opposed to everything good, and inclined to nothing but evil while in a state of unregeneracy. The understanding, at the same time, maybe clear, strong, and speculatively right. It is not this, therefore, but the will must be changed. Hence, regeneration is said to be giving a new heart, a heart of flesh, a pure heart, etc.

The understanding, indeed, is sometimes spoken of in a moral view, as being enlightened or darkened, according to the character of the man. But this is never spoken of in this manner, with reference to the intellect merely, or the understanding as distinct from the will.

It is allowed, however, that in consequence of regeneration. The heart may be more disposed to pursue the knowledge of religious truth, and excite the mind to more vigorous pursuit of it; but this does not prove that regeneration immediately affect the understanding. No new truth is conveyed by it. No new faculty is implanted, nor is any one immediately strengthened.

Question 187 [252]. Is regeneration effected by light?

Answer 187. Regeneration is not effected by light, for a illumination does not take place, but in consequence of regeneration. The illumination of which the Scripture speaks evidently does not precede regeneration, but always implies it.

Knowledge merely never can change the heart. If they could, the heart would of consequence, grow better the faster knowledge is increased. In regeneration, a new principle is implanted, a new taste and relish for divine things. But this knowledge could never effect. As the taste of any of the productions of nature could not be excited by describing the nature and properties of that, so neither can a taste for spiritual beauty in glory be exercised by knowledge, however perfect.

Question 188 [253]. What do you mean by the physical operation of the Spirit in regeneration?

Answer 188. Man is represented as being by nature dead in a moral view. He cannot, therefore, give life to himself as anymore than it first. He could give himself natural life. No exertion which man can make would ever produced a change of heart. Nor can any means, either of internal convictions or external applications of the word and ordinances, ever affected. The change. Therefore, is immediately wrought by the Spirit of God as Adam's mind was at first formed. In this change. There is no medium made use of, as in natural generation. Means may be used to prepare the mind, but the change itself is effected without means, and by the immediate operation of the Spirit.

Question 189 [254]. Is the subject of regeneration active or passive in it, or in what sense is he both?

Answer 189. In that act of the Spirit by which a man is regenerated, he doubtless is passive, for the supposition is it is an effect not in the least produced by himself, but by the Holy Spirit. A man is no more active than he was when created. But the moment he is regenerated, he may be active. Indeed, the distinction more properly arises from the order of nature. A man, in order of nature, is not active in regeneration, before he is passive. He may be passive, however, before he is active. But whether in all cases, there is a distinction in point of time, is perhaps, not easily to be determined. A man is active when he puts forth holy exercises. Where a principle exists, it is natural to expect the operation of that principle.

Question 190 [255]. Whence arises the necessity of regeneration?

Answer 190. The necessity of regeneration arises from the depravity of the human heart. The heart is represented as dead in trespasses and sins, not only partially so, but totally. Were depravity only partial, and improvement upon the remaining good principle might be sufficient. But now it is wholly opposed to every holy exercise and inclined to evil continually. There is no power in man, evidently, to regenerate himself. Indeed, he has no real disposition for the exercises which necessarily result from regeneration. Unless, therefore, he be regenerated. He never can be happy. Nor is it possible to overcome the total depravity of man's heart, but by regeneration.

Question 191 [255]. Is not the physical operation of the Spirit, and the passivity of the subject under the operation of regeneration, inconsistent with the moral agency of the subject?

Answer 191. The real and immediate act of the Spirit, in regeneration, does not appear to be any more consistent with the free agency of the subject than the production of Adam's soul was consistent with his free agency. Taking either of these acts simply, regeneration or the production of Adam's soul, the action of the subject is not supposed. Neither free agency nor moral agency, then, is properly concerned in regeneration.

It does not appear that man in regeneration is any more of a free agent or moral agent, then he would be if a new sense should instantaneously be added. No more than if a man born without the sense of tasting should have it at once infused.

The acts of the will, however, previous to the existence of this effect, were contrary and opposed to it. But the very idea of regeneration is that in the act of the itself there is no opposition, for the will is supposed to be perfectly submissive. No real exercise of the will, however, is to be supposed in the case. The actual exercise of the principle is that which is moral and free.[51]

Question 192 [257]. What is true love the God? And what is the primary foundation of it?

Answer 192. The dignity, excellence, or moral worth of any being in proportion to the degree which it exists, merits the love and esteem of other beings. And it is the infant worthiness of God lays his creature under infinite obligations to love him. True love to God, then, is that which arises from a sense of this excellence. It is an attachment to the character of God, a delight in pleasure in it. Were God and him moral and evil being, he would not merit love, but hatred. In the same proportion as he was evil and wicked, he would be detestable and odious to all holy beings. But he is at an infinite remove from this, and the affection, exercised towards him ought to be at an infinite remove from hatred. The infinite excellence and worthiness of God, therefore, is the primary foundation of love to him.

As God is not only infinitely the greatest being, but infinitely the best and excellent being, and indeed, the foundation and fountain of all being and excellence, it is evident, he merits the supreme love of his creatures. Their love, comparatively speaking, ought to be absorbed in him.

This love cannot be the love of gratitude merely, for that presupposes some favor. This does not. True gratitude, however, will necessarily flow from it. It is not a love to God, because he is thought to love us and to do as good. Love to him, on this account merely, is not properly love to him, but to something else. For the supposition is were it not for this love of his in this good he bestows, our love would not exist.[52]

Question 193 [258]. What is true benevolence to men?

51. Supplement, p. 385; *Answer 191*. This question was misunderstood. It respects the acts of the soul. They are doubtless free.

52. Supplement, p. 385; *Answer 192*. Benevolence to God ought to have been mentioned and explained.

Answer 193. True, benevolence to men is that love which flows disinterestedly, without any confined considerations of cells and self-interest. It is disposed to regard and will well to being in general, and to individuals in particular, according to their worth and excellence, and so far is consistent with the general good.

Question 194 [259]. What is repentance unto life? And how distinguished from legal repentance?

Answer 194. That repentance, which is unto life, implies a knowledge of sin, its nature and tendency. Through the glass of the law sin is seen to be infinitely odious and abominable. It is seen to be contrary to the pure and holy nature of God, destructive of his government and all moral good. With this sight of sin is inseparably connected a hatred, of abhorrence and detestation of it, because the consequences to the sinner are evil, but because in its nature and tendency, it is malignant, odious, and abominable.

The true penitent not only views sin to be what it really is, but sees himself to be a sinner, dead in trespasses and sins. He sees that the thoughts of the imagination of his heart have been evil continually. In this view of his sinfulness, he loathes and abhors himself, and repents in dust and ashes.

That which is generally denominated legal repentance is consistent with all hearty love of sin. It is only the consequences, the punishment which attends sin that is disagreeable. This kind of repentance implies some sense of sin, but not a true sense. The sinner would willingly continue in sin were it not for the consequences of it. But on account of the consequences he may wish to avoid it. Remove them, therefore, and he would freely and wholly pursue sin.

Question 195 [261]. This true repentance implied that some are sorry, that we have committed those sins which we have committed?

Answer 195. True repentance implies a trust and confidence in God, and in the dispensations of his providence. It implies a sense of his superintendence and government. The true penitent must also be sensible that God suffers nothing to take place, but what on the whole is best: and that therefore, the sins he has committed must, on the whole have been for the best, when overruled by God. In this view, he will not be sorry that he has committed them. He will, however, have that morning in sorrow for sin, which implies and abhorrence of it, of himself on account of it, and which will lead him to forsake every appearance of sin.

Question 196 [261]. What is saving faith? And how distinguished from historical and doctrinal faith, and from the faith of miracles?

Answer 196. Saving faith implies unbelief and assurance of divine truth in general, and especially of that which immediately relates to salvation. It implies a sense of our helplessness and undone the state by nature, and the only way of salvation in and through the Lord Jesus Christ. It more especially consists in a firm trust and reliance upon Christ, and a renunciation of our own righteousness. It evidently is represented as consisting in acts of the will. "But to as many as received him, to them gave he power to become the sons of God, even to them that believe on his name." John 1.12. Here receiving Christ, which consists in an act of the will, is spoken of as being the same as believing on him. Trusting in him, also, implies an act of the will and is also an act of faith. "That we should be to the praise of his glory, who first trusted in Christ." Ephesians 1.12.

Saving faith necessarily implies the existence of other graces, likewise. By this faith Christ dwells in the hearts of believers. "That Christ may dwell in your hearts by faith." Ephesians 3.17.

Historical faith is that which, with doctrinal faith and that of miracles, exist in the understanding more properly than in the heart. Historical faith respects the facts related in the gospel. The understanding fully assents to their authenticity. Doctrinal faith respects the various sentiments and doctrines of revelation. This faith also may be a full assent of the understanding to the truth of those things. The faith of Miracles seems to be a firm belief that God has effected, or will, by immediate interposition, effect miraculous events.

The great difference between saving faith and this is, that is seated more especially in the heart. These are seated in the understanding. None but the Christian possessed that. These the worst of men, and even the devils may possess, in a high degree.

Question 197 [264]. Have all a warrant to exercise an appropriating faith?

Answer 197. An appropriating faith seems to be a faith which supposes Christ died for him in particular who possessed it. This no one has a warrant to suppose who really has not faith. If he believes he has faith, when he has not, he believes a lie.

Question 198 [264]. Is an appropriating faith a saving faith?

Answer 198. A saving faith has already been described to be a trust and reliance upon Christ, and a renunciation of our own righteousness, to be also attended with the other exercises of grace. But an appropriating faith does not necessarily imply this. A man may believe, Christ died for him, in particular, and yet be self-righteous, destitute of a reliance and trust in Christ, and wholly in love with sin. If a saving faith consisted in an appropriating faith, and the former did not exist, but in consequence of the latter, a man must believe a thing to be true before it really is so. He must believe he is interested in Christ, in order to be thus interested. But this would be inconsistent and absurd. If this be the only faith necessary, a man may possess faith and yet continue in the greatest wickedness. This is evident from fact. But surely the gospel gives no encouragement for such a faith as this.

Question 199 [265]. Is there a specific difference between common grace and special grace?

Answer 199. Grace is the operations of the Spirit in awakening, convincing in reforming the sinner. Special grace is the implantation of a new principal, and the producing of new and holy exercises. The former may exist with a love of sin and hatred of the divine character. The latter is not consistent with either of these. There is evidently, therefore, a specific and essential difference.

Question 200 [265]. What is pardon of sin?

Answer 200. Pardon of sin does not consist in forgetting a man has sent Erie it, nor does it consist in a formal declaration of pardon and reconciliation. It consists rather, in treating the creature, as if he never had sinned, or as if his sins were really forgotten. Before, he was treated as a sinner, and exposed to infinitely more dreadful treatment in the future world. Now, he is treated as the friend of God, and heir of eternal happiness.

Question 201 [266]. What is justification?

Answer 201. Justification does not consist in a formal declaration or pronouncing of a man to be righteous, and perfectly unbelievable in the view of the law. But it consists rather in treatment. A man who is justified is treated as if he had never sinned, or at least as if he were really righteous. It consists therefore, in pardon, and exemption from the sentence and punishment of the law, and also a title to positive happiness, even the happiness of heaven and eternal glory.

Question 202 [267]. Is justification from eternity?

Answer 202. If justification consists in treatment, and this arises from certain qualifications of the person justified, then he is not treated the highest until he is possessed of those qualifications: for God surely does not treat a person as if he were justified before he really is so. The qualifications of a Christian which entitled him to justification, evidently are not from eternity. Nor are they generally from the first period of man's life. "And such were some of you: but he are washed, but ye are sanctified, that ye are justified in the name of the Lord Jesus, and by the Spirit of our God." 1 Corinthians 6:11. This passage evidently represents those to whom it was addressed as having been once in the situation in which they were neither washed, sanctified nor justified. And by the arrangement we should naturally suppose that in the order of nature justification takes place after the beginning of sanctification.

Question 203 [268]. What is the meritorious cause of justification?

Answer 203. The meritorious cause of justification cannot be the sinner's own righteousness, for he evidently cannot fulfill the demands of the law. "For as many as are under the works of the law, are under the curse: For it is written, Cursed is every one that continueth not in all things which are written in the book of the law, to do them." Galatians 3.10.

The Scriptures everywhere represent the atonement. Christ has made as the meritorious cause of justification. "He is the end of the law for righteousness to everyone that believeth." Romans 10.4. "Being justified freely, through the redemption that is in Jesus Christ. Whom God hath set forth to be a propitiation, through faith in his blood, to declare his righteousness or the remission of sins that are passed, through the forbearance of God. To declare, I say, at this time his righteousness: that he might be just, and the justifier of him that believeth in Jesus." Romans 3.24–26.

Question 204 [269]. What is the influence of faith to justification?

Answer 204. Faith unites the believer to Christ, and entitles him to the blessings promised in the gospel. In consequence of this union, the believer is treated as if he were really one with Christ. He is pardoned and justified for the sake of Christ, and in regard to the atonement he has made.

Justification, as before observed, is the treatment of the believer as if he really were just. This treatment consists partly in communicating the various exercises of grace and of various degrees of holiness. One of the exercises of grace is faith. This therefore, is itself a part of justification.

Faith may also be considered, as evidence of a man's being justified before God. When a man is fully confident of his possessing a true and saving faith on the Savior, he is equally sure of his justification.

Question 205 [270]. In what sense is the believer one with Christ?

Answer 205. The believer is one with Christ so far as the union of affection and interest in and make them so. There is a mutual return of affection, and the interest of Christ is also the interest of the believer.

The believer is, in some respects, treated as if he were really one with Christ. He receives many blessings in consequence of Christ's atonement, as if he had personally wrought out this atonement.

Question 206 [270]. Is the believer, in justification, viewed and considered as one with Christ, and really thought by God to be one with him?

Answer 206. God never views, considers or thinks things to be different from what they really are. Otherwise, he would view, consider, and think things to be contrary to the truth. But this surely would be a great reflection upon his discernment, knowledge, or integrity.

Now the believer is no more one with Christ in point of real literal oneness than any two persons are one, no more than a woman is really and truly one with her husband. There is a similar oneness between Christ and the believer, as between a man and wife. But this is not a personal oneness. It is a oneness of affection and interest.

Question 207 [271]. What is the true idea of the imputation of the righteousness of Christ the believer?

Answer 207. The idea of the imputation of the righteousness of Christ to the believer is, that the believer is treated as if you were really righteous in strict law, or as if he were really possessed of the righteousness of Christ. The righteousness of Christ can no more really be transferred from him to the believer than any other property, no more than his knowledge, wisdom, and the like. One may have a moral quality, either evil or good, similar to that of another, but this property or quality can never be transferred from one and be made personally and really another's in the same sense that any of his own natural properties are his. So neither can the righteousness of Christ be imputed by such a kind of transferring.[53] But God treats the believer in the manner as he would if he really possessed this righteousness.

Question 208 [272]. Is the believer considered by God as possessed of the righteousness of Christ? Or does he think that the believer possessed that righteousness?

53. Gelston excises: God never sees things but as they really are, he never sees it to be in this sense, imputed.

Answer 208. It has Artie been observed that the believer is not really possessed of the righteousness of Christ. But only, in consequence of it, is treated as if he really were. Now it is evident, God does not see, consider or think things to be different from what they really are. He who knows all things surely knows the truth of this matter. And surely he is not so inattentive as to think or consider things to be different from what he knows them to be.

Question 209 [273]. Is justification a declaration that the believer stands right with respect to the divine law?

Answer 209. The believer does not, considered in himself and with respect to the real truth of things, stand right with respect to the divine law. Justification, therefore, is not a declaration that he does stand right. If it were, it would declare that which is not true.

Question 210 [273]. Is not free pardon included in justification as an essential part of it?

Answer 210. Pardon in justification appear in some respects to be the same. They both consist in treatment. Justification is treating the believer as if he really were righteous. Pardon is treating him as if he never had offended, or as if his sins were all wiped away or forgiven.

Justification, however, extends farther than pardon. The actual communication of good which could not be really merited, were the person really righteous, may come under the head of justification.

Question 211 [274]. Is the justification of the believer a judicial and legal act or an act of sovereign grace?

Answer 211. If justification were a judicial and legal act. It must be because the believer is just and right in the view of the law, and because, had no atonement been made, he would not justly have been condemned by the law. But this is not the real case with the believer. He is condemned by the law, and justly. Notwithstanding all Christ has done and suffered, were it not for the grace and mercy of God, the believer would still suffer the penalty of the law. The act of justification must, therefore, be an act above or beside the law, or it must be a sovereign act. If it were no sovereign act, but a judicial and legal act, it must be something which God could not but in justice perform. But this is contrary to the express declarations of Scripture. "Being justified freely by his grace." Romans 3.24. "Therefore, we conclude that a man is justified by faith without deeds of law." Romans 3.28. "For if

Abraham were justified by works, he hath whereof to glory, but not before God." Romans 4.2.

Question 212 [275]. Has the believer, on account of the righteousness of Christ, a right to demand justification as justly and legally do him?

Answer 212. If the justification of the believer being not a judicial or legal act, then he has no right to demand justification as justly and legally due to. If he had a right, then he might demand justification and it would not be by grace, but would contradict those passages which make the whole a matter of grace.

Question 213 [276]. Is the believer, even after he is justified by faith, condemned by the divine law?

Answer 213. It will forever remain that the believer has send, in no instance will ascend and be so removed from a person as for it to be truly said that person is not guilty of the sin which he once committed. With respect to this sin, then, he stands condemned by the law, for that condemneth for every transgression. The same may be said of every sin. The believer has committed. If he were not condemned by the law. He would stand right with the law. And if so, he would have a right to claim exemption from the punishment on the footing of the law. Of consequence, there would be no grace in the case.

Question 214 [277]. In what sense, then, is the believer free from the law?

Answer 214. The believer is free from the law. So far as that he will not suffer the penalty of it. It is the punishment of the law threatening from which the believer is redeemed. But with respect to the requirements of the law, he is still holden by them, and condemned in every instance of breaking it.

Question 215 [277]. How are full satisfaction and free pardon consistent?

Answer 215. Full satisfaction is paid so far as the honor of the law and the dignity in support of government require, but it is not paid him such as sense as that anything can be demanded by the believer in point of justice. God, therefore, is under no obligation of justice to accept of the atonement. And if he did, it must be free and sovereign. The pardon, then, he bestows must be free and what the believer cannot demand on the footing of justice.

Question 216 [278]. Is the sinner forgiven before he repents?

Answer 216. Forgiveness is universally represented in Scripture as following repentance and not proceeding it. "Repent ye therefore, and be converted, that your sins may be blotted out." Acts 3:19. But if forgiveness had already taken place, it would not have been proper to exhort them to repent that they might be forgiven, but because they had been forgiven. Besides, it would be converting the natural order of things, and in a measure supersede the necessity of repentance.

Question 217 [278]. Is forgiveness granted on account of the sinner's repentance?

Answer 217. Forgiveness is granted in consequence of repentance. Or by the constitution of the gospel, the sinner is entitled to forgiveness when he sincerely repents. This however is not because repentance merits forgiveness. Aside from the sovereign mercy and grace of God, the sinner, notwithstanding all his repentance, however sincere, would still be exposed to the expression of the divine displeasure, and might justly be punished with the full demerit of his sins. Forgiveness, therefore, is not properly granted on account of repentance, but on account of the atonement which Christ has made for sin, and in consequence of repentance, according to the gracious constitution of God.

Question 218 [279]. Does forgiveness extend to future sins?

Answer 218. It has already been proved that forgiveness follows repentance: It cannot then extend to future sins. A man surely does not repent of the sin before he commits it. His forgiveness then cannot extend to any future sins.

Besides, forgiveness must presuppose things to exist which have no existence. This would be absurd. It would be directly contrary to truth to treat a man as if he had committed certain sins, when in reality he had not committed them.

Question 219 [280]. Is the sinner forgiven by God's absolute goodness or grace without satisfaction?

Answer 219. The Scriptures nowhere represent the forgiveness of the sinner as by God's absolute goodness or grace, but in consequence of the satisfaction of Christ. "In whom we have redemption through his blood, the forgiveness of sins, according to the riches of his grace." Ephesians 1.7. Though forgiveness be according to the riches of grace, it is not grace, independent of redemption through the blood of Christ. Had it not been for this redemption of Christ, the grace here mentioned would not have existed. It is not, therefore, absolute. "And be ye kind one to another, tenderhearted, forgiving one another, even as God for Christ sake hath forgiven you." Ephesians 4.32. Here, forgiveness is said to be for the sake of Christ. It must, therefore, be in consequence of the satisfaction he has made. "In whom we have redemption through his blood, even the forgiveness of sins." Colossians 1.14.

Besides, if the sinner be forgiven by the absolute goodness or grace of God, then the atonement was unnecessary. If so, God has unnecessarily been at an intimate expense for the salvation of mankind, when the whole might have been accomplished without any expense at all.

> Question 220 [281]. If the sinner had, of his own accord, repented and become perfectly holy, could he have been forgiven without the satisfaction of Christ?

Answer 220. The sinner, by repentance and a future holy life, would never atone for the least of his past offenses. It would be no more than what he is under obligation to perform, and therefore would never repair the damage his sins produced. But for God to receive the sinner to favor and forgive him without a satisfaction would never support the honor and dignity of his law and moral government. If the sinner could have been pardoned on condition of repentance and a future holy life, nothing was necessary, but to bring them to this, and the way would be prepared for forgiveness. The atonement which Christ has made would, therefore, have been altogether unnecessary.

> Question 221 [282]. Is the faith by which a believer is justified a mere speculative assent?

Answer 221. The faith by which the believer is justified is doubtless a saving faith, and this has already been described to be something more than a speculative assent. It is everywhere represented as seated in the heart and connected inseparably with the affections. Romans 10.9.

> Question 222 [283]. If I imply love, which is a moral exercise or a work, is not the believer justified by work? He is justified without the deeds of the law.

Answer 222. Faith in some sense is a work. It is a duty and implies the exercise of love, which is the fulfilling of the law. But it is not a work or fulfilling of the law in such a sense as to become meritorious. The believer, however strong and operative his faith, is destitute of anything which could recommend him to favor, considered in himself and aside from the atonement which Christ has made. Though, therefore, he be justified by that which may properly be considered as a work, yet it is not on the footing of strict law, but of grace.

Question 223 [284]. In what sense is the believer justified by works?

Answer 223. The believer is justified by works, not as performed to recommend him to the favor of God, but as by the constitution of the gospel they are necessary to his salvation. They also evidence the believer's justification.

Question 224 [284]. How do you reconcile James's account of justification with Paul's?

Answer 224. The design of James seems to be to prove that faith is an operative principle, and that the various exercises of grace necessarily flow from faith. And therefore, where the various works or grace is peculiar to the Christian do not exist, we may inferred there is no justification. On the contrary, where they do exist and appear in life, this is an evidence of justification.

Paul seems to place justifying faith in opposition to works of the law, to that which is performed with a view of merit. In the sight of God, faith, or any other act of obedience performed, as a covenant of works or with respect to the law, has nothing which can be meritorious. The design of Paul, therefore, seems to be to prove that faith can never, as a covenant of works, merit the favor of God.

Question 225 [285]. Exhibit your proofs, that James means justification in the side of God?

Answer 225. That James means justification in the side of God is evident from what he says of Abraham. The justification of Abraham was doubtless in the side of God. For his believing God "was imputed to him for righteousness: and he was called the friend of God." James 2.23. If the word justification is not used by James with a meaning similar to that of righteousness, then the instance he brought of Abraham would not properly illustrate the matter it was designed to.

Question 226 [286]. Will not this scheme of justification derogate from the grace of God in it?

Answer 226. If this were a justification according to the covenant of works, a legal justification, and that which the law strictly requires should take place, then it would derogate from the grace of it. Indeed, there would be no grace at all. In the case. But the justification is not of this kind, as has been already proved. It does not, therefore, derogate in the least from the grace of it.

Question 227 [286]. Is sanctifying grace at all needful to any man, unless it be with respect to that which is his duty and in respect to which he is without excuse?

Answer 227. Sanctifying grace is not needful as belonging to a covenant of works. It is needful, however, as it is a man's duty, that without which he is without excuse, and without which, according to the constitution of the gospel, he cannot be saved. It is needful, also, to evidence a man's justification. On no other accounts does it appear to be needful.

Question 228 [287]. What is the sum of man's duty? And what the effect produced by the sanctifying influences of the Spirit? Matthew 22.37–40; Hebrews 8.10.

Answer 228. The sum of man's duty is love. "Love is the fulfilling of the law." Romans 13.10. "Thou shalt love the Lord thy God with all thy heart, and with all thy soul, and with all thy mind. This is the first and great commandment. And the second is like unto it, Thou shalt love thy neighbor as thyself. On these two commandments hang all the law and the prophets." Matthew 22.37–40.

The effect produced by the sanctifying influences of the Spirit are a new and holy principle, together with the various exercises which flow from this. Those who are favored with these are treated by God as his, and has his peculiar people. All the blessings of children are conferred upon them. "For this is the covenant that I will make with the house of Israel after those days, saith the Lord, I will put my laws into their mind, and right them in their hearts: and I will be to them of God, and they shall be to me a people." Romans 8:10.

Question 229 [288]. Can that holy volition in us which is wholly. The effect of divine power be wholly our act, and our duty? Deuteronomy 10.10; 30.6; Ezekiel 18:31; 36:26.

Answer 229. If the volition be an act of our minds, however it be produced, it still is ours. Nothing more is necessary to make the volition wholly hours, then for us to will, to put forth an act. If we were operated upon as a machine is by mere natural powers, Galician would be no duty. But this is not the case. We are influenced by arguments and motives. It is our duty, therefore, to be influenced by the most proper motives. Disappears from the express commands of Scripture. "Circumcise therefore, the foreskin of your heart, and be no more stiff-necked." Deuteronomy 10.16. Here, those who are spoken to are commanded to do this, as if the act were their own, which also fully implies a duty. The same, however, is said to be done by God. "And the Lord thy God will circumcise thine heart, and the heart of thy seed." Deuteronomy 30.6. "Cast away from you, all your transgressions, wherein ye have transgressed, and make you a new heart, and a new spirit." Ezekiel 18.31. "A new heart also will I give you, and in the spirit will I put within you, and I will take away the stony heart out of your flesh, and I will give you an heart of flesh." 36:26. From these different passages. It appears evident that the same things are a duty and per form by those who are the subjects of the duty, as their own personal act, and yet are also said to be performed by God.

Question 230 [289]. How can it be made to appear that unbelief is a sin? And that all errors in moral matters are of a criminal nature?

Answer 230. Unbelief implies enmity of heart to God and the Savior, which without doubt must be a sin. Besides, faith is a duty and expressly enjoined. The want of it, therefore, is a breach of duty. Where faith is not, love does not exist. But the want of love is a direct breach of the moral law. "Because of unbelief they were broken off." Romans 11.20. "Take heed, brethren, lest there be in any of you an evil heart of unbelief." Hebrews 3.12. "If ye believe not that I am he, ye shall die in your sins." John 8.24.

All errors, in moral matters, arise from the corruption of the human heart and its opposition to the truth. Were mankind sincerely disposed to seek for and to receive it, doubtless they would be exposed to those errors which now prevail. That therefore which is the occasion of error is a sin.

Question 231 [291]. Will the wicked, the heathens, Jews, infidels, and errorists of every kind be without excuse at the day of judgment?

Answer 231. If the errors of mankind, arise from the corruption and wickedness of their hearts or from a criminal blindness, then doubtless they will in this respect be without excuse. And if they are not interested in Christ, they will in every respect be without excuse. Where ever they belong, whatever be their nation or religion. "Neither is there salvation in any other: for there is none other name under heaven given among men, whereby we must be saved." Romans 4.12. Christ, at the day of judgment, will say to all who were not interested in him. "I never knew you: depart from me, ye that work iniquity." Matthew 7.23.

Question 232 [291]. What is the essence of true virtue or holiness?

Answer 232. That which the law requires is true virtue or holiness. This is love, therefore: for "love is the fulfilling of the law." Romans 10.13.

The first and foundational exercise of love is benevolence to being in general. This is meant by love to God and our neighbor. And this is the fulfilling of the law. "Thou shall love the Lord thy God with all thy heart and with all thy soul, and with all thy mind. This is the first and great commandment. And the second is like unto it, thou shall love thy neighbor as thyself. On these two commandments hang all the law and the prophets." Matthew 22.37–40. This benevolence is the union of heart, and attachment to being in general. This is properly, the principal from which the other kinds of love, such as complacence, gratitude, and esteem, necessarily flow. A man who is not possessed of this love of benevolence may have other kinds of love in a certain sense and of a certain kind. A man may take complacence and objects which are pleasing to the taste of his mind, and yet have no holy complacence. So he may have a kind of gratitude for favors received, and esteem for the character and properties of another, and yet be destitute of true virtue. But that complacence, which arises from universal benevolence is exercised only towards the proper objects of complacence. The existence of a holy complacence presupposes the existence of holiness in moral beauty, and this alone is the object of a holy complacence.

Esteem and gratitude, also, which arise from a principle of benevolence will never be exercised in a virtuous manner, but on their proper objects.

Question 233 [293]. Is there no virtue in the exercises of natural conscience, the moral sense, natural compassion, natural generosity, or natural affections?

Answer 233. The various exercises of natural conscience, the moral sense, natural compassion, natural generosity, or natural affections, when directed by benevolence may become virtuous. But, unless they be accompanied with a principle of holy love or universal benevolence, they are possessed of no virtue, but may become a vice. Indeed, considered in themselves. They do not appear to have any more virtue in them than the various exercises of animal instinct.

Question 234 [294]. What do you mean by self-love?

Answer 234. Self-love is a supreme and ultimate regard to self and the private can find interest of self. It subordinates the general good and every individual good, however great to its own private interest.[54]

Question 235 [294]. What do you say concerning this definition of self-love: "A love of our own happiness"?

Answer 235. The definition of self-love that is "A love of our own happiness" is ambiguous and indeterminate. In everyone there is naturally a love of happiness and aversion to misery. But this principle is capable of various directions. A man may place his happiness in promoting the general good. He may do this to the hazard of his own private interest, ease, comfort and reputation. As this is his happiness, so he may and will doubtless love this. But on the contrary, if instead of this is sacrifices and subordinates of the general and every other individual good to his own private interest, ease and comfort, his own happiness, and of consequence, the love of his own happiness, would be something totally distinct from that in the former case. The definition, therefore, is capable of two very different constructions, and unless further explained will not determine anything with respect to the nature of self-love.

Question 236 [295]. Is not self-love the root of all virtue?

Answer 236. Self, according to the definition already given, is directly opposed to the general good. It is tendency is to sacrifice a greater, even an infinite good, to its own private interest, however small. But this surely cannot be virtue: Nor can it be the root of virtue. Virtue is a principle which is disposed to promote the greatest possible increase of happiness. But self-love is disposed to promote only a small degree of happiness, and this at the expense of a much greater good.

Besides, that love which in Scripture is represented as the root of all virtue is not defined self-love, but love to God and our neighbor. That charity, which is the end of the commandment is that which "seeketh not her own," and of consequence, can not be self-love. 1 Timothy 1.5 and 1 Corinthians 13.4.

Question 237 [296]. Are the voluntary exercises of self-love positively sinful?

54. Supplement, p. 386; *Answer 234.* Self-love is a regard to that happiness which consists in the gratification of the sensual appetites, the pleasure of riches and honors of this world. It is no the love of body and soul, properly. For, these are sometimes sacrificed to indulge it.

Answer 237. The voluntary exercises of self-love are evidently of the moral kind, and therefore either positively holy or positively sinful. They are not holy, for they are directly contrary to that love which is the fulfilling of the law and which is real holiness.

Besides, self-love is everywhere in Scripture represented as positively sinful. It is said that in the last days "Men shall be lovers of their own selves." 2 Timothy 3.2. And this is evidently considered as something positively sinful.

Indeed, in the disposition is implied necessarily an opposition of the heart to the general good, which is but another phrase for enmity and hatred of the general good. What ever stands in competition with the interest of self, it opposes and hates, though it be the greatest possible moral worth and happiness.

Question 238 [297]. Does self-love proceed from an original and peculiar bias or principal?

Answer 238. Mankind evidently possess the principle of self-love originally. The first moral exercises of their hearts proceed from this principle. The peculiar and distinguishing bias of their hearts is to seek their own private happiness, for naturally we are "Lovers of pleasures more than lovers of God." 2 Timothy 3.4.[55]

Question 239 [298]. As distinguished from selfishness can self-love be subordinated to the general good?

Answer 239. Self-love, properly defined, is selfishness and is opposed to the general good. But if it be meant a love of happiness and an aversion to misery, this principle of nature may be subordinated to the general good. A man's happiness may consist in promoting the general good. And this may require a sacrifice of oneself and his private interest.[56]

Question 240 [298]. Does the sinner love himself more than assigned loves himself?

55. Supplement, p. 386; *Answer 238*. The questions means whether self-love proceeds from some principle originally in man or his at the foundation of all corrupt or original principles.

56. Supplement, p. 386; *Answer 239*. Selfishness may not be subordinated to the general good because [it is] always opposed to it. Self-love may, because those things in which it consists may not be indulged only when agreeable to on coinciding with the general good. A well-regulated self-love is justifiable.

Answer 240. The sinner loves himself supremely. The saint loves God supremely. The former regards himself and his own interest as the most important. The latter regards himself and his individual interest and happiness as infinitely small and inconsiderable.

Question 241 [298]. Is the enmity of the sinner against God disinterested?

Answer 241. The enmity of the sinner is altogether of the selfish nature, and therefore interested. It arises from an apprehension of God's being opposed to him and his interest. All the sinner supposes God is friendly to him and is aiming at his highest good, he may feel reconciled to God and exercise the kind of love to him. But whenever he becomes acquainted with the character of God and his own true character, his heart rises in enmity and hatred, and the reason is because while in his own present character. He knows it is not for his own interest in happiness for God to be such a being is he really is.

Question 242 [299]. What you mean by "disinterested love"?

Answer 242. Disinterested love is an affection directly contrary to that of self-love or selfishness. Disinterested love is that principle which is regulated by the general good. It seeks a private good, no farther than it appears to be consistent with general good. It however, this poses a man to seek his own good, so far as it does not interfere with a greater. For by promoting his own, thus far, he at the same time promotes the general good. It is not, therefore, of such a nature as totally to exclude self, but to treat one's own interest according to its real value and importance.

As self-love has a certain interest in view, so has disinterested love. The former is infinitely small. The latter is infinitely great. Self-love regards its object and interest in the confines of self. Disinterested love is not confined to one or a small number of objects that takes in being in general, and is therefore universal benevolence.

Question 243 [300]. Is God to be loved disinterestedly?

Answer 243. Disinterested love is that which regards, beings, according to their real worth and importance. As God, therefore, is the greatest and best of beings. He is worthy of the most pure and this interested love. If we love him merely because he loves us and does good to us, we are actuated by no higher principle than self-love.

Question 244 [301]. If a man love God directly and disinterestedly at all, will he not love him supremely?

Answer 244. There are but two kinds of love, which are radical principles. One is self-love. The other is disinterested love. Self-love never influences a person to any direct love of God, but only on account of some benefit received or expected. But if God be loved directly and disinterestedly, it is not measured by regard to self, but the excellence and worthiness of God. Since, therefore, he is infinitely more excellent and worthy of love that any other be or all other beings he merits the supreme love of his creatures, and will actually be thus loved.

> Question 245 [302]. Are the voluntary exercises of natural compassion, natural generosity, natural affection, and all voluntary exercises in the unregenerate positively sinful?

Answer 245. A natural disposition to pity compassion, generosity, natural affection, and the like appear to be of the instinctive kind, and considered aside from voluntary exercises of the will, do not appear to be of the nature of virtue or vice. But where there are voluntary exercises, whether of those kinds or any other, they are of a moral nature and therefore are either wholly or sinful. If they are not of the benevolent kind. They must evidently arise from a principle of selfishness, and therefore, be sinful. And if they are positive in real acts of the will, they are as positively sinful. Now it is evident from Scripture. The unregenerate have no moral, voluntary exercises which are holy, but on the contrary, are positively sinful. "The carnal mind is enmity against God: for it is not subject to the law of God, neither indeed can be." Romans 8.7. Hence, it was said, "Every imagination of the thoughts of his heart was only evil continually." Genesis 6.5. "Whatsoever is not of faith is sin." Romans 14.23. But the supposition is that those exercises referred to in the question are not of faith. They must therefore be sinful.

> Question 246 [303]. What do you mean by moral obligation?

Answer 246. A man is said to be obliged to do the things when there is some cause, which induces him or actually compels him to do it. Thus, a man who is in prison for debt is obliged from a natural necessity to continue there until his creditor or the law will release him. A man who has sufficient to discharge his debts is obliged punctually to pay them to avoid the confinement of a prison. This is an obligation of the civil kind. A man is also frequently said to do many things for the sake of his reputation, emolument, preferment and the like. In all cases, there is something supposed which either actually does, or ought to excite, induce or constrain to such and such actions.

Those kinds of obligation mentioned above are not immediately of a moral nature, though a man may act as a moral agent in each of the cases. Moral obligation respects that faculty of man for the exercise of which he is a subject of praise or blame. It implies the existence of duty, and something the neglect of which would be wrong. In this case, as well as all others, there is some reason, ground or cause, which enforces or constitutes the obligation. And this renders the agent accountable according to his compliance or noncompliance with his duty, or which is the same, the obligation under which you was placed.

Question 247 [304]. What is the primary foundation of moral obligation?

Answer 247. The tendency of an action to produce the greatest possible degree of happiness appears to be the primary and real foundation of all moral obligation. What ever other foundation be supposed, the inquiry may still arise, why it is considered as the foundation? or, what are the reasons and grounds of this? And then we must recur back to its tendency to happiness. For if an action tends to more misery than happiness, it surely can never be right and obligatory. But on the contrary, that which is calculated to promote happiness, on the whole, is right and fit and obligatory on this account.

Question 248 [305]. Is the knowledge of the will of God necessary to moral obligation gesture?

Answer 248. It does not appear, but that the same foundation of moral obligation would exist, where the will of God unknown, as now does. There would be the like tendency in actions there now is, and mankind would therefore be under the like obligations.

Question 249 [306]. Is the will of God itself, or his moral perfections, the primary foundation of moral obligation?

Answer 249. The will of God cannot be the foundation of moral obligation for in the order of nature, we may suppose something antecedent to this, and on which the will itself is founded. It is the tendency of actions to produce such and such sins, which is the reason why God wills them. Were not the will of God, holy, just, and good. It is not conceived his creatures would be under an obligation of the moral kind to obey it. That, therefore, which makes it such also establishes the obligation.

Nor are the moral perfections of God. The foundation of moral obligation. Notwithstanding these, there is still a tendency in actions. And were the moral character of God different from what it really is, still mankind would be under an obligation to act agreeably to the tendency of actions to produce happiness. Neither the will nor perfections of the being. Make an action right and morally obligatory, which, on the whole, was calculated to promote more misery than happy.

Question 250 [307]. Is the knowledge of the existence of God necessary to moral obligation?

Answer 250. If mankind can but become acquainted with the nature and tendency of actions, this would be sufficient, though they had no knowledge of the existence of God. This is evident from the real state of those who are either partially or wholly ignorant of his existence. They doubtless are under obligation to acquaint themselves with him and knowledge of his perfections, and to treat each other with justice and benevolence.

Question 251 [308]. Is the existence of God itself necessary to moral obligation?

Answer 251. Though there were no God, still the tendency of actions among mankind would be the same. Some actions would still be calculated to promote happiness, and others misery. There would, likewise, be still a general good: and this so far is known ought to be pursued.

Question 252 [308]. Is God himself free from moral obligation?

Answer 252. Wrong, though done by God, could never become right. Were he a malevolent being. We should find no difficulty in supposing he ought to become holy and do that which is right. And though he is now a good being, were he wants to do that which, on the whole was not best, it is evident this single instance would be wrong, and so far, deface is character. He therefore, is under obligation to do that which is best on the whole and right.

Question 253 [309]. If the tendency of an action to happiness be the primary foundation of moral obligation, will not follow that natural good, is more valuable and important than moral good?

Answer 253. The value of moral good, arises from its tendency to promote happiness. If it were not calculated to promote this it would neither be valuable nor important. In moral good consists the happiness of holy beings. It is in the exercise of holy dispositions and tempers that good beings enjoy happiness. If this happiness be called natural good, then it will not be easy to distinguish between that natural and moral good referred to in the question.

Question 254 [309]. What other foundations of moral obligation have been invented and published?

Answer 254. Some have supposed the moral fitness and propriety of things to be the foundation of moral obligation. Others have found the did on the divine will, others again on the divine attributes. Some have founded moral obligation on utility, and others on a social compact. And others have founded on truth.

Question 255 [310]. In what sense do the unregenerate desire to be regenerated? And in what sense can they pray for regenerating grace?

Answer 255. The unregenerate may desire and pray for regenerating grace as that which they know to be necessary to avoid misery, and the only way to happiness. They cannot, however, pray for it in sincerity and an acceptable manner. Nor do they desire it on its own account, and on account of that happiness which is connected with it. The happiness they would prefer is of a very different kind. And could they be sure of escaping the punishment to which they see themselves exposed, they neither would desire nor prayed for regenerating grace.

Question 256 [311]. Is it the duty of the unregenerate to pray for regenerating grace?

Answer 256. The unregenerate, while such, cannot pray with that temper and disposition which all ought to possess. Now, surely it is not the duty of any, however bad, to pray with unholy hearts. The first and immediate duty is to be renewed in the spirit and temper of their minds. To say that the unregenerate may pray for regenerating grace seemed to imply that they may at least continue unregenerate until they had that prayed, and that it was right to pray in an unholy manner. It is evident, while unregenerate, they cannot pray in any other manner. It is their duty, therefore, to pray, but to pray with a temper, which implies and results from regeneration.

Question 257 [311]. Do the unregenerate desire the happiness of heaven?

Answer 257. The unregenerate have no direct and real desire for the happiness at. They are in their hearts opposed to such a happiness. That happiness for which they have a real and hearty desire is very different from the happiness of heaven. Were they to have their choice, they would forever prefer the happiness of this world to that. They do not, therefore, desire the happiness of heaven on any other act found, but to secure them from the misery of hell.

Question 258 [312]. What is the utmost which the unregenerate do in the use of the means of grace?

Answer 258. The unregenerate can do nothing, which is of the holy nature, for nature cannot act above itself. A corrupt tree cannot bring forth good fruit. The external actions of the unregenerate may be naturally good, or such as if the heart were right, would be acceptable. Indeed, it is the want of a heart conformed to the law of God, which renders all they do unacceptable. And were this right, they would be accepted without regard for the external appearance. They do nothing, therefore, to any saving in really good purpose.

All they do is unholy and will forever be so until their hearts are renewed. They may, however, do things which are calculated under the influence of God to more a sexually awakened and convinced them of their situation and the badness of their hearts. What they do may also render the probability of their salvation still greater.

Question 259 [313]. Is any real duty done by the unregenerate in the use of the means of grace?

Answer 259. If the unregenerate do-nothing, which is acceptable in the side of God, they do nothing which can properly be called duty. The very idea of duty is something which is right and fit, and which, when done, it is acceptable. Their prayers are said to be an abomination, and their plowing, sin. Isaiah 1.13; Proverbs 21.4.

Besides, if they can do that which is real duty while unregenerate, it must be because there is still some remaining goodness and him. But this would destroy the doctrine of told depravity, and set aside the necessity of regeneration which are abundantly asserted in Scripture.

Question 260 [314]. Are all the voluntary, external actions of the unregenerate positively sinful?

Answer 260. The external actions, separately considered, contained neither the nature of virtue, nor vice. It is from the state of the will, or a man's voluntary exercises, aside from the external actions that a man's real character is determined and it is the voluntary exercises of the will which properly is either simple or holy.

But, that the voluntary exercise of the will in the unregenerate are positively sinful is abundantly evident from the passages which proved the doctrine of total depravity. Indeed, every action or exercise of the will is either positively sinful or positively holy. There is no medium between these. Nor are there any which are indifferent, or which are partly one, and partly of the other.

Question 261 [315]. Do the unregenerate grow better in the use of means?

Answer 261. If the unregenerate in the use of means are more and more awakened, they evidently sin against greater light, and of consequence, their sin must be proportionably aggravated. There is nothing date due, while in the state, which can be considered as possessing any thing gracious or holy, for the supposition considers them unholy. And if their convictions and awakenings be increased that they become more clearly acquainted with their own real character and the character of God, they are in the will be equally greater. They do not, therefore, grow better, but worse or more sinful and wicked.

Question 262 [316]. What is the immediate duty of the unregenerate? And to what are they to be exhorted?

Answer 262. The immediate duty of the unregenerate is written in and be converted. If it were not, there would be some excuse for their continuance, at least for some time, in impenitence. But if they die in impenitence, what ever may have been there awakenings and conditions, they will be found without the least excuse.

As repentance is the immediate duty of the unregenerate, it is this to which they are to be exhorted. If they are exhorted to anything short of this, they are exhorted to that which is no real duty, for that which does not imply repentance cannot be acceptable with God, and therefore, is not duty. Hence, we find that the direction given in Scripture to the awakened were such, as implied or expressed this. "Repent and be baptized." Acts 2.38. "Repent and be converted." 2.19. "Repent of this thy wickedness." 8.22. These were the general exhortations which we find to have been given in such case.

Question 263 [317]. What is the real advantage of an assiduous use of means to the unregenerate?

Answer 263. An assiduous use of means is calculated to promote convictions and to bring the awakens to a clearer sense of their guilt, their lost and helpless condition. This also is the way in which God usually visit sinners.

Question 264 [317]. To whom are the promises of the gospel made? To the regenerate or unregenerate?

Answer 264. The promises of the gospel do not appear to be made to any but the regenerate. They appear evidently to be connected with no exercise, but what imply the real existence of grace. Hence, when it is said, "Ask, and it shall be given you: seek and ye shall find: knock, and it shall be opened unto you." Matthew 7.7. These are exercises with which all the blessings of the gospel are connected. While unregenerate, the sinner is dead in sin, an enemy to God, and at real enmity against him. In this situation, he cannot please God. Nor surely does God indulge him in this by promising things to him while in a state of unregenerate state. On the contrary, the reason why the unregenerate do not receive is because they ask amiss. James 4.3.

Besides, if promises were made to them, it would seem as though there were something good in them, and therefore, that they were not totally depraved.

Question 265 [318]. Are there no encouragement given to the unregenerate? And what are they?

Answer 265. The encouragements given to the unregenerate arise principally from the general methods of God's providence and the increasing probability of their salvation. This evidently is a greater probability that those who live under the light of the gospel will be saved, then those who are totally ignorant of it. So also those who are in the diligent use of means are more likely to become awakened than those who are totally regardless and neglectful. And the awakened are far more likely to be met with by God, than the stupid and unconcerned.

Question 266 [319]. How do you prove the saint's perseverance?

Answer 266. 1. The love with which God loves the Saints is everlasting love. "Yea, I have loves the with everlasting love." Jeremiah 31.3. "Having loved his own, which were in the world, he loves them unto the end." John 13.1. These passages fully prove that the love of God, to the saints is not of a temporary nature, and such as depends upon uncertainty. But if it were possible for Saints to fall from grace, it would not be true that in all instances, those whom he loved it, loved to the end. Though he might love some to the end, yet others, he would love to the short time.

2. The doctrine of perseverance is evident from the union of the believers to Christ. You it is not a union of political kind, which may be of a short in temporary duration, but of a real affection and attachment of heart. "Abide in me, and I in you. If ye abide in me, and my words abide in you, ye shall ask what ye will and it shall be done unto you." John 15.4, 7. "But the anointing which ye have received of him, abide in you: and ye need not that any man teach you: But as the same anointing teaches you, of all things, and his truth, and is no lie: and even as it hath taught you, ye shall abide in him." John 2.27.

3. The perseverance of the saints is evident from the continuance of the principle implanted in regeneration. "Whosoever is born of God does not commit sin, for his seed remaineth in him and he cannot sin, because he is born of God." John 3.9. "Being born again, not of corruptible seed, but of incorruptible, by the word of God, which liveth and abideth forever." 1 Peter 1.23.

4. The doctrine is also evident from the indwelling of the Holy Spirit as a sanctifier. "He that believeth on me, as the Scripture hath said, out of his belly shall flow rivers of living water. But this spake he of the spirit, which today that believe on him, should receive." John 7.38, 39. "But whosoever drinketh of the water that I shall give him, shall never thirst, but the water that I shall give him, shall be in him a well of water springing up into everlasting life." John 4.14.

5. Christ is represented as making continual intercession for the saints which doubtless is effectual, and will therefore, ensure their perseverance. "Wherefore he is able also to the uttermost to save them that come unto God by him, seeing he ever liveth to make intercession for them." Hebrews 7.25.

6. The doctrine is still more evident from numerous other declarations of Scripture directly to the point. "All that the Father giveth me, shall come to me, and him that cometh to me I will in no wise cast out." John 6.37. "And this is the Father's will, which hath sent me, that all of which he hath given me, I should lose nothing, but should raise it up again at the last day." Verse 39. "And I give unto them eternal life, and they shall never perish, neither shall any pluck them out of my hand." John 10.28. "Who are kept by the mighty power of God through faith unto salvation." 1 Peter 1.5. "Being confident of this very thing, that he which hath begun a good work in you, will perform it until the day of Jesus Christ." Philippians 1.6.

Question 267 [322]. Can you make it appear that the promises of the gospel mean more than that those who persevere shall be saved?

Answer 267. The promises are not expressed with a condition of salvation in the case of perseverance. But it as much respects the perseverance of the saint, as his salvation. In the passage last quoted, it is expressly said, "He which hath began a good work in you," that is the saints to whom the Apostle was addressing himself, "will perform it unto the day of Jesus Christ." This is evidently expressed without any condition, and is a promise of actual perseverance. But if he suffers some finally to fall from grace, he will not in these instances perform what he had begun agreeably to the promise. The like construction is the most natural for the chief of the texts introduced above. "For the gifts and calling of God are without repentance." Romans 11.29. But if God should elect, justify, and sanctify his saints, and then suffer them to fall away, his conduct would in this case be agreeable to other parts of conduct in his providence, where he is said to repent.

Question 268 [323]. Is assurance attainable by saints in this life?

Answer 268. Good that assurance is attainable is evident both from the nature of the change which is wrought and the effects of totally distinct from holiness, corruption from grace, self-love and the love of God, sorrow for sin on its own account, and sorrow for it on account of the punishment which is due to it. There is evidently in all of these cases a specific difference. If therefore, one kind of exercises are discoverable. It is difficult to conceive why the other should not be: If a man may know when he is under the reigning power of sin. It is difficult to conceive why he should not know when he is under the will of grace.

But the Scriptures abundantly proved the doctrine. "These things I have written unto you, that believe on the name of the Son of God; that ye may know that ye had eternal life." 1 John 5.13. "And hereby we do know that we know him, if we keep his commandments." 1 John 2.3. "We know that we have passed from death unto life, because we love the brethren." 3:14. "Wherefore the rather, brethren, give diligence to make your calling and election sure." 2 Peter 1.10.

Question 269 [325]. Is assurance is essential to faith?

Answer 269. Many without doubt are possessed of faith who are destitute of assurance. This is evident from what we have reason to conclude, by appearances among mankind. It is also evident from the Apostle's directing those who were already possessed of faith, to make their calling and election sure, as if they had not already attained to assurance. Besides, if assurance were essential to faith. It must be because it constituted, at least, a part of true faith, and then he who had the greatest assurance would have the strongest evidence of his faith. But this would place the strongest title to faith in the power of deluded hypocrites and enthusiasts.

Question 270 [326]. By what means is assurance to be obtained?

Answer 270. That of which a real Christian would wish to be assured is, that he is actually possessed of grace. This is a principle which is of an operative nature, and produces effects in the life. There are certain exercises which are the genuine effects of it, and which cannot possibly proceed from any other principle. Wherever these are discoverable. There is at the same time, the same evidence that grace is there an actual existence. The way, therefore, for a Christian to obtain that assurance is by his sanctification. Hence it is that the Apostle John made this a foundation of his and their assurance, to whom he wrote. They were assured that they knew Christ, because they kept his commandments, and because they loved the brethren.

Question 271 [327]. What is the Witness of the Spirit? And is it mediate or immediate?

Answer 271. The Witness of the Spirit is that effect which he produced in the Christian by sanctification. He gives him that temper and produces those exercises which one discovered are evidences that he is a child of God. "The Spirit itself beareth witness with our spirit that we are the children of God." Romans 8.16.

There is no intimation in Scriptures that the Witness is immediate nor does there appear to be any necessity that it should be. All the advantages derived from it [are] assurance, considered merely as a Witness, and this is obtained mediately. Witness is one who gives in the testimony, and this testimony, when viewed in a proper light and seemed to be true, amounts to. So great evidence in favor of the truth as to produce a real conviction and assurance it. But this is all mediate.

Question 272 [328]. What is the Seal of the Spirit?

Answer 272. The Seal of the Spirit appears to be of much the same import with the Witness of the Spirit. By the seal must be meant the impression which is made. And this is made in several graces which are produced in the Christian, or rather, these are the impression or the seal itself. "After that ye believed, ye were sealed with that holy spirit of promise." Ephesians 1.13. The meaning seems to be that after a man once becomes a Christian, progressive sanctification is carried on by the Holy Spirit, and this, properly viewed, is an evidence in favor of that man's good estate as infallible as the seal upon a deed is of the authenticity of that deed.

Question 273 [328]. Do all real Christians know the time of their conversion?

Answer 273. There appear to be many Christians, and some who are eminently so, who cannot determine the day, or perhaps the year of their conversion. This we should suppose would more peculiarly be the case with those who are converted in child. Even with some who have arrived to a maturity of judgment and memory, the change may not be so striking, and so particularly noticed at the time, as in the future to be recollected. There evidently is a great difference, in this respect, in the operations of the Spirit.

Question 274 [329]. Do all real Christians certainly know that they are converted at all?

Answer 274. There appear to be some Christians who never in this life attained a certain knowledge of their conversion. Through their whole lives, they are full of doubts and fears. That this may be the case is evident from the method in which assurance is attained. This depends on the nature of the evidence and the person's peculiar method of receiving evidence. If the gracious exercises of a Christian be small, seldom, and much clouded with corruption, his evidence will be proportionably feeble. And if he be naturally disposed to hesitation, doubt and uncertainty, and to form conclusions unfavorable to himself, he may not give the real evidence of his good estate its proper way. Both of these may operate, through the life, and prevent a man's ever attaining to a certain knowledge of his conversion.

Question 275 [330]. Are great awakenings and convictions of conscience, followed with great joys and comforts, and attended with texts of Scripture extraordinarily suggested to the mind, proofs of real conversion?

Answer 275. A person may have great awakenings and convictions of conscience, and these be attended with great joy and comfort, and yet never be the subject of real conversion. This appears to have been the case with Herod and those represented by the stony ground hearers in the parable of the sower. Matthew 13. He may also have texts of Scripture extraordinarily suggested to the mind, and yet been totally destitute of every gracious principle. The devil may be suffered to do this, and most probably does actually do it in many instances. Neither of these things is real grace, and that which is not a real act of grace ought never to be considered as a proof of it.

Many appear to have the greatest awakenings and convictions, joys and comforts, and pretend to many extraordinary suggestions; and, after all, fall away and the last error of them becomes much greater than the first.

Question 276 [331]. Is the state of the righteous and the wicked between death and the resurrection a state of sensibility? And how do you prove it?

Answer 276. Those passages of Scripture which favor the idea of the state of sensibility between death and resurrection respect the righteous more generally than the wicked. Yet if one are in a state of sensibility, doubtless, the others are, likewise. Some of the passages, however, refer to both, and those are sufficient to support the doctrine.

"For me to live is Christ, and to die is gain." Philippians 1.21. If, however, the Apostle after death had been in a state of his ability, death would not have been gained. "For I am in a strait betwixt two, having a desire to depart, and to be with Christ, which is far better." Philippians 1.23. This determines why it was better to die and why he desired: that is, because he would be with Christ. But if he were not to be with Christ until the resurrection, it would by no means have been better: for he would then have experienced this happiness, whether he died when he desired to or fifty years afterwards. "For in this week groan earnestly, desiring to be closed upon with our house, which is from heaven." 2 Corinthians 5.2.

"That he may take part of this ministry and Apostleship from which Judah by transgression fell, that he might go to his own place." Acts 1:25. This seems clearly to intimate that Judas had been gone to his own place, which doubtless was a state of sensibility. "Even as Sodom and Gomorrah, and the cities about them in like manner, giving themselves over to fornication, and going after strange flesh, are set forth for an example, suffering the vengeance of eternal fire." Jude 7.

The parable of the rich man and Lazarus in Luke 16 evidently is in favor of the doctrine. What Christ said to the thief on the cross, we may be sure, he never would have said where there are no state of sensibility and immediately after death. "Today, shalt thou be with me in Paradise." Luke 23.43.

"And when he had opened the fifth seal, I saw under the altar, the souls of them that were slain for the Word of God, and for the testimony of which they held." Revelation 6.9. These are fully represented as in the state of sensibility. "And they cried with a loud voice, saying, how long. Oh Lord, holy and true, dost thou not judge and avenge our blood on them that dwell on the earth?" Verse 10. "And they sang a new song, saying, Thou art worthy to take the book, and to open the seals thereof: for thou wast slain, and hast redeemed us to God by thy blood, out of every kindred and him, and people, and nation." Revelation 5.9. "And the smoke of their torment ascendeth up for ever and ever." 14:11. In these several passages. The righteous and the wicked are represented as being already in a state of sensibility. 2 Corinthians 5.

Question 277 [334]. How do you prove the resurrection of the body, and a general judgment?

Answer 277. The doctrine of the resurrection of the dead end of the general judgment are with many others, peculiar to the Scriptures, and such as the light of nature would never have taught: for it is by the gospel alone that life and immortality are brought to light. 2 Timothy 1.10. But both are here abundantly asserted.

"For since by man came death, by man came also the resurrection of the dead." 1 Corinthians 15.21. "The trumpet shall sound, and the dead shall be raised incorruptible, and we shall be changed. For this corruptible must put on incorruption, and this mortal must put on immortality." 1 Corinthians 15.52, 53. "The dead in Christ shall rise first." 1 Thessalonians 4.16. "Marvel not at this: for the hour is coming in the which all that are in the graves shall hear his voice: And shall come forth, they that have done good, unto the resurrection of life, and they that have done evil unto the resurrection of damnation." John 5.28, 29. These passages fully prove the doctrine of the resurrection. Others might be adduced, particularly Paul's preaching it at Athens, Acts 17:32, but these are sufficient.

The doctrine of the general judgment is supported with equal clearness. "Before the Lord, for he cometh, for he cometh to judge the earth: he shall judge the world with righteousness, and the people with his truth." Psalm 96.13. "Because he hath appointed a day wherein he will judge the world in righteousness, by that man whom he hath ordained, whereof he hath given assurance unto all men, in that he hath raised him from the dead." Acts 27.31. The same truth is more strongly evident from the representation given of the general judgment by our Lord himself. Matthew 25.31–46.

Question 278 [336]. How do you prove the immortality of the soul?

Answer 278. The immortality of the soul has been argued by mere reason, from its immateriality, its fondness for existence, dread of annihilation, its hopes of immortality, and its capacity for a constantly accelerating improvement. But it is from the Scriptures alone that we derive clear light on the subject, and arguments which may be defended upon with certainty. "But is now made manifest by the appearing of our Saviour Jesus Christ, who hath abolished death, and hath brought life and immortality to light through the gospel." 2 Timothy 1.10. Here immortality is expressly asserted. "For this corruptible must put on incorruption, and this mortal must put on immortality." 1 Corinthians 15.53.

The doctrine of the souls immortality may also be proved from the eternal duration of the happiness of the righteous, and misery of the wicked: for if these be eternal the soul must be made immortal to you to enjoy the one, and suffer the other. "And these shall go away, into everlasting punishment: but the righteous into life eternal." Matthew 25.46. "And many of them that sleep in the dust of the earth shall awake, some to everlasting life, and some to shame and everlasting contempt." Daniel 12:2. "For God so loved the world, that he gave his only begotten Son, that whosoever believed that in him, should not perish, but have everlasting life." John 3.16. "Who shall be punished with everlasting destruction." 2 Thessalonians 1.9.

Question 279 [338]. Will the secret sins of the righteous be made public at the day of judgment?

Answer 279. The sins of the righteous are frequently so connected with the sins of the wicked, that it seems difficult to conceive how the latter should be revealed, and not at the same time expose the former. This will hold with respect to all their sins, where connected. And if any are exposed, no reason can be given. Why others or all should not be. The sins of the wicked will all probably be made public. Some of the secret sins of the righteous have already been made public, and some wise and important reason may exist to occasion the publication of others at the day of judgment. It may serve to heighten, in the view of all holy beings, the greatness and excellence of God's grace and mercy, because, "were sin abounded, Grace did much more abound." Romans 5.20.

"In the day when God shall judge the secrets of men, by Jesus Christ." Romans 2.16. This passage does not make any distinction, with respect to their being revealed between the sins of the righteous and the wicked. Doubtless, when the sentence is pronounced at the day of judgment reasons will be given for the sentence. This is evident from the representation of our Savior, respecting the process. Matthew 25. And if the sentence of the wicked is founded on their secret, as well as open sins, then some, at least, of the sins of the righteous will also be exposed. Ecclesiastes 12.14.

Question 280 [340]. Do the saints in heaven know anything that is done on earth?

Answer 280. Since there is intercourse between the Angels and the saints in heaven, and since the former from the nature of their employment are acquainted with things on the earth, we should naturally conclude they would communicate information of these things to the latter. Besides, the saints are represented as being acquainted with many things done on the earth. "I say and to you that likewise joy shall be in heaven over one sinner that repenteth, more than over ninety and nine just persons which need no repentance." Luke 15:7. Though it is not said the saints experienced this joy, yet we may rationally conclude they are in dull, just with a participation in it; and, therefore, are made acquainted with the repentance of sinners on the earth. "And I cried with a loud voice, saying, how long, O Lord, holy, and true, dost thou not judge and avenge our blood on them that dwell on the earth." Revelation 6.10. These are evidently represented as being acquainted with things on the earth.

Question 281 [341]. How do you prove that the institution of the Sabbath is of perpetual obligation?

Answer 281. That the institution of the Sabbath is of perpetual obligation appears from its being inserted in the Decalogue. That it properly belongs to the Decalogue has been disputed, but the contrary, it is presumed, has never been proved. There evidently were then commandments given at Mount Sinai on the two tables. But if we expunge this we must split up one of the others to make to of it, for which we have not the least authority. Besides, it is extremely unlikely that this would have been intermixed with the moral precepts into united in one, without being discovered. If then, it belongs to the first table of the law. It is equally binding with the other moral precepts which are evidently perpetual.

Besides, the reason given at the promulgation in the amount is such as applies in every age of the world. The reason is, "For in six days the Lord made heaven and earth, the sea, and all that in them is, and rested the seventh day: wherefore the Lord blessed the seventh day, and hallowed it." Exodus 20.11. Also, the use and importance of the Sabbath will probably perpetually exist, and we may rationally conclude, therefore, that it is obligation is perpetual.

The perpetuity of the Sabbath may be argued from the example of Christ and his apostles. He always honored the Sabbath, and his followers appeared always to consider a seventh part of time as holy. Though the date was changed under the Christian institution, yet one day and seven was constantly capped. Nor did any of the writers in the New Testament ever give intimation, but that the fourth commandment was equally binding with the others.

> Question 282 [343]. Had a you prove that the Sabbath is changed from the seventh to the first day of the week?

Answer 282. It may with propriety be observed that the fourth commandment does not so properly confined the Sabbath to a certain day, as to a certain portion of time. The object of it seems to be to require the sanctification of the seventh part of time. When it was first instituted, most probably, directions were given when the reckoning should begin, and therefore when the first Sabbath should be. This then would equally establish the succeeding sabbaths, unless God were pleased to make an alteration in this respect. This he doubtless might do, consistently with everything expressed in the institution. It is said, "six days shalt thou labor, and do all of thy work. But the seventh day is the Sabbath." Exodus 20:9, 10. But this might have been said had any other day of the seven been appointed. The first day of our civil week, counting from the Sabbath, is the seventh day, it is the seventh part of time, and may fully come under the institution.

It has been supposed, and perhaps not without reason, that some intimation of the change is given in the Old Testament. "This is the day which the Lord hath made: we will rejoice and be glad in it." Psalm 118.24. The passage seems to refer to the time of Christ's exaltation, which was immediately upon his resurrection, and this was on the day As the Christian Sabbath. In the latter part of the verse seems to intimate that it should be a day celebrated on this account, which is a work peculiar to the Sabbath. But however this passage be received, there is in the New Testament sufficient authority for the change. This will arise from the directions and intimations given respecting the duties and exercises of the day, and the example of the Apostles.

"Concerning the collection for the saints, as I have given order to the churches of Galatia, so, do ye. Upon the first day of the week let every one of you lay by him in store, as God hath prospered him." 1 Corinthians 16.1, 2. This evidently supposes that the religious assemblies at Corinth and Galatia were on the first day of the week, and therefore, we may conclude this was their Sabbath. "I was in the Spirit on the Lord's day." Revelation 1.10. This was someday, doubtless, which was known peculiarly by that name, and no one day, more than any other can with any propriety be called the Lord's except the Sabbath. As this is a day appropriated, peculiarly to divine worship, it may properly in distinction from other days be called the Lord's. Most probably it is called the Lord's for a similar reason, that the sacrament is called the Lord's Supper. The Apostles evidently met on this day, for the purposes of religious worship, and attended to exercises which are properly the exercises of the sabbath. "Then the same day at evening, being the first day of the week, when the doors were shut where the disciples were assembled for fear of the Jews, came Jesus and stood in the midst, and saith unto them, Peace be unto you." "And after eight days. Again, his disciples were within." John 20.19, 26. These passages, taken together, make it evident. It was the practice of the disciples to meet for the purposes of religious exercises on the first day. "And upon the first day of the week, when the disciples came together to break bread, Paul preached unto them." Acts 20.7. Here both the administration of the Lord's Supper and preaching were on this day, which are duties most especially of the Sabbath.

Question 283 [346]. How do you prove that public worship ought to be attended on the Sabbath?

Answer 283. That public worship is to be attended on the Sabbath is evident from express declarations of Scripture and the example and practice of Christ and his disciples. In the Old Testament appears to have been expressly enjoined, and doubtless was considered as included in the commandment itself. If so, then it is still obligatory. "You shall keep my Sabbath, and reverence my sanctuary: I am the Lord." Leviticus 26.2. This seems to intimate very plainly that the sanctuary was to be visited on the Sabbath, which must have been for public worship. "And it shall come to pass, that from one new moon to another, and from one Sabbath to another, shall all flesh come to worship before me, saith the Lord." Isaiah 66.23. This still more plainly and extensively enjoins public worship on the Sabbath. And it may be here observed also that the Psalms in general appear to be calculated for public worship, and if this be the case. No reason can be given why the Sabbath is not the most proper and suitable time. Indeed, the ninety-second Psalm was expressly composed for public worship on this day.

Christ and his followers honored this day with their attendance at public worship, and in such a manner as to fully convince us that it was instituted by God. Luke 4.16. Acts 20.7.

Question 284 [347]. Which evening is to be kept as part of the Sabbath?

Answer 284. It appears clearly that the Jewish Sabbath began at ease and, if so, we have every reason to suppose the Christian Sabbath ought likewise to begin, then. Theirs was established by divine authority, and as the same institution is still continued, only on a different day of the week, it seems as though the like regulations, respecting the length of the time and the beginning of it, ought still to continue unless some intimations had been given to the contrary, which it is presumed never were. "From even until he then shall ye celebrate your Sabbath." Leviticus 23.32. It is also worthy of remark, that in speaking of natural day, the evening is always placed before the morning, in the Old Testament, and likewise the new. "In the first month, on the fourteenth day of the month at even, you shall eat unleavened bread until the one and twentieth day of the month at even." Exodus 12.18. From this we may conclude, as the fourteenth day of the month began, and the twentieth ended at even, that other days, and consequently their months universally began then. But this is still further evident. "And that even, when the sun did set, they brought under him all that were diseased, and them that were possessed with Devils." Mark 1.32. But this, they would not have done had not their Sabbath, then ended. We may, therefore, conclude it also began at sun set. It appears, likewise, that Nehemiah commanded the gates of Jerusalem to be shut when it began to be dark before the Sabbath that it might not be profaned. Nehemiah 13.19.

Question 285 [349]. What is the foundation of the duty of prayer since God is immutable?

Answer 285. The original and real foundation of prayer is our dependence upon God. He is able, were it most fitting and best on the whole, to bestow blessings upon us without our asking for that. He has perfectly knows what we need before we present our supplications, as afterwards. And though he grant what is prayed for, it is not because of any merit in the prayer which could lay him under obligations to do this. Nor does he grant or refused in consequence of any change of mind, but he beforehand. It knew what he should do. The design of our prayer, therefore, cannot be to produce any real effect upon God. But the design of it must be, to produce and affect upon the creature, upon him, who is the subject of prayer.

Prayer is calculated to promote an humbling sense of our dependence, and to fit us for the reception of favors with gratitude, and also to encourage a spirit of devotion.

Question 286 [350]. How do you prove that family prayer is the duty?

Answer 286. The reason or ground of family prayer is that they are jointly dependent on God, have a union of interest, and wants, and also, that it is calculated, more especially in point of example to convince children and servants of their dependents and duty.

"Pour out thy fury upon the heathen that know the not, and upon the families that call not upon by name." Jeremiah 10.25. This fully implies that the families who called not on the name of God, were extremely guilty, and merited a distinguished punishment. "Likewise ye husbands, dwell with them, according to knowledge, giving honor to the wife, as unto the weaker vessel, and as being heirs together of the grace of life, that your prayers be not hindered." 1 Peter 3.7. By "your prayers" seems to be meant the joint prayers of man and wife, or family prayer. And the expression in the passage seems to suppose that prayer would without doubt be made, as a duty well known and practiced.

Question 287 [351]. Ought we to pray for perfection in this life

Answer 287. It appears from the Word of God, and the universal conduct of his providence, that he does not bring any of his creatures to perfection in this life, and that it is not his will. They should arrive to it here. To pray for it, therefore, would be to pray for something, which we know to be contrary to the will of God, which is rebellion, and which on this ground is not justifiable and right.

Question 288 [351]. What is the nature of the Christian church?

Answer 288. The Christian church consists of a body of professing Christians, united for mutual fellowship, and to communicate mutual assistance to each other, especially in watching over one another in brotherly love. This, however, applies rather to the church militant and visible.

Question 289 [352]. Who are fit for communion in the church?

Answer 289. Those are properly fit persons for communion in the church who are possessed of those qualifications, peculiar to the true and real disciples of Christ. The idea of a Christian church is an assembly of Christians. But nothing short of faith and repentance is sufficient to denominate a man a real Christian. Some doubtless, may appear to possess these qualifications who are, in reality, totally destitute of them. Still, however, where a credible profession is made, accompanied by a moral and regular life, it is the duty of the church to receive such. The reason of this arises from our incapacity to judge of men's hearts and the principles by which they are actuated.

Question 290 [352]. Ought we to have universal charity for all professing Christians?

Answer 290. So long as the outward conversation of professing Christians is regular and apparently conformable to the gospel, it is our duty to entertain charity for them. But when they become irregular and regardless of the Christian duties of the gospel, it does not appear that we are bound to exercise charity for such. Unsound this on principles appears to be manifestly I just ground of respecting the soundness and genuineness of their profession.

Question 291 [353]. Ought we to think that all sects of Christians are right?

Answer 291. The New Testament manifestly in a variety of places represents some who profess Christianity as far from being right. And it generally has laid down marks by which we are enabled frequently to judge with respect to those who are censured and condemned. Such as teach "doctrines the commandments of men," who teach "things which they ought not, for filthy lucre's sake," are clearly not to be thought right. Matthew 15.9. Titus 1.11. If now it be evident that whole sects come under this description, they are equally to be considered as wrong. 2 Timothy 2.18.

Question 292 [354]. What is the nature and import of baptism?

Answer 292. Baptism is of the nature of a sacrament. Its import is that it is a token of the covenant standing of the believer with God, that he fulfills the covenant at least thus far.

Question 293 [354]. How do we prove infant baptism?

Answer 293. Baptism appears to be a mode of dedication. And as the children of a man are, in a certain sense, is to dispose of it seems to very proper that he should have the power of dedicating, and a reasonable duty to dedicate, his children to the Lord. Baptism evidently comes in, as a substitute for circumcision, and this incontestably was performed upon children. The object of circumcision was evidently to dedicate their children, and in a peculiar and distinguishing sense, to denominate them the Lord's. Hence, he says to some in the days of Ezekiel, "moreover, thou hast taken thy sons and died daughters, whom thou hast borne unto me, and these hast thou sacrificed unto them to be devoured." Ezekiel 16.20.

The direction in the New Testament is general respecting baptism, and may apply to incidents as well as adults. "Go ye, therefore, and teach all nations, baptizing them in the name of the Father, and of the Son, and of the Holy Ghost." Matthew 28.19. It is very probable, also, that when the

Apostles baptized the whole households particularly mentioned, there were some children among them. Particularly were baptized the families of the jailer, Lydia and Stephanus. Acts 16.13, 33; 1 Corinthians 1:16, 7:14.

Question 294 [355]. Does infant baptism alone give a title to all other privileges of the church?

Answer 294. Properly infants are not in covenant, but their parents. Baptism is rather a matter of dedication. They are not, therefore, baptized on account of any relation they sustained to the church, as members, but in consequence of their parent's church membership. If then, they are neither in covenant nor members of the church, they are not entitled to the other church privileges.

Question 295 [356]. What is the nature and import of the Lord's supper?

Answer 295. The Lord's supper is a sacrament, and designed to commemorate the sufferings and death of Christ. In partaking of the bread and wine, in a worthy and acceptable manner, the communicants partake also, in a spiritual manner, of the body and blood of Christ. They become interested in the benefits of Christ's atonement.

Question 296 [356]. Are the same qualifications necessary for and attend on both sacraments?

Answer 296. The two sacraments are seals of one and the same covenant. This is the covenant of grace, and requires one thing uniformly, that is regeneration. For an attendance upon either of the sacraments, therefore a man ought to be the subject of this. And nothing more than this can be required. It is evident, then, that the qualification which will render a man a fit candidate for one sacrament, will also for the other.

Question 297 [357]. What are the rules and what the end of church discipline?

Answer 297. The rule for a private Christian to act towards an offending brother is contained in Matthew 18:15–18. When he has taken proper steps, in private, if his brother remain refractory, he is to tell the matter to the church. The discipline, by way of punishment, consists in a suspension from privileges, and sometimes a total exclusion from communion and fellowship.

Question 298 [357]. What is a just matter of discipline and excommunication?

Answer 298. Irregularity of behavior is properly a just matter of discipline. When a man openly ask inconsistently with his profession, he becomes liable to the discipline of the church, and if he remained obstinate and pertinacious, he becomes liable to excommunication.

Question 299 [358]. Is heresy a just matter of excommunication?

Answer 299. "A man that is an heretic, after the first and second admonition, reject, knowing that he is such, is subverted and send this, being condemned of himself." Titus 3.11. This passage decidedly determines the excommunication of an heretic.

Question 300 [358]. Is Universalism a just matter of excommunication?

Answer 300. The doctrine opposite to Universalism is so clearly revealed that it seems a man must willfully shut his eyes against the light who can from sentiment become a Universalist. Universalism is not only not taught in the Bible, that it is contrary to some of its fundamental doctrines. It is even subversive of the most alarming in serious doctrines, is calculated to promote and indulge stupidity and countenance every kind of wickedness. On these accounts, therefore, it is heretical, and is a just matter, if obstinately persisted in, of excommunication.

Question 301 [359]. Is marriage a sacrament?

Answer 301. Marriage is a divine institution, but does not appear to contain anything of the nature of the sacrament. "A sacrament is an holy ordinance constituted by Christ, wherein by sensible signs, Christ, and the benefits of the new covenant are represented, sealed, and applied to believers." The institution of marriage has no reference to Christ for the benefit procured by your. Nor are any promises annexed to it of a spiritual kind.

Question 302 [359]. In what case may divorce take place?

Answer 302. The Scripture is explicit with respect to divorce, though it says, but a little on the subject in the New Testament. "Whosoever shall put away his wife, except it be for fornication, and shall marry another, committed adultery, and who so marries her which is put away doth commit adultery." Matthew 19.9.

Question 303 [360]. May a man marry his wife's sister?

Answer 303. "Thou shall not uncover the nakedness of thy brother's wife: it is thy brother's nakedness." Leviticus 18.16. Here, a woman is prohibited. The marrying of her husband's brother, and why it should not equally operate with respect to a man's marrying his wife's sister, it is presumed no satisfactory reason can be given.

Question 304 [360]. May an uncle marry his niece?

Answer 304. "Thou shalt not uncover it. The nakedness of thy father's sister: she is thy father's near kinswoman." "Thou shalt not uncover the nakedness of dying mother's sister: for she is by mother's near kinswoman." Leviticus 18.12, 13. If now, a man may not marry his aunt, it is presumed no authority can be urged to support a woman's marrying her uncle.

Question 305 [360]. Is polygamy unlawful?

Answer 305. The design of the deity appears evidently in creating but only a male and one female at first and in keeping up so great an equality among the sexes. But polygamy is directly contrary to this. It is also calculated to produce jealousies, alienation of affections, animosities, voluptuousness, in men, abasement and degradation of one half of mankind, and neglect of family government; together with the corruption of the children's morals and neglect of their education. "So then, if while her husband liveth, she be married to another man, she shall be called an adulterous." Romans 7.3. If a woman, by taking a second husband, while the first is living, then in a similar case we may reasonably suppose the man would become an adulterer. "Whosoever shall put away his wife shall, except it for fornication, and shall marry another, committeth adultery." Matthew 19:9. If a man committeth adultery, when he marries while his wife is living, but divorced from him, he may with still greater propriety, be considered as committing adultery if he marries another while he has one undivorced, and whom he has not the least right to divorce.

Question 306 [362]. What is the character of a good minister of Jesus Christ?

Answer 306. The most important, necessary, and extensively useful qualification of a good minister of Jesus Christ is that he be a good man; that he firmly and heartily believe the doctrines of the gospel and that he experiences the power of religion on his heart. Such are the duties and trials of a faithful minister of the gospel, that he appears to stand in peculiar need of a lively and vigorous exercise of religion.

To become of a good minister of Jesus Christ and to become faithful, a man must be thoroughly acquainted with the important doctrines of the gospel and the various duties of his station. He must be ready and willing to perform everything incumbent on him in this profession and must be cheerful, active, and laborious. He must discharge all the important duties of his station with impartiality and fidelity. In his preaching, he must be "plain, searching, and sentimental."

Question 307 [363]. Have you reason to think that you are possessed of the spiritual part of this character of a good man of Jesus Christ.

Answer 307. I professed to entertain a hope that I am possessed of that part of a minister's character which denominates him a Christian. I have however, to lament that this hope is greatly clouded with doubts and fears. These operate so greatly as produce many discouragements and scruples about the propriety of entering upon the profession of the ministry. It seems as though I should never be able to support the dignity becoming so important a character, and with advantage to the interests of religion. Under these and other discouraging reflections I am ready at times to relinquish the study until my hopes are more strongly confirmed. But again, I reflect, it is rather my duty to be thankful and resigned. In the whole, if I know my own feelings, I think I am desirous to be useful in the world. I feel an attachment more peculiarly for the profession of the ministry and am disposed to enter upon it at a proper time, though with timidity and anxious apprehensions.

Question 308 [364]. To whom does the performance of ordination belong?

Answer 308. Ordination of ministers is everywhere in the New Testament represented as belonging to the elders or presbyters. They were at first ordained by the Apostles and authorized by virtue of this office communicated to them to ordain others. Timothy was ordained, "with laying on of the hands of the presbytery." 1 Timothy 4.14. He is also cautioned to, "lay hands suddenly on no man." 1 Timothy 5.22. This doubtless means, he should not, as an elder, be hasty in ordaining anyone. Titus also, who was an elder, had the power of ordination. Titus 1.5. And in no case do we find it performed and directions given for it to be performed except by the Apostles or Elders.

Questions 309 [364]. May a man preach as a candidate before he is ordained?

Answer 309. The design of ordination appears to be to invest a man with power to administer the sacraments and to perform the duties of a pastor. It seems to be designed to establish a man in the ministry, by divine authority, to keep up a standing, regular order of the clergy, and to prevent intrusions. None then, has the right to take this office upon him without being regularly introduced. No one has right, previous to a regular introduction to administer the sacraments, or to conduct as a pastor of a particular the church or the church in general.

It does not appear, however, but that a person with permission may preach, previous to his ordination. There is nothing in the New Testament, which appears to disprove this. On the contrary, some things are rather in favor it. "And God hath set some in the church, first Apostles, secondarily, prophets, thirdly, teachers, after that miracles, then gifts of healings, helps, governments, diversities of tongues". 1 Corinthians 12.28. What order of men those were, who were denominated helps who possess the power and office referred to, we are not told. Some things would rather lead us to conclude, that they were preachers, not ordained. We have no account of the ordination of Apostles. It is pretty evident he was not ordained before he commenced a preacher. He, being instructed with respect of the Savior by the baptism of John preached boldly. And when he was instructed more fully by Aquila and Priscilla, we are not informed but that he still continue to preach without any further introduction. In Achaia, he said to have helped them much. Possibly, he helped them much in the office denominated helps in the passage recited above. Acts 18.25–27. What is said, respecting Mark, would rather lead us to suppose, he was not an ordained Bishop, but rather a helper who was yet under the direction of others, and not possessed of that independence which belonged to a Bishop. Yet it is evident, he had something to do in the ministry; most probably, he preached, but could not administer the sacraments and perform those parts peculiar to a Bishop or Pastor. Acts 15.37; 2 Timothy 4:11.

It seems that Stephen and Philip preached. But we have no account that either was ordained, as a Bishop or Pastor, but only as Deacons. If then, these might preach, without an ordination to that end, it does not appear but that others may at the present day. Besides, Timothy is directed to lay hands suddenly on no man. 1 Timothy 5.22. This manifestly was designed to prevent hasty and incautious ordinations, before a man's abilities and fidelity in the ministry were proved. And if a Deacon must first be proved before he is invested with this inferior office, as appears from 1 Timothy 3:10, then surely a Bishop who's office in every respect is far more important, ought more especially and more fully to be proved. And the most effectual method of trying and proving a man in this respect is often a proper examination of his principles and knowledge to license him as a candidate, and afford him an opportunity to bring forward his talents into actual and public exercise. This appears to be the safest for the church and nothing appears to be directly against it in the Bible.

Question 310 [368]. If we hold that ordination belongs to the Elders must we also maintain that the line of ordination has never been broken?

Answer 310. If the line of ordination had once been broken it does not appear that the succeeding ordinations by those who had not themselves been ordained would be valid. It seems necessary, therefore, to maintain, there has been a regular succession of ordained elders. An assertion of this, however, is all that is necessary. If it be doubted, the burden of proof lies upon those who call the assertion in question. The church was never under obligations to keep records or prevent unfounded surmises and doubts.

Question 311 [369]. In what does the happiness of heaven consist?

Answer 311. It is abundantly represented in Scripture that God has prepared a place for the residence of the saints after death. "For he," that is Abraham, "looked for a city which hath foundations, whose builder and maker is God." Hebrews 11.10. "In my Father's house are many mansions, if it were not so, I would have told you. I go to prepare a place for you." John 14.2. "I appoint unto you a kingdom as my Father hath appointed to me, that ye may eat and drink at my table, in my kingdom and sit on thrones, judging the twelve tribes of Israel." Luke 22.29–30. "Then shall the Kings say unto them on his right hand come, ye blessed of my Father inherit the kingdom prepared for you from the foundation of the world." Matthew 25.34.

The inhabitants of heaven are exempted from the various troubles and evils of life. "There remaineth therefore a rest for the people of God." Hebrews 4.9. "They rest for their labors." Revelation 14.13. "God shall wipe away all tears from their eyes." Revelation 7.17; 21.4. It does not partake in the sensual enjoyments of this life. "For when they shall rise from the dead they neither marry nor are given in marriage, but are as the angels in heaven." Mark 12.25. "They shall hunger no more, neither thirst anymore, neither shall the sun light on them, nor any heat." Revelation 7.16.

The saints in heaven will experience the happiness of being made perfectly holy. "To the general assembly of the firstborn, which are written in heaven, and to God the judge of all, and to the spirits of just men made perfect." Hebrews 12.23. "We know that when he shall appear we shall be like him." 1 John 3.2. "Nevertheless, we, according to his promise, look for the new heavens and a new earth, wherein dwelleth righteousness." 2 Peter 3.13. "And shall be in nowise enter into it anything that defileth, neither whatsoever worketh abomination or maketh a lie." Revelation 21.27.

In addition to this, it may be observed, the knowledge of the saints in heaven will be greatly increased and perfected. "Blessed are the pure in heart for they shall see God." Matthew 5.8. "I will that they also whom hast given, be with me where I am, that they may behold my glory which though hast given me." John 17.24. "Now we see through a glass darkly, but then face to face, now I know in part then I shall know even as also I am known." 1 Corinthians 13.12. Then the reality, excellence, and importance of Divine things will appear in a more striking and joyful light. In proportion as their knowledge increases, their joy will increase. And as new objects will constantly be presenting themselves, in their capacities constantly enlarging, their happiness will also be constantly increasing.

Again the happiness of heaven will be everlasting. "We have a building of God a house not made with hands, eternal in the heavens." 1 Corinthians 5.1. "And so shall we be with the Lord." 1 Thessalonians 4.17. "That they may obtain the salvation which is in Christ Jesus, with eternal glory." 2 Timothy 2.10. "To an inheritance incorruptible and undefiled, in that fadeth not away, reserved in heaven for you." 1 Peter 1.4.

Question 312 [372]. Why is holiness necessary to the enjoyment of the happiness of heaven?

Answer 312. The reason why holiness is necessary to the enjoyment of the happiness of heaven is that this happiness consists in holiness; in the holy exercises of holy being. Were an unholy being admitted, it would be no joy or happiness to him, for he would abhor and perfectly disrelish it. It would be directly contrary to every feeling of his heart. Instead of being happiness to him it would misery.

Question 313 [372]. What are the essential or fundamental doctrines of Christianity?

Answer 313. The most essential doctrines of Christianity are: 1. That there is one God, the creator, preserver, and ruler of all things; that he is possessed of all possible excellencies and perfections. 2. That this one God subsists in three divine persons. 3. That he has made a declaration of his mind and will in the Scriptures of the Old Testament and New Testament. 4. That he has decreed whatsoever cometh to pass. 5. That though man was at first made upright, he apostatized and fell from this primitive state of holiness and happiness into a state of sin and misery. 6. That mankind became totally depraved. 7. That God has made an atonement, and offers salvation to mankind, on certain conditions. 8. That to experience this salvation, a man must be regenerated, and become the subject of faith, repentance, and the various graces of the gospel. 9. That mankind are of themselves morally unable to regenerate themselves or put forth any of these exercises and that if ever they become the subjects of them, it must be by the energy of Divine power. 10. That those who are born again by the Spirit of God shall persevere in holiness and finally be made happy. 11. That after death departed souls continue in a state of sensibility. 12. That there shall be a general resurrection, where the bodies shall be raised and reunited with their souls. 13. That as there are two set of characters in this world, the wicked and the righteous, so there will more eminently appear this distinction at the general judgment. And that sentence shall be pronounced in a more public manner, agreeably to their different characters and what they before have experienced the wicked will be fixed in everlasting misery and the righteous in everlasting happiness. 14. That God has established a church in the world, appointed officers, and favored it with peculiar privileges. 15. That he has heretofore upheld the church from its first establishment, and will uphold it to the end of the world.

Bibliography

Ahlstrom, Sydney. *A Religious History of the American People*. 2nd ed. New Haven, CT: Yale University Press, 2004.

Anderson, Glenn Paul. "Joseph Bellamy (1719–1790): The Man and His Work." Ph.D. diss., Boston University, 1971.

Bellamy, Joseph. *A Blow at the Root of Antinomianism of the Present Age*. Boston, 1763.

———. *The Great Evil of Sin, as It Is Committed against God*. Boston, 1753.

———. *The Law, Our School-Master*. New Haven, 1756.

———. *True Religion Delineated*. Boston, 1750.

———. "True Religion Delineated." In *The Works of the Rev. Joseph Bellamy, D.D. Late of Bethlehem, Connecticut, with a Memoir of His Life and Character*, edited by Tryon Edwards, Vol. 1, 3–360. 2 vols. Boston: Doctrinal Book and Tract Society, 1850.

———. *The Wisdom of God in the Permission of Sin, Vindicated*. Boston, 1760.

Bezzant, Rhys. "'Singly, Particularly, Closely': Edwards as Mentor." *Jonathan Edwards Studies* 4.2 (2014) 228–47.

Brietenbach, William. "Piety and Moralism: Edwards and the New Divinity." In *Jonathan Edwards and the American Experience*, edited by Nathan O. Hatch and Harry S. Stout, 177–204. New York: Oxford University Press, 1989.

Boardman, George Nye. *A History of New England Theology*. New York: Randolph, 1809.

Conforti, Joseph. *Samuel Hopkins and the New Divinity Movement: Calvinism, the Congregational Ministry and Reform in New England between the Great Awakenings*. Grand Rapids: Christian University Press, 1981.

Cooke, Parson. "Edwards on the Atonement." *American Theological Review* 2.5 (1860) 97–120.

Crisp, Oliver D. "Divine Retribution." *Sophia* 42.2 (2003) 35–52.

———. "The Moral Government of God: Jonathan Edwards and Joseph Bellamy on the Atonement." In *After Jonathan Edwards: The Course of New England Theology*, edited by Oliver D. Crisp and Douglas A. Sweeney, 78–90. New York: Oxford University Press, 2012.

———. "Penal Non-Substitution." *Journal of Theological Studies* 59.1 (2008) 140–68.

———. "Penal Non-Substitution." In *A Reader in Contemporary Philosophical Theology*, edited by Oliver D. Crisp, 299–327. London: T. & T. Clark, 2009.

Cooley, Daniel. "The New England Theology and Atonement." PhD Thesis, Trinity Evangelical Divinity School, 2014.

Cooley, Daniel, and Douglas A. Sweeney. "The Novelty of the New Divinity." In *Diversity and Controversy in the Reformed World of the Eighteenth Century*, edited by Michael A. G. Haykin and Mark Jones. Göttingen: Vandenhoeck & Ruprecht, 2018 (forthcoming).

Dexter, Franklin Bowditch. *Biographical Sketches of the Graduates of Yale with Annals of the College History*, Vol. 4, *July 1778–June 1792*. New York: Holt, 1907.

Edwards Jr, Jonathan. "Remarks on the Improvements Made in Theology by His Father, President Edwards" and "Thoughts on the Atonement." In *Works of Jonathan Edwards D.D., Late President of Union College*, Vol. 1, edited by Tryon Edwards, 481–508. Andover, MA.: Allen, Morrill & Wardenwell, 1842.

———. "Three Sermons on the Necessity of the Atonement and Its Consistency between That and Free Grace in Forgiveness." In *The Atonement: Discourses and Treatises by Edwards, Smalley, Maxcy, Emmons, Griffin, Burge and Weeks, with an Introductory Essay*, edited by Edwards Amasa Park, 1–42. Boston, 1859.

Edwards, Tryon. "Memoir." In *The Works of the Rev. Joseph Bellamy, D.D. Late of Bethlehem, Connecticut, with a Memoir of his Life and Character*, 2 vols., vii–lxv. Boston: Doctrinal Book and Tract Society, 1850.

Eig, Jonathan. *Get Capone: The Secret Plot That Captured America's Most Wanted Gangster*. New York: Simon and Schuster, 2011.

Evans, William B. *Imputation and Impartation: Union with Christ in American Reformed Theology*. Studies in Christian History and Thought. Eugene, OR: Wipf and Stock, 2008.

Franklin, Benjamin T. *History of Long Island*. New York: French, 1839.

Ferm, Robert L. *Jonathan Edwards the Younger (1745–1801): A Colonial Pastor*. Grand Rapids: Eerdmans, 1976.

Foster, Frank Hugh. *A Genetic History of the New England Theology*. Chicago: University of Chicago Press, 1907.

Gambrell, Mary Latimer. *Ministerial Education in Eighteenth-Century New England*. New York: Columbia University, 1937.

Giddings, Minot D. *The Giddings Family*. Hartford, CT, 1882.

Guelzo, Allen. *Edwards on the Will*. Middletown, CT: Wesleyan University Press, 1989.

Harountunian, Joseph. *Piety Versus Moralism: The Passing of New England Theology from Edwards to Talyor*. 1932. Reprint. Eugene, OR: Wipf & Stock/The Jonathan Edwards Center at Yale University, 2006.

Harrison, Fosdick. *A Discourse Delivered . . . at the Funeral of Rev. Maltby Gelston*. New Haven, CT, 1857.

Hopkins, Samuel. *Life and Character of the Late Rev. Mr. Jonathan Edwards*. Boston, 1765.

———. *A System of Doctrines contained in Divine Revelation*. Boston, 1793.

Hume, David. *An Inquiry concerning Human Understanding*. London, 1748.

Kling, David. "New Divinity School of Prophets 1750–1825: A Case Study in Ministerial Education." *History of Education Quarterly* 37.2 (1997) 185–206.

Kuklick, Bruce, ed. *American Religious Thought of the 18th and 19th Centuries*. New York: Garland, 1987.

Kvanvig, Jonathan L. *The Problem of Hell*. New York: Oxford University Press, 1994.

Levering, Matthew. "Jonathan Edwards and Thomas Aquinas on Original Sin." *The Ecumenical Edwards: Jonathan Edwards and the Theologians*, edited by Kyle Strobel, 134–40. Aldershot, UK: Ashgate, 2015.

Lewis, David. "Do We Believe in Penal Substitution?" In *A Reader in Contemporary Philosophical Theology*, edited by Oliver D. Crisp, 328–34. London: T. & T. Clark, 2009.

Miller, Perry, John E. Smith, and Harry S. Stout, eds. *The Works of Jonathan Edwards in 26 Volumes*. New Haven, CT: Yale University Press, 1957–2006.

Minkema, Kenneth P. "Jonathan Edwards on Education and His Educational Legacy." In *After Edwards: The Courses of the New England Theology*, edited by Oliver Crisp and Douglas Sweeney, 31–50. New York: Oxford University Press, 2012.

Ogden, James De Peyster. *An Address Delivered . . . Union Hall, Jamaica, Long Island*. Jamaica, NY, 1842.

Packer, James I. "What Did the Cross Achieve? The Logic of Penal Substitution." *Tyndale Bulletin* 25 (1974) 3–46.

Park, Edwards Amasa. *The Atonement: Discourses and Treatises by Edwards Jr, Smalley, Maxcy, Emmons, Griffin, Burge and Weeks, with an Introductory Essay*. Boston, 1859.

———. "An Introductory Essay." In *The Atonement, Discourses and Treatises by Edwards, Smalley, Maxey, Emmons, Griffin, Bunge and Weeks*, edited by Edwards Amasa Park, vii–lxxx. Boston: Congregational Board of Publication, 1859.

———. "Questions of the Two Edwardses for Their Pupils in Theology." *Bibliotheca Sacra* 39 (1882) 367–81.

Post, Stephen. "Disinterested Benevolence: An American Debate over the Nature of Christian Love." *Journal of Religious Ethics* 14 (1986) 356–68.

Rudisill, Dorus Paul. *The Doctrine of the Atonement in Jonathan Edwards and His Successors*. New York: Poseidon, 1971.

Smith, H. Shelton. *Changing Conceptions of Original Sin: A Study of American Theology Since 1750*. New York: Scribner's Sons, 1955.

Stephens, Bruce M. "An Appeal to the Universe: The Doctrine of the Atonement in American Protestant Thought from Jonathan Edwards to Edwards Amasa Park." *Encounter* 60.1 (1999) 55–72.

Stowe. *Oldtown Folks*. Boston: Houghton Mifflin, 1869.

Tindal, Matthew. *Christianity as Old as Creation, or The Gospel, The Republication of the Religion of Nature*. London, 1730.

Valeri, Mark. *Law and Providence in Joseph Bellamy's New England: The Origins of the New Divinity in Revolutionary America*. Oxford: Oxford University Press, 1994.

Verill, Dorathy Maltby, ed. *Maltby-Maltbie Family History*. Newark, NJ, 1916.

Warch, Richard. *School of the Prophets: Yale College, 1701–40*. New Haven, CT: Yale University Press, 1973.

West, Stephen. *The Scripture Doctrine of the Atonement, Exposed to Careful Examination*. New York: Dodge, 1809.

Williams, Gary. "A Critical Exposition of Hugo Grotius's Doctrine of the Atonement in De Satisfactione Christi." D.Phil thesis, Oxford University, 1999.

Wright, Conrad. *The Beginnings of Unitarianism in American*. Boston: Star King, 1955.

Index

(Subjects keyed to questions)